MY EXPERIENCES AT
NAN SHAN AND PORT ARTHUR

LIEUT.-GENERAL NIKOLAI ALEXANDROVITCH TRETYAKOV,
COMMANDING 5TH REGIMENT.

[*Frontispiece.*

MY EXPERIENCES AT
NAN SHAN AND
PORT ARTHUR

WITH THE FIFTH EAST SIBERIAN RIFLES

BY

LIEUT-GENERAL N. A. TRETYAKOV

TRANSLATED BY A. C. ALFORD, R.A.

EDITED BY CAPTAIN F. NOLAN BAKER, R.A.

WITH MAPS AND ILLUSTRATIONS

The Naval & Military Press Ltd

published in association with

FIREPOWER
The Royal Artillery Museum
Woolwich

Published by
The Naval & Military Press Ltd
Unit 10 Ridgewood Industrial Park,
Uckfield, East Sussex,
TN22 5QE England
Tel: +44 (0) 1825 749494
Fax: +44 (0) 1825 765701
www.naval-military-press.com

in association with

FIREPOWER
The Royal Artillery Museum, Woolwich
www.firepower.org.uk

*In reprinting in facsimile from the original, any imperfections are inevitably reproduced
and the quality may fall short of modern type and cartographic standards.*

Printed and bound by Antony Rowe Ltd, Eastbourne

PREFACE

In 1909 there appeared in the Russian military journal, "Voenny Sbornik," twelve articles from the pen of a distinguished Russian officer.

The writer—Lieutenant-General (then Colonel) Tretyakov—as commander of the Western Section of the Defences had taken a prominent and gallant part in the historic struggle for the possession of Port Arthur.

His narrative—of which this work is a translation—placed before his countrymen, in simple and intimate language, his experiences at Nan Shan and within the beleaguered fortress. The impression created throughout Russia was deep and immediate.

No more touching and direct appeal to judge its beaten heroes sympathetically and fairly has ever been made to a nation. Six thousand miles from the Fatherland the author's regiment, the 5th Siberian Rifles—and many another—fought to the death for God and the Czar. This plain tale is a fitting record of their soldierly devotion. As such we offer it to English readers, assured that every page must bring home the conviction that here we have the actual history of the fighting line—as perhaps nothing else in our language gives it.

We follow the fortunes of the General's own unit,

we live with his men amidst the bloodstained wreck of their trenches on 203 Metre Hill, losing all thought of the general conduct of the attack and defence of the fortress—in a word, we are transported from the dry bones of military history to the living realities of the battlefield.

To the soldier these annals afford example after example, deeply interesting and instructive, of military cause and effect. In theory a specialist's business, here we see laid bare the foundation on which stands scientific siege warfare. The infantry soldier's readiness to die makes possible the rôle of the gunner and the sapper—his blood cements their work.

From the historical point of view these pages exemplify the rare incident of a writer of the beaten side giving to the world an opportunity of comparing his account with that of the victor—not years after the strife, but while the sword is yet barely sheathed. The student of war will doubtless fully appreciate the value of such contemporary history.

In Semenov's " Rasplata " we have a bitter lament for " what might have been." The psychological contrast is now before us—a commander who rarely criticizes, but, instead, shows us every one cheerfully doing his best to make bricks without straw.

In him the British soldier will recognize a brother-in-arms, whose unassuming character and cheerful self-restraint in the midst of adversity must appeal to his national instincts.

This is perhaps hardly the place to enter upon a critical discussion of the strategy and tactics of the conflict, but we cannot refrain from reminding the

reader that in this great siege we beheld the remarkable spectacle of an army sacrificing itself to secure
for its fleet the command of the sea. No more
eloquent testimony to the value to an island power
of that command has ever been presented.

In conclusion, we add a short biographical sketch
of the author, and we take this opportunity to
acknowledge with gratitude his most kind and invaluable assistance in the translation and illustration
of the work.

Lieutenant-General Nikolai Alexandrovitch Tretyakov was born in the Simbirsky Government in 1856.
Educated in Moscow, he passed through the Con-
stantine Military School and the Engineer Academy
before being gazetted in 1875 to the 6th Sapper Battalion as Second-Lieutenant.

On the outbreak of the Russo-Turkish War he
accompanied this battalion to the front, and, volun-
teering to serve in the 4th Battalion before Plevna,
took part in that famous siege, and was the first to
enter the Turkish stronghold by the Grivitsa road,
which he did at the head of a company of sappers.
He was rewarded for his services with the 3rd Class of
the Order of Stanislav and the 3rd Class of the Order
of Anne, together with the rank of Staff-Captain.

At the conclusion of the war Staff-Captain Tretyakov passed through the Nicholas Engineer Academy,
and was then appointed to the command of a company in a sapper battalion stationed at Kiev. Re-
taining this post for eight years, he attained the rank
of Lieutenant-Colonel in 1893, and in the same year
was sent to the Far East at the head of an East

Siberian Engineer battalion. During the Boxer
Rising he helped to fortify the Nan Shan position,
and was present at the capture of the Taku Forts,
afterwards joining in the advance on Pekin. General
Lincivitch marked his appreciation of the good work
done in this campaign by Lieutenant-Colonel Tretyakov by recommending him for " the gold sword."
This honour was followed by appointment to the
command of the 5th East Siberian Rifle Regiment,
and for the next two years he was engaged in protecting the railway from Pekin against the attacks of
the Hunhutzes, and was again decorated, this time
with the 3rd Class of the Order of Vladimir.

On the conclusion of the Russo-Japanese War the
Czar conferred upon him the much-coveted " George
Cross," the 1st Class of the Order of Stanislav, the
1st Class of the Order of Anne, and the rank of Major-
General. On his return to Russia he commanded
the 3rd Sapper Brigade at Kiev until, on promotion
to the rank of Lieutenant-General, he became
Inspector-General of Engineers in the Kiev District.

F. N. B.

Note.—The notes and explanations throughout
this work are by the Translator or Editor.

COPY OF LETTER FROM GENERAL TRETYAKOV TO THE TRANSLATOR

JELIESNOVODSK,
July 16*th*, 1909.

Dear Sir,

I have been rather long in answering your letter, as it was forwarded to me here from Kiev.

I hasten to inform you that, not only have I no objection to your translating my articles into English, but I am very glad of it, as it is to the interest of the Russian Garrison that all the circumstances of the defence of Port Arthur should be fully stated; and I take this opportunity of thanking you beforehand for undertaking the task.

I remain,
Your most obedient servant,
N. TRETYAKOV.

CONTENTS

CHAPTER I

CHAPTER II

CHAPTER III

CHAPTER IV

CHAPTER V

CHAPTER VI

CHAPTER VII

CHAPTER VIII

CHAPTER IX

CHAPTER X

CHAPTER XI

CHAPTER XII

LIST OF ILLUSTRATIONS

PLATES OF TRENCHES

MAPS

MY EXPERIENCES

AT

NAN SHAN AND PORT ARTHUR

CHAPTER I

Arrival of the 5th Regiment at Chin-chou—Rumours of war—Declaration of war—Restoring the fortifications on the Nan Shan position —Watching for the Japanese—First signs of the enemy—A reconnaissance in force—Fighting to the north of Chin-chou, May 16.

THE Staff of the 5th East Siberian Rifles, with the 2nd, 3rd, and 4th Companies, arrived at Chin-chou on April 1, 1903. The regiment, for the past three years, had been stationed at various points on the Yellow Sea, engaged in guarding from the attacks of the Hunhutzes the railways rebuilt by our railway battalion in conjunction with the 1st East Siberian Sappers, the unit which I commanded during the Boxer campaign.

The regiment began to settle down at Chin-chou and to transfer its baggage there from Novokievsk, after which, the men having first been housed, some large buildings were run up for the accommodation of the horses and transport vehicles, both of which were in a splendid condition, notwithstanding the wear and tear of the campaign just gone through.

1

Our two-wheeled carts were all in good repair; the horses I had bought from the Germans at Tientsin, when they offered for sale a magnificent lot of animals, brought at enormous cost from Austria and America, and, though costing us only about 80 roubles * per head, one could not speak too highly of them. I handed over our former small horses to our mounted scout detachment,† which, owing to some misunderstanding, was without any. Thus, the best-equipped unit of all our forces in China, we spent the whole of the summer of 1903 at Chin-chou.

Throughout that summer we were worried by the Hunhutzes, and not only were the scouts constantly engaged in encounters with these brigands, but we were also obliged to send out strong detachments, as the police and scouts combined proved insufficient to deal with them. The authorities at home knew very little about all this, since the local commanders refrained from sending in reports about the Hunhutze bands. Seeing that the police could not cope with them, I personally took all measures in my power against them; but when I spoke to the commandant about taking further steps, saying that I could not understand why he did not call in the help of the regular troops, the answer was always the same : "My dear Colonel, the authorities think

---

* Somewhat less than £8 at the rate of exchange of 9·5 roubles to the pound sterling.

† The term "scout detachment" is used in all official accounts, and will be used throughout this work, to denote a detachment, either mounted or on foot, composed of volunteers ("okhotnik") and attached to various regiments. All Russian volunteers were thus organized.

that we do nothing at all, or else suspect us of pusillanimity; there has already been some unpleasantness about it, and the civil governor has flatly refused to make any report to the Viceroy." So the people had to pay more and more tribute per head, and the Hunhutzes threatened our military posts as well as those of the Chinese police. In the end we had regular pitched battles with them, and the scouts and various regiments in the Kuan-tung Peninsula, as well as the 5th Regiment, lost a considerable number in killed and wounded.

" What's their little game ? " we asked.

" Ah ! " said some ; " the Chinese say that there are Japanese among them."

" But what are the Japanese after ? "

" They say they are going to fight *us*. Our people from Shanghai tell us that the Japanese officers speak to ours about nothing but politics : ' You,' they say, ' must take Persia under your protection ; but we will have Korea, which we have tried to obtain for centuries.' "

At the end of the summer we received orders to prepare quarters for all the companies of our regiment (except the 6th, which was at Pi-tzu-wo), and in August they all arrived. From the first moment of the concentration of the regiment it became clear to us that relations with Japan had become strained, and that a rupture might be expected. Soon after we heard it rumoured that the 3rd Battalion was going to join us, and then we heard that they were forming a 7th Rifle Division in Port Arthur. The officers spoke of war, but as, according to those who ought to know, the Japanese could only put 300,000 men into the field, we all felt quite confident. However, when it became known that General Kashtalinski's division was going to the Yalu, we did not feel quite the same assurance, since it would be very difficult to defend Port Arthur with only two divisions. French officers, we heard, were greatly surprised that we did not think seriously of war when we really were on the very eve of it. It must be admitted that, while contemplating the peaceful aspect of Port Arthur, we did indeed forget that we were living on the edge of a volcano.

The awakening came on the night of February 8–9, when I was roused up and given a telegram from General Glinski, on opening which I rubbed my eyes as I read :

" The Japanese fleet is fifty miles from the coast and making for Port Arthur. Be on the alert."

" Well," I thought to myself, " there is nothing to fear ; our fleet will soon make an end of theirs."

I do not know why, but we always believed in the invulnerability of our fleet, more especially since we heard that the Admiralty had refused to buy from Argentina the two splendid armoured cruisers *Nisshin* and *Kasuga*, saying that we were strong enough without them. (This may be a misconception, but I am speaking of what we heard at the time.)

Having sent for the commander of the 1st Scout Detachment, I told him to proceed to Kerr Bay and the Ta-ku Shan Peninsula, to keep a look-out on the shore. I then lay down, and was just dozing off when they called me again. Another telegram

from General Glinski ; it only contained three words :
" War declared. Glinski." This did not worry me
very much. " Let them come first and destroy
our fleet, and then they can land in Southern Korea,"
I thought to myself.

However, I sent the detachment, and with it
ten mounted scouts to act as orderlies. Early in
the morning I went out on to the Nan Shan position,
where, as I had expected, all the trenches and batteries were in a ruined condition, and in the winter,
when the ground was as hard as rock, it would be extremely difficult to restore the fortifications. Returning from the position, I met an officer coming out of
Port Arthur, who told me that three of our battleships
had been blown up suddenly by Japanese destroyers.*

This news was a great shock to me. A landing
was now possible, not only in Southern Korea, but
even in our rear, and it was absolutely essential to
hurry on with the strengthening of the position.
But now we had nothing whatever to work with,
and so I had to collect all the tools available in the
town, which, thanks to the help of Captain Preegorovski, a very smart and energetic officer, was done
remarkably quickly. I told off working parties,
who set to work to restore the advanced trenches,
but the frozen earth would not yield, and the shovels
only served for throwing up the lumps of soil loosened
by the picks.

Our first recruits and reservists arrived on Feb-

* Accounts received on the Nan Shan position were probably
greatly exaggerated, as something of the nature of a panic ensued
upon the first Japanese torpedo attack (see Official History, Part III.,
pp. 10 *et seq.*). Two battleships and one cruiser were injured in this
attack.

ruary 16, and had all to be thoroughly drilled. According to our mobilization plans all the companies of the regiment, except the 1st,* should be at the disposal of the officer commanding, and orders were given accordingly, and the 5th and 6th Companies immediately called in, the latter having all this time been engaged with the Hunhutzes. The town of Chin-chou became so crowded that I quartered about half the companies in barracks behind the Nan Shan position, and had the regimental baggage transferred to Port Arthur, where I had hired a private house for its storage, the authorities having refused to give us Government buildings.

Some mounted scouts were sent out to watch the shore under the command of Major Pavlovski, commandant of the Gandzalinski district, and a section of rifles was also allotted to him under Acting Ensign † Shiskin of the reserve, as he had complained that the Hunhutzes had become so daring as to be threatening his quarters. We ourselves watched Kerr Bay and the bays adjoining by establishing posts and a chain of mounted scouts, the practice of hunting up the Hunhutzes being abandoned.

Now began a period of activity such as I had never before experienced in the whole of my service. We fortified the positions, brought up stores, instructed the recruits and reservists, of whom more than half the regiment was now composed, and, lastly, kept a look-out for the enemy, for which latter duty two hundred men were required daily. All this

---

* This company formed part of the Legation Guard at Pekin.

† An "Acting Ensign" is a senior non-commissioned officer who has done his service with the colours, and ranks next to an Ensign in the Reserve, and, like him, wears officer's uniform.

made the situation of the regiment a very difficult one, the more so, as the enemy was free to effect a landing between Chin-chou and Port Arthur, and cut us off from the fortress. For these reasons I considered our situation not only difficult, but dangerous.

The 3rd Battalion arrived on April 2. They were a fine lot of men. I quartered them in the town, and disposed the old companies in the villages situated in front of the position.

Major * Schwartz, an engineer officer, was attached to us to help us with the fortifications, and had brought money with him for the hire of workmen. From this time, too, we began practising manœuvring on the position while yet the enemy gave us a short respite, which we endeavoured to make the most of.

Sixty versts † from Port Arthur, on the isthmus joining the southern part of Kuan-tung to the mainland beyond, and occupying half the breadth of the isthmus, is some high ground cut up lengthwise and crossways by a number of deep ravines, which mark the well-known Nan Shan position.

In the last China campaign, ‡ there being a danger of Chinese troops moving on Port Arthur from the north, this position was turned into a vast series of fortified batteries by Colonel—now General—Kholo-

---

* Though the rank of Major does not exist in the Russian Army, it is used in this translation to denote the Captain Commanding a Battery, Company, or Squadron, in contradistinction to Captain, which term must be understood as applying to a Russian Staff Captain, a rank corresponding to the rank of Second-Captain formerly existing in the British Royal Artillery.

† Sixty versts is roughly forty miles, one verst being equal to 1,166 yards.

‡ This refers to the Boxer rising (see Official History, Part II., p. 16).

dovski, and when the sapper battalion, of which I was in command at that time, came up to the position to complete its fortification, all the commanding points were found to be crowned by batteries, armed with heavy guns. We set to work at the time to build trenches for the infantry, a work already partially done on the right flank, whereupon we built two redoubts in front of the batteries in advanced positions, and one central one near Battery No. 13.

All these fortifications, now almost completely in ruins, had to form part of our present line of defence. I was put in command, and Schwartz and myself set to work to restore the forts. I was told that the 5th Regiment would have to defend the position against the Japanese, and I recognized at once that we had not sufficient men. Having carefully calculated the minimum numbers required to hold these works, I arrived at the conclusion that for a more or less successful defence it was necessary to have at least three regiments. (The peninsula was 3 versts across, * with 2 versts of shallow water on either flank, increasing to 8 versts at low tide.)

In front of the position, and 2 versts from it, stood Chin-chou, a town surrounded by an old Chinese wall, 3½ versts in length, and proof against field-artillery fire. It would be extremely difficult to storm the wall in face of artillery fire from the main position, and as also it gave good cover from the enemy's rifle and gun fire, it was decided to occupy

---

* This seems to be underestimated, as the Official History gives 4,400 yards as the breadth of the position. The author evidently means that at low water the *whole* breadth of the peninsula was 8 versts, which agrees with other accounts.

GUN-PITS.

the town as an advanced post. It did, in fact, cover
the front of the position, and it would be a difficult
matter to attack the heights beyond without having
first taken it. The state of affairs became, however,
more complicated, as at least two companies were
necessary for the defence of the town, thus leaving
us only nine companies for the main position.

We were ordered to defend ourselves to the last
drop of blood. When I told General Fock of the
difficulty of defending the position with one regiment,
which was not even up to full strength, he replied :
" Do you know, if I were in your place, I should say
to my commanding officer : ' Leave me only two
companies, and I shall know better how to die with
them than with a whole regiment.' " From this I
concluded that, instead of a successful defence, he
had some other object in view, the nature of which
I could not then fathom.

It was, in fact, impossible to defend this position
successfully. The enemy's fleet could make an
appearance on both flanks and at the rear. Our
opponent, moreover, had vastly superior numbers,
and his batteries eventually spread out in a circle
which commanded the crowded mass of our guns on
the Nan Shan heights, while the absence of a sufficient
number of bomb-proofs and cover for reserves completed the difficulties of the position of the defenders.
We built field bakeries, and dug wells on the position,
and, as the possibility of a landing in our rear was
realized, we were ordered to fortify the rear as well
as the front, which is really saying that the position
assumed the nature of a fortress.

I had indicated the position lying immediately

to the south of the Nan Shan position as being an incomparably better one. On it we could have met the enemy, while he was in the act of filing across the isthmus, on a broad front and with a numerous and well-placed artillery, our flanks on this position being protected from any action on the part of the enemy's fleet. General Kholodovski's idea, however, prevailed, perhaps because the work needed to carry it out was almost completed (they did not realize that to restore the fortifications and to build new ones was practically one and the same thing). Be this as it may, the constant talk about the Nan Shan position had made it so popular, that for many its very name became a "mascot." The view and field of fire from it were certainly splendid, and I took good care to see that the defenders should feel that the position could be successfully held, and satisfied myself that they felt confident of their capability to do so.

Continuing incessantly to fortify the position, the 5th Regiment watched the shore 30 versts to the north by mounted and infantry Scout detachments, sometimes employing the regular companies on this service. We received orders every day by wire to be on the alert and to watch for a landing, and I did everything possible to prevent being taken by surprise. Half of the mounted detachment I sent to Pi-tzu-wo, the most likely point for a landing, and all the mounted scouts of the 14th Regiment were sent to the same locality to watch the coast. A section of a company, under an officer, and ten mounted scouts were sent to Godzarlin * to watch

* On the Pi-tzu-wo road, but not shown on map.

Terminal Point. In Kerr Bay and Deep Bay was Lieutenant Vaseeliev with the 1st Infantry Scout Detachment, and ten mounted scouts, and on a headland in Sulivan Bay a post of twenty-five sharp-shooters and six mounted scouts, while the shores of Chin-chou Bay were guarded by the men occupying the town. From Godzarlin up to the position I had distributed a flying post of the 2nd half of the Mounted Scouts, ten of whom I kept with me for orderly duties.

At this time the regiment was disposed as follows : in the town of Chin-chou, the 10th Company under Major Goosov, the 3rd Scout Detachment under Captain Koudriavtsev, and a mixed force of sixty men under Lieutenant Golenko, an officer who had distinguished himself against the Hunhutzes. The 3rd Company occupied the village of Lu-chia-tun, in front of the centre of the position, while the 2nd Company was in the village of Ma-chia-tun, in front of the right flank, and the 6th Company in the village of Ssu-chia-tun, behind the left flank, the remainder being quartered behind the centre of the position. Major Schwartz, with about a dozen men, was quartered in some shelters in the centre of the position. All the regimental and officers' baggage was stored near the position and in Port Arthur. Lieutenant-Colonel Eremeiev, who had voluntarily joined the regiment from the reserve, and whom I had personally known at the Academy and the Engineer College, I appointed commandant of the town.

As soon as the men of the regiment had settled down in their various quarters, work on the position was pushed forward with feverish haste. Every day thousands of Chinese * and soldiers worked at it; they brought up building material, constructed obstacles, dug wells, and the soldiers concurrently underwent musketry and field training; and all this at a time when we expected a landing every moment either in front or in rear. As the regiment might have to withstand a regular siege, we set to work to make splinter-proofs for storing food, supplies, and small-arm ammunition, though the means at our disposal were very limited. We had in hand no more than 60,000 roubles, and so we only made two splinter-proofs, neither of them remarkably long or broad, and began the construction of four wells without, however, much hope of finding water. The cold weather hampered us sadly. The soil was frozen hard, and our shovels and picks, of which we only had a limited supply, kept on breaking. The companies occupying the town, too, worked hard at putting it also into a state of defence. It was proposed to strengthen the existing caponiers and the corners of the town wall, and to build bomb-proofs for the protection of the reserves against splinters.

The enemy was evidently waiting for something, and we felt more secure every day. We improvised an entertainment hall from one of the barrack rooms, decorated it as well as we could, and put a gramophone in it; hence our dinners and suppers went off in right merry style. We used to get a lot of people coming out to see the position, and gladly received them, as we got news from them of what

---

* Official accounts state that as many as 5,000 Chinese coolies were employed.

was going on in the outside world. Of course, one could not be sure that the information was exactly correct, but, such as it was, it generally emanated from the staff. The majority of our informants held the opinion that we should never see a shot fired, and that the whole action of the war would be limited to sea fighting and the occupation of the southern part of Korea by the Japanese, as the latter could never raise more than 300,000 men, and, when our battleships had been repaired, we should smash up their fleet and they would have to make terms. No one doubted that our fleet *would* destroy the Japanese navy, because our naval commanders were more active than the Japanese, our sailors infinitely better at gunnery, and, finally, our ships' armour was very much stronger, as it was " annealed." * Our naval experts told us all this. No attention whatever was paid to the fact that the Japanese had five first-class battleships while we had only two, † and that torpedo craft, of which the Japanese possessed a hundred, had not yet proved their full power of independent action. Our informants did not say how they had come by their knowledge, but they always laid particular stress on the bravery of our sailors.

" Never mind if you do see drunken sailors on shore, nor how rudely officers may answer to any

---

* As a fact the armour of the Japanese ships built in England was as good as any of its date, all of it being hardened in accordance with modern processes.

† General Tretyakov was evidently still under the impression that three Russian battleships had been *blown up*. The Russians had in reality four first-class battleships still unharmed—*Petropavlovsk, Pobieda, Poltava,* and *Peresviet.*

remark addressed to them—on shore ; on their ships they cultivate an iron discipline."

If any one stated that the Japanese fleet was considerably stronger than ours, our tellers of fairy tales would contemptuously answer, especially if the individual was a naval man : " A lot you know ! Why do you think the Government refused to buy the *Nisshin* and *Kasuga* from Argentina ? Because we are strong enough without them ; otherwise they would not have refused such a purchase." And we listeners, satisfied with such arguments, were quickly laughing and joking and telling stories. I always sat at the head of the table, and it was a pleasure to me to listen to the stories and watch the happy faces of those round me, many of whom felt no forebodings then of the destiny awaiting them.

While fortifying the position we made some experiments on the effect of rifle fire directed against targets sheltered by loopholed parapets, as compared with that against targets in the open. It always happened that at a range of 200 yards the effect was considerably greater against loopholed targets, while at longer ranges the latter suffered most. Since, in addition, we ran the risk of hostile shrapnel, we also experimented with this type of fire, and found that 20 rounds at a range of 1 verst put out of action half the defenders of the earthwork, when they stood in the open on the glacis. It was therefore decided to make loopholes everywhere and to provide the detachments with plank overhead cover, which, with General Fock's approval, was carried out on the succeeding days.

Senior officers frequently visited the position.

General Kondratenko came out before we started working, and said that we must occupy the town as strongly as possible. Generals Fock and Nadyein were frequently with us, sometimes staying two or three days. General Fock talked a great deal with the officers, giving his opinion on the way of defending the position and ground in front of it. He thought of meeting the enemy in front of the position, near the villages lying to the north of Mount Sampson, and we often went out reconnoitring with him, and thoroughly studied the ground, but though he insisted on the necessity of fortifying it, we had no means of doing so. The general, it seems, had not told off the regiments of his own division to any work. Only the 5th Regiment continued working, and the nearer the time of our meeting with the enemy approached, the further advanced and stronger became our field works. Judging from what I heard from superior officers, it was *not* intended to defend the Nan Shan position stubbornly ; hence they would not let us have enough money for its fortification, and they sent up no artillery. But the closer our meeting with the enemy impended, the more I became convinced that the position *would* be stubbornly defended.

From certain remarks of General Fock it seemed as if it was not necessary to make a stubborn defence. The general, for instance, once said to me : " You know that less heroism is required to defend this position than to retreat from it. Those who do not understand the true position of affairs are beginning to call General Fock a traitor ! "

Indeed, it was impossible not to fear a landing of the Japanese in rear of the position simultaneously with a landing at Pi-tzu-wo, and this was so obvious that the position was ordered to be fortified in rear. The regiment was in a bad way, and I felt downhearted at not being able to carry out many of General Fock's suggestions as to the fortification of the position and the means of defending it.

Attaching great importance to the grazing effect of shell, General Fock insisted that the defensive line should be continued right down to the foot of the Nan Shan Hills. Without making a single exception, without taking into consideration that the slopes of the hills were long and gentle, and served as a most difficult obstacle to an attacker, and also completely losing sight of the fact that by carrying our trenches down to the foot of the hills we exposed our companies to fire from the opposite hills, and thus assisted the attackers, he stuck to his point and insisted on our extending our line to a total frontage of 8 versts. In speaking of them, he called our top tier of trenches "swallows' nests," and always added: "You, of course, are glad to put your regiment right up under the sky!" I at once pointed out to the general that he had completely ignored the fact that the heights formed a natural and difficult obstacle to pass, that every inequality in the ground below (of which there were many) gave the enemy cover from our fire, and that shot bursting on graze would not have any effect; that we had only one regiment with which to defend the position, and that we ought to make our dispositions with due regard to this unpleasant circumstance. Upon this, General Fock lost his temper, exclaiming that only traitors placed their men under the artillery fire of the enemy, and that the intervals between men in trenches should be 20 paces, or certainly not less than 10 paces, and then there would be no swallows' nests for them to occupy. I answered that if we should place our unseasoned troops, the majority of whom were recruits and reservists, at 20-paces interval, each one would feel himself isolated and thrown out before an advancing foe without any support, and it might prove that in the moment of need he would be without the moral support of his commander. At the same time I did not lose the opportunity of saying that we had but eleven companies in the regiment, and that if they were spread out over a frontage of 8 versts I should have a very weak line of defence, liable to be broken through at the slightest pressure, and if I were to keep only one company in reserve, which was absolutely indispensable, I should then have a large gap in the line absolutely unoccupied; was a stubborn defence possible under these circumstances? Of course, I understood that General Fock, by throwing his firing line well forward, wished to lessen their losses from the enemy's rifle and shrapnel fire. Granted, this was important, and was quite feasible at the beginning of the battle. If I had had only a few reserves with which to strengthen threatened points, I should have had nothing to urge against the 20-paces interval even. But there were no reserves told off for the 5th Regiment, although General Nadyein told me that I should be supported, and that the 15th Regiment would be posted near Ta-fang-shen * ; but when

---

* The 13th, 14th, and 15th Regiments were actually posted in rear of the 5th during the battle, but did little to support it.

2

I asked him, "Then, when they are needed, I can use them?" he said: "You want to command a whole division then, do you?" On the whole, therefore, the plan of action at Nan Shan was not very plain to me. One thing was at length clear—I had it from General Kondratenko—that we must defend the position to our last drop of blood, and to this end I prepared both officers and men. We began to make field kitchens in the trenches; we brought up provisions to the position and put them in bomb-proofs, cleared the ground for bivouacking in places covered from the enemy's fire, and built shelters for the men in the trenches themselves and in the fortifications.

The enemy made no sign, the weather was splendid, and we peacefully continued our work of constructing cover from shrapnel fire and of preparing obstacles.

From the end of February the enemy's ships constantly appeared in Deep and Kerr Bays; luckily we had already set up a telephone there and connected it with the Naval Observing Station, of which the gallant and enterprising Naval Lieutenant Ditchmann held charge. There was a certain amount of firing from the Japanese ships and an attempt to land from one of their gunboats, but our men drove them off. In view of this, the scouts under Lieutenant Kragelski were reinforced by the addition of some mounted scouts under Lieutenant Sietchko, and on March 7 Major Stempnevski (jun.), with the 7th Company, was sent to Kerr Bay. Two mountain guns, under Lieutenant Naoomov, were sent with the 7th Company. This detachment was formed from the 5th Regiment; the horses were taken from the transport, the guns we had brought with us from China, and the drivers were our own men, but the officers and gun detachments were sent out from Port Arthur.

General Nadyein wished to acquaint himself personally with the position of affairs in the two bays, and on March 23 I accompanied him to Kerr Bay. While still some way off, we saw three large Japanese ships and five destroyers. On arriving we found the 7th Company and our two guns on the position. They were so disposed as to be able to sweep the entrance to Kerr Bay and to oppose the enemy's advance if he effected a landing on the end of the Ta-ku Shan Peninsula, where we had two weak advanced posts. The Japanese shells pitched as far up as the ravine behind which the company had taken cover, and the Japanese gunners fired even on single individuals if they exposed themselves for a moment.

We were told that our artillery (two small 32-mm. guns forming the section under the command of Naoomov) had done some excellent practice on the enemy's destroyers, which had consequently retreated from the bay. General Nadyein came to the conclusion that the enemy intended to land in the bay, and gave me some orders in case this should prove to be the case. It was 12 versts from the bay to the position, and 24 to the end of the Ta-ku Shan Peninsula. In the event of a landing, I was to support the 7th Company and the scout detachments with a battalion. If, however, they had wished to force a landing in considerable strength, the whole of the 5th Regiment would not have been able to prevent it.   To oppose a landing is a very difficult business, and here the rugged coast added considerably to the difficulties of the defender.   The bays cut right into the coast-line, and the hills made inter-communication exceedingly difficult.   Having enticed the defenders to some point off the shore by a small feint landing, or by threatening a landing in force, the attacker could, in a quarter of an hour, make a sudden rush from another point, where he could then land without any opposition on the part of the regiment defending the shore.   For this reason we did not hope to prevent a landing, but thought that the defence of the position would considerably delay the enemy's advance on Port Arthur.

More than all I feared a landing in Dalny Bay, which was eminently suited for such an enterprise. Such a landing would divide the strength of the garrison, and would free the enemy from the necessity of an attack on the Nan Shan position.   Under cover of the great guns of the fleet a landing was possible at all places where the depth of water was sufficient for the large ships to come in close enough for effective gun fire.

Having inspected the bay and the detachment, we, accompanied by shots from large naval guns, returned to the position untouched.   On the following day the 7th Company and scout detachments beat back a small attempt at a landing, for which the officers were recommended for high orders, which, however, they never received.   Lieutenant Ditchmann sank one of the enemy's ships ; I myself went to Kerr Bay and saw two masts projecting from the sea.

About this time, *i.e.* March 24, the Nan Shan position was armed with artillery, and we awaited the enemy with light hearts, thinking that our artillery, consisting of 56-mm. and 6-in. short guns, were superior to the enemy's field pieces. When, however, we continued to complain that one regiment was insufficient for defending the whole position, our commanders reassured us by saying that the enemy would not attack the position from all sides at once, but would choose one special point for the assault. I did not ask for explanations, as this view appeared to be sound enough. About April 2 General Smirnov came out, and, in a fearful rain-storm, inspected the whole position ; he seemed surprised that the position was fortified to the south as well. I explained to him that we anticipated an attack from the rear, as the enemy could land behind Dalny. Having told me that I must construct a large redoubt behind the position, in order to cover a retreat, the general went to Dalny.

On the night of May 4 one of our scouts came up with a report from Major Pavlovski that a Japanese squadron had appeared north of Terminal Point,* and was landing an army. On the morning of the 5th, it was reported that a Japanese fleet of thirty-nine transports, † covered by three large warships, one of which flew the Admiral's flag, was landing troops near the mouth of the Ta-scha River, and in a bay to the north ; about a battalion was said to have already landed. We immediately reported

---

* See Note 3 at end of book.

† See Official History, Part II., p. 11. This news must have come from some of Colonel Rantsov's cossacks.

this to higher authority, whereupon the regiment occupied its positions and did not leave them day or night.

Captain Andreievski was ordered to watch the movements of the enemy closely, and from this time forth to the end of the siege our mounted corps were in touch with the Japanese. A large force, with cavalry and guns, had been disembarked, and soon after we received a telegram to the effect that a landing had also taken place near Pi-tzu-wo.

On the night of May 5 three wounded men of the Mounted Scout Detachment, two of the 14th Regiment, and one of ours, were brought in. The enemy had sent out his magnificently mounted cavalry from the eastern to the western shore towards the railway. It was said that a battalion, to which had been added a mounted scout detachment, with which we never obtained touch, had detrained at Shih-san-li-tai station, having come from General Kuropatkin's army.

General Fock decided to make a reconnaissance in force, as nobody knew the exact strength of the troops which had landed. The enemy's cavalry, in very considerable numbers, strengthened by infantry and Hunhutzes,* completely screened from us the landing points and the early movements of the Japanese. It was reported that they were moving towards Shih-san-li-tai, and that their landing place had been strongly fortified.

Towards evening on May 8 all the regiments

* It seems unlikely that any of these marauding bands were assisting the Japanese. It must be remembered that the Russians had no good word for the Japanese at this time.

of the division, except the 15th which was with Stessel in Port Arthur, and I with my two battalions, moved out along the road leading towards the place of the landing, and all had to pass the night in positions detailed to them along that road. Having reached their allotted destinations, the regiments received further orders to continue their night march, the object of which was, apparently, to sweep the stretch of country to the southeast of Shih-san-li-tai station (this operation was termed "Manœuvre" in the order). The enemy, in unknown strength, was somewhere between Changchia-tun and Shih-san-li-tai. Up to the time our regiments had occupied their positions, our scouts had reported nothing trustworthy about the enemy, and I expected to meet them every minute. The 5th Regiment, like all the others probably, was ordered: "At 1 a.m. to move from its bivouacs and be at dawn at height No. so-and-so." I did not know what to do; all our maps had the names of the villages defaced, the contours were scarcely marked, none of the heights of the various hills were given, and how to find, at night, a certain unknown height No. so-and-so, which might be a good 10 versts from where we were, was too much for me. I must add, too, that we had no guides with us; no amount of money could buy them. So I repaired to General Fock with my doubts. The staff had already settled down to sleep, and fatigue and the certainty of the forthcoming battle had made them all very irritable. Be it said, however, to the honour of the staff, they realized fully the difficulties of the night march, and an order was sent out immediately, postponing the time of the advance until 3 a.m., when they knew that the dawn would just begin to break, forgetting, however, that the dawn comes very quickly, and that it is quite dark till just before the sun actually rises. It was decided that the chief of the staff would himself guide the leading column. Returning to my staff, I gave the necessary orders, and tried to get some sleep, but I could not, as one alarming thought followed upon another. Should we succeed in reaching height No. so-and-so ? What if the enemy suddenly fell upon our rear from Chang-chia-tun, or our flank from Shih-san-li-tai, or the surrounding country (all was quite possible) ? It was doubtful if we could make good our retreat to our positions at Nan Shan, the more so, as the road from Chang-chia-tun to Chin-chou had been left absolutely unprotected by us. These thoughts were justifiable in view of the fact that the enemy had landed from forty transports north of Terminal Point, under our very noses, and, supposing there was a battalion in each, that meant forty battalions to our eleven or twelve.

At 2 a.m. I got up. Every one was sound asleep. Reaching the men's bivouacs, I saw them served out with a pound of meat and a large quantity of bread ; they had no tea, as orders had been given that fires were not to be lighted, and from this it was clear that General Fock expected a brush with the enemy. About 3 a.m. the battalions stood to arms, but, as it happened, there was some delay, and the chief of the staff did not turn up until 5 o'clock, when we at last made a start.

LIEUT.-COLONEL BIELOZOR, KILLED AT THE BATTLE OF NAN SHAN.

[p. 25

I was put in command of a detachment consisting
of the two battalions of the 5th Regiment and a
battery under Lieutenant-Colonel Romanovski. We
started off well enough, but the trouble was that the
horse of the chief of the staff was a particularly good
one, and the column fell considerably behind him ;
the country was very intersected and covered by a
regular network of roads, and very bad ones at that.
The chief of the staff, leading the way with his map,
forgot to leave guides at the cross-roads, the result
being that the column stopped when it came to a
cross-road, not knowing which direction to take.
We lost a lot of time owing to these halts, but we
nevertheless preserved the right direction. (I do
not mention the order of march, as that was as usual :
skirmishers, advanced guard with mounted scouts,
and main body.)

To the north and north-west was our screen of
scouts, and as they constantly showed themselves on
the skyline we kept wondering: "Are not these
the enemy's scouts ? "   Two hours had already passed
since we started, and we had gone down into a wide
valley, when Lieutenant-Colonel Bielozor, commanding the 2nd Battalion, came up to me and drew my
attention to the peculiar movements of our artillery.
Instead of following us, it had moved off to a height
lying on the left flank of our line of march ; behind
it was a chain of skirmishers from the rear of our
column, and behind this line compact companies.
Not understanding its doings, I galloped up to the
battery, and in the midst of the moving columns,
unaccompanied by his staff, I saw General Fock.
I had hardly got up to him, when he shouted to me :

"What kind of a company commander have you got? See how he lets that battery get in front of him; he is a perfect fool! Such officers are a curse to us!" I answered that I would overtake the company at once, but I wished to know what was happening, as the battery under my command was going off somewhere, and I had not been informed of it. "That is its right position," answered the general, pointing to the hill the artillery were making for. "Then we are going to stop there?" "No," replied General Fock; "we are going on farther under cover of this battery."

I then saw that, far ahead of the battery, our dense columns were advancing, apparently attacking some one. The regiment advancing on the left of my column had sent out a line of skirmishers to the flank on one side of our advance, and I learnt that they had noticed a hostile column in a hollow on our left flank. It turned out that this was a company of that regiment which had advanced on Shih-san-li-tai from the south, and occupied the position covering Chin-chou from the Shih-san-li-tai side.

"Form a reserve for the attackers, and with one company occupy the hill towards which the head of your column is moving," ordered General Fock. I galloped off to comply with this order.

This advance went on for an hour. We occupied a succession of positions, but it was very noticeable that our men did not take full advantage of the ground, but rather tried not to lose touch with each other. It was all right when the officers were actually keeping them together, but what would happen when they were not there to do so? Our men are

not accustomed to act on their own initiative, and
a long skirmishing line does not permit of the officers
directing their men by voice and example. It was
lucky that we were the defenders and not the
attackers!

While occupied with these thoughts, I heard the
" assembly " sounded by our buglers; our men
remained where they were, but the commanders
hurried off to the general, who had called them by
this signal. The enemy had not been encountered;
he was at Chang-chia-tun, or perhaps to the north
of Shih-san-li-tai. The operation had been thought
out in great detail by the general. For me it was
remarkable in that we had manœuvred under the
enemy's very nose, while contemptuously leaving
him also in the rear. After a short halt we returned
to the position with the men singing loudly. *

After this expedition we received an order which
brought home to me the exactness with which General
Fock gauged the situation. His directions were
clear and fully conformed to the real state of affairs.
Here are some characteristic paragraphs of the order:
" God save us from those commanders who wait
for orders in the heat of battle: they won't
get any given them, so let them get that idea out
of their heads." Or: " I ask all company and battalion commanders, as soon as they meet the enemy,
to raise their heads, open their eyes, and keep their
ears shut. Believe me, your eyes are everything: your
ears won't help you much, though, unfortunately,
this is not a generally accepted idea. Even an old

* The Russian soldiers invariably sing on the march, when the
band is not playing.

captain of twenty-two years' service will, during manœuvres, begin to prick up his ears like a hare so as to catch some order from his commander; but his commander is dead, or is himself engaged with something else." These golden rules are worthy of a place in every book on tactics, and in all regulations on the general direction of an action.

Immediately after our return our scouts brought us news that the enemy was near Shih-san-li-tai station in small numbers, and massed on the shores of the bay, a little to the south of Chang-chia-tun. This was about May 11, and from this time onward our scouts had daily skirmishes with the enemy.

General Fock remained true to his decision to meet the enemy in front of the Nan Shan position. We only roughly knew the enemy's strength, so he decided to carry out another reconnaissance in force, and again moved his forces forward to the villages of Chang-chia-tun and Shih-san-li-tai, and thus blocked the line of the enemy's advance southward along the Pu-lan-tien and Nan Shan road. All the regiments of the 4th Rifle Division, except the 15th, were employed; our eight companies were in the advanced guard; the 3rd and 4th at Shih-san-li-tai, and the 6th and 8th, and the 3rd Scout Detachment at Chang-chia-tun, our 3rd Battalion being placed in the interval between these two detachments. The positions to be occupied by us were well studied beforehand. The companies moved out and took up their positions. On the night of May 15, and the morning of the 16th, other troops with guns moved off, two batteries were placed near the railway bridge on the road to Pi-tzu-wo, and one (Romanovski's) with the regimental half-battery under Second-Lieutenant Sadykov on the hills above Shih-san-li-tai. After our battalions had occupied their positions an order came from General Fock that our 3rd Battalion, under the command of Colonel Dounin, was to return to the position. In order not to give the enemy a chance of working round behind us, I was ordered to move the 7th Company and the scout detachment with Lieutenant Naoomov's two guns through the space between the shore of Kerr Bay and Mount Sampson to the old Chinese fortifications, and to form half the 9th Company as a reserve to the 7th, but I myself was left on the position with three companies.

At daybreak on May 16 I went to Battery No. 13,* and had an excellent view of the engagement † and the movements of our troops. Our companies and guns were already in position on the left flank. The other regiments were moving round towards the foot of Mount Sampson in a south-westerly direction, and the head of the column had just reached the hill, when heavy rifle fire broke out, and Lieutenant-Colonel Romanovski's and the bullock battery on the left began to speak. In five minutes the fire of these batteries had become awful, and thick smoke completely hid them from my view (this smoke was caused by bursting Japanese shells). After half an hour, when the tail of our main column had

* Battery No. 13 is situated in rear of the centre of the Nan Shan position.

† In our Official History (Part II.) this action is briefly described as an engagement with General Nadyein's rearguard, but it is evident that two separate reconnaissances were made on May 8 and 16 respectively, and that no rearguard was left as indicated in that report.

passed Mount Sampson, the batteries on the right
flank opened fire. Firing continued for an hour
from both flanks, and we followed the course of the
fight most intently. I was very much afraid that
the enemy would try to get round our rear, but the
7th Company was silent, and its commander reported
that no movement was noticeable in his front. The
fire on the left flank began to slacken, and carts
and stretchers were seen moving from that direction.
Half an hour later I noticed Romanovski's battery
on the road from Shih-san-li-tai, followed by our
bullock battery, both moving towards us at a
walk. An orderly from the left flank came up
and reported that we were retreating, but he had
not seen the Japanese infantry, having only observed
that the Japanese had swept our battery with shells,
thereby silencing it and compelling it to retreat behind the hill. At the same moment that the batteries
on the left flank moved, I saw that the reserves
had occupied a shoulder of Mount Sampson facing
the village of Shih-san-li-tai. Dense lines of skirmishers quietly lay on the crest of this ridge, allowing
the guns, and subsequently the skirmishers of our left
flank, to pass through them. From this I concluded
that the enemy was pressing our right and that
General Fock thought that we could not hold our
ground, and had, therefore, strengthened his left
flank, which had, so far, not been assailed by the
Japanese. After another hour had passed, our
retreating lines came into view from behind Mount
Sampson, and the guns near the railway bridge
opened a terrific fire. The rifle and gun fire behind
Mount Sampson continued, now weaker, now

stronger, till at last the lines of reserves, passing through the left flank, quickly collected and began to retreat on our position. I expected to see the Japanese in pursuit, but none appeared. At last the batteries on the right flank retired and our companies followed in their wake, but still the Japanese did not pursue. It was now that I saw a picture of a truly wonderful retreat, in which our men marched in column as at manœuvres. The left flank had already reached our position, when General Nadyein came in wounded in the hand, and Lieutenant-Colonel Romanovski with a wound in the leg. The situation naturally gave rise to a good deal of questioning and surmise. It appears that Second-Lieutenant Sadykov, who commanded our bullock battery, had himself gone to the assistance of Lieutenant-Colonel Romanovski and commanded his half-battery to the end of the engagement.

CHAPTER II

Further account of the actions at Chang-chia-tun and Shih-san-li-tai—
Preliminary skirmishes round Chin-chou—The battle of Nan Shan,
May 26, 1904.

OUR regiments went on to Ta-fang-shen, while the
enemy's troops found themselves facing the Nan Shan
position, all ready and prepared to meet them with
a hail of shell and bullets. However, they did not
show themselves as yet, and everything retained
its usual aspect. On the night of May 17 it was
reported at the advanced posts that the enemy had
occupied the pass near the railway bridge and was
forcing back our advanced detachments with small
bodies of infantry, a cross fire being kept up all
that night. Next, a report came in from the left
flank to the effect that the enemy was pressing the
outpost line on that side ; in proof of which a few
wounded were brought in. It thus became evident
that the Japanese were drawing closer round the
Nan Shan position. Reports received in the morning made it clear that the Japanese had occupied
all the heights lying in front of the Nan Shan position
and were engaged in fortifying themselves on them.
We could not, however, see any definite signs of
them, as they were careful not to venture out from
the shelter of the hills in front, save that towards

midday we were able to locate earthworks on
the hill near Shih-san-li-tai about 7 versts from
our position. On closer examination we discerned
certain works somewhat nearer, which were without
doubt infantry trenches, and on which our long-
range guns immediately opened fire. Our shells
did not reach the more distant line, but at once
succeeded in stopping work on the nearer trenches.
Fire on the enemy's works was kept up, off and on,
all that day.

In view of the fact that one regiment was insufficient to defend the whole position, as well as the
ground lying to the front of it, I asked General Fock
to send me two infantry scout detachments from the
13th and 14th Regiments. My request being granted,
the outpost line, on the following night, consisted
of four infantry detachments and one mounted. All
this night a cross fire was kept up with the Japanese
posts, which pressed our men so hard that I had to
strengthen the line on the right flank by a half-
company (supplied by No. 2 Company). Our
outpost line ran as follows : from the shores of Chin-
chou Bay to the town wall of Chin-chou, with patrols
out to some distance in advance of the wall, from
the town to Nan Shan railway station, and from there
to Hand Bay. During the night the Japanese drove
us out of the old Chinese fortifications beyond Kerr
Bay, inflicting some losses—a few killed and many
wounded. Our opponents threw out such a strong
screen that our men were not able to penetrate it at
any point so as to see what they were doing behind,
and, as we were thus left in complete ignorance as
to their numbers and dispositions, I had to be guided

3

by the knowledge gained at the time of the action of Chang-chia-tun, which information I cannot do better than give in the words of Lieutenant-Colonel Saifoolin, who commanded a portion of our right flank, and from whom I had the following story of the engagement :

" Our companies were disposed in the following order : I, with the 8th Company, occupied a hill near a ruined tower on the left side of the nullah along which runs the road to Godzarlin ; the 6th Company occupied the crest on the right side of this nullah ; and the 3rd Scout Detachment, under Captain Koudriavtsev, occupied a hill on the extreme right flank of the line and somewhat in front of the 6th Company. The mounted scouts were sent out in front as skirmishers. Hardly had day broken, when our scouts reported that the enemy was moving in considerable force along the road from Godzarlin and nearer ; following hard upon this report there came in view, in front of out right flank, dense Japanese lines, with their left flank resting on Mount Sampson, and firing commenced at once at very long range. The enemy did not hurry in his advance, but developed such a terrific rifle fire that a great number of our men were placed *hors de combat.* Not having any companies in reserve, I sent for help to a battalion of the 14th Regiment, which was formed up in our rear, and one company of this battalion (commanded by Suvorov), posted by itself behind our right flank, started to move up to us, but halted and commenced firing without joining our line. This continued for an hour, during which time the enemy's troops advanced without check

LIEUT.-COLONEL SAIFOOLIN, COMMANDING 2ND BATTALION, 5TH
REGIMENT.

p. 34]

until they were 400 paces, or less, from our scouts and the 6th Company; their strength being about fifteen companies. Meanwhile about forty Japanese companies were turning our left flank. Our losses in the 6th Company and among the scouts were already considerable. In the former the commander was wounded and the sergeant-major and thirty men were killed; while of the latter about one-half were *hors de combat*, including the commander. Not seeing any sign of reinforcements, we sent to ask what was to be done. At this time the enemy began to turn our right flank also. No one came to our assistance, our companies were melting away, and the enemy was continuing to advance. I gave the order to retire, and, under a terrific fire, we got back almost to the railway bridge, where our artillery covered us, opening such a deadly fire on the enemy's lines that they came to a standstill and then took cover in the folds of the ground. The order was then given for a general retreat, whereupon we retired behind the town and ultimately to the main position."

At Shih-san-li-tai, on the left flank, a fearful artillery fight took place with rather disastrous results for us. In Romanovski's battery all the officers were put out of action, and he himself was wounded, as were also nearly all the men of the gun detachments, so that there was no one to bring up ammunition, and volunteers from the 3rd Company had to be called for. Things reached such a pass that Romanovski himself loaded a gun; the adjutant of the brigade, who had been sent off with an order, was killed by a shell. But the enemy not being strong in infantry on that flank, did not press an advance, so that our losses in the 12th Company were only four men, and in the 3rd but a few more.*

There seems to have been some misunderstanding about this retreat. The following day I went to the divisional headquarters with my report, and, while there, General Fock sent for General Nadyein, who commanded the detachment engaged at Shih-san-li-tai.†

" Why did you retire ? " said General Fock, turning to him.

" On your order, your Excellency," replied General Nadyein.

" What order ? I never gave any order."

General Nadyein thereupon produced a note, signed by Lieutenant-Colonel Romanovski, in which it was clearly stated that General Fock had himself ordered the retreat. Lieutenant-Colonel Romanovski, having been sent for, stated that General Fock had actually ordered him to write the note. General Fock was quite at a loss to understand this, but gave orders that for the future, on important occasions, only orders signed by him in person were to be obeyed.

On May 21 General Stessel came out to the position. He was apparently very dissatisfied with the result of the late engagement, and when he heard that Major Gomsiakov, the commander of the 6th Company, had been left wounded on the field of

* In Part II. of the Official History (p. 43, par. 2) the estimated losses were 150 officers and men killed and wounded. For the Russian estimate, see following page.

† The Official History gives General Nadyein as the commander during the battle, but General Fock himself conducted the action, General Nadyein being in command of the left flank.

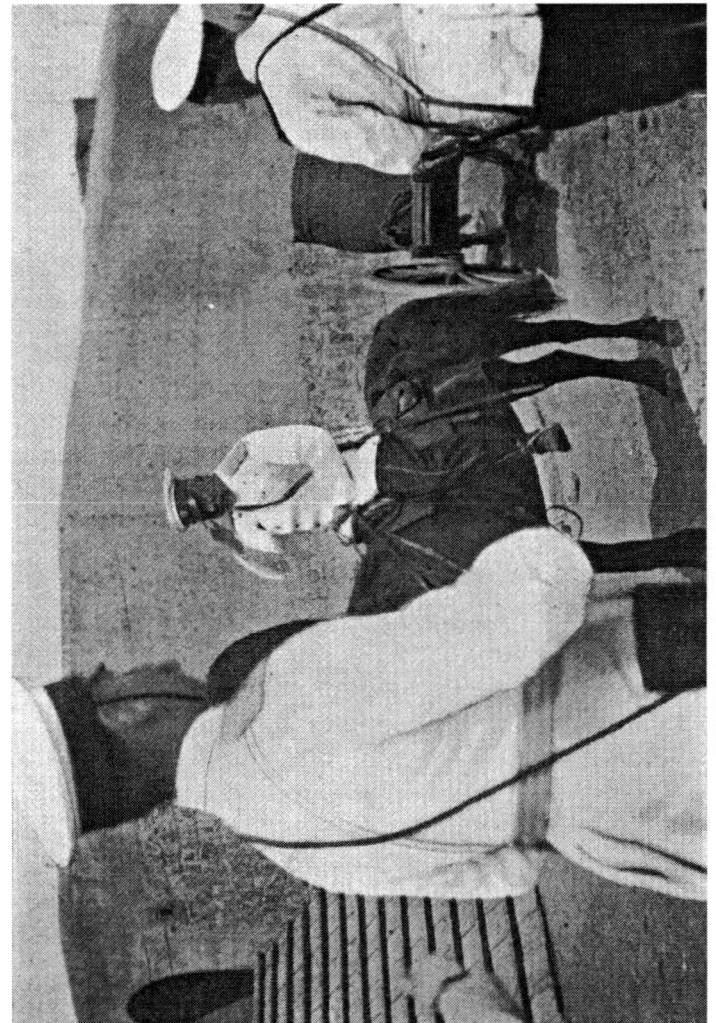

GENERAL STESSEL, INSPECTING ONE OF THE FORTS.

p 36.]

battle, his displeasure knew no bounds ; he addressed the 6th Company in severe terms, removed the next senior officer, Captain Sichev, from the command of the company, and said that he was not to be recommended for any reward.

As a matter of fact, neither the company nor the officer was at all deserving of this rebuke. Major Gomsiakov had been taken away in a Chinese cart, and subsequently a horse had been procured for him on which to ride to the dressing station. Being, however, unable to mount, an ambulance wagon was sent for, but meanwhile he sent back the men who had brought him, saying that they were needed in the firing line, and he awaited the arrival of the wagon with a soldier of the Medical Corps. About this time the retreat commenced, and Major Gomsiakov gave his sword to the man and told him to go away, saying : " You can't help me, and if you remain they will kill you, and perhaps they want you in your company." Major Gomsiakov was taken prisoner by the Japanese, and died from his wounds.

The engagements at Shih-san-li-tai and Changchia-tun cost us about 100 men in killed and wounded.

Having inspected the position, General Stessel went on to Chin-chou, which was already being attacked by the enemy from the northern side. When we rode into the gates bullets had begun to whistle along the streets, but the general, having gone as far as the old Chinese temple, turned back and reached the position again without hurt.

Our men slept in the trenches and batteries, the outpost line consisting of a screen of scouts and a line of sentries detailed from the companies occupying the trenches. I dreaded a night attack, which might very well be successful owing to our lack of defenders, and I was the more afraid because the enemy did not hurry himself, but seemed to be minutely studying the defences. We thus had to be keenly on the alert.

Early in the morning of May 22 we heard heavy rifle fire opening under the walls of the town.* We could not see the enemy from the position, but the town commandant informed me by telephone that the Japanese were preparing for an assault. I had no fear of the town being taken, since we had 400 men there and had filled sixty sand-bags with powder ready to explode when the enemy got close to the walls. Besides this, at the request of the commandant, I had reinforced the garrison with half the 9th Company under its commander, Major Sokolov. Though it would be impracticable to take the town without a heavy artillery preparation, it would be quite feasible to pass round it and proceed to attack the adjoining position from the right flank. So we quietly followed the course of the action and watched for targets for our artillery, but none appeared. The first attack on the town was beaten back easily, but the enemy effected a lodgment on the north-western side, where he was completely covered by the town wall from fire from the direction of the position. From this time the rattle of rifle fire round the town did not cease. As an advanced

---

* The attack on Chin-chou here mentioned as taking place on May 22 is not given in any of the official accounts, the first mentioned being that of May 25, which is *also* described here. These two may, however, be one and the same, owing to confusion of dates.

point of the position the town certainly began to fulfil its intended rôle in the operations.

It is a great pity that we did not take steps with a view to the stubborn defence of the Nan Shan position. Even assuming that such determined defence was risky, as the enemy's troops could effect a landing to the south of the position, and so cut us off from Port Arthur, they would, on the other hand, have had to run considerable risk themselves in landing under our very eyes. They had, indeed, already thrown considerable forces against us from the north, and it would, perhaps, have been difficult for them to have sent another force (about two divisions) against the Port Arthur garrison. Therefore, I say with the greatest assurance that, had we decided to defend the Nan Shan position stubbornly and had armed our batteries with heavy guns, supplementing our guns of position with, say, a brigade of field artillery, we should have held the enemy before Nan Shan for a long time and perhaps have compelled him to have recourse to sapping operations. During the time thus gained, the garrison of the fortress would have been enabled to put its works into a better state of defence than that in which they actually were left in consequence of lack of time.

The enemy made constant assaults on the town, but always without success.* Once the Japanese sappers brought up a huge charge of gun-cotton to the gates, but our marksmen killed those who tried to place it, and brought the charge into the town. Continuing his operations, the enemy placed a

* See Official History (Part II., p, 20).

battery on the slopes of the hills overlooking the town, and fortified the heights near Shih-san-li-tai. The care displayed in doing this surprised us. We tried to impede the work by fire, but the range was far too great for our guns.

On the evening of May 22, a 6-inch Schneider-Canet gun was brought on to the position, and I decided to place it in the central redoubt, where it would command the bays on both flanks. Starting at once to get it into its allotted position, a whole company worked day and night on the 23rd and 24th mounting the gun, and on the 25th it was just ready to be placed on its carriage, when a heavy bombardment commenced and greatly hindered the work.

From the time of our retreat from the positions at Shih-san-li-tai and Chang-chia-tun to the Nan Shan position we hardly had a moment's peace; constant small night affairs in the outpost line, and the nightly expectation of a big attack, compelled us to have half our men on the alert. I never once undressed, or took off my boots; messages kept on coming in, and hardly gave me a chance of closing my eyes. Such was the strain that we were quite worn out.

On the morning of the 25th the enemy began a terrific bombardment. We were all at our posts, and replied with heavy artillery fire, suffering, however, little damage during this bombardment; none of our guns were touched, though it was impossible to work at mounting our big gun of position. We had several hit, including Boochatski, commanding the 11th Company, who was severely wounded.

I must mention an incident with a kite. Why it was brought on to the position, I do not know, as we could observe the movements of the enemy perfectly from the top of our hill, and without incurring the risk of being dashed to the ground. The party who brought it, with Mr. Kourelov, a very brave man, decided to fly it at the very height of the bombardment. The kite reached a great altitude, and, of course, immediately attracted the attention of the Japanese, with the result that a hail of shrapnel burst over the heads of the daring detachment, and, to avoid unnecessary losses, I ordered them to bring the kite down. Thank God ! neither a man of the detachment nor Mr. Kourelov was touched.

The Battle of Nan Shan *

I spent the night of the 25th–26th with my adjutant and orderly officer on Battery No. 13 in a bombproof, which was placed high up, but nevertheless capable of protecting us from the enemy's field-artillery fire. Everything was quiet in the evening, but at about midnight the enemy began to move ; our outposts reported that they heard guns moving, and our posts on the right flank were driven back by advancing infantry. The weather was shocking—it was pouring with rain and there was thunder in the air. Foreseeing that the enemy would make an attack on our right flank and, if successful, would surround the town, and not wishing to make him a present of the four hundred men in it, who were indispensable to me on the position, I sent an order to the commandant, Lieutenant-Colonel Yermeiev, not

* See Map I.

to allow himself to be surrounded, but to retreat from the town on to the position while the southern gates were free, and to man the trenches on our left flank. The enemy attacked the town about 3 a.m., but, being unsuccessful, began to surround it, when the commandant passed out through the south gate and fought his way back to the position. One section, which was late in getting through the gate, jumped down from the wall, a height of 9 feet, and effected its retreat. But in the darkness the men did not reach the positions to which they had been assigned, and, instead of the whole of the 10th Company, only two sections, under Second-Lieutenant Merkoulev, reached the point they had been ordered to defend. The remaining half-company,* under Major Goosov, and half of No. 9 Company, under Major Sokolov, occupied the empty trenches near Redoubt No. 8. Some of the 3rd Scout Detachment occupied the lower tier of trenches of this redoubt, but the majority of them got to their proper positions on the left flank.

Our dispositions were as follows : the 2nd Company held the extreme right flank from No. 2 Redoubt ; the 2nd Scout Detachment was near the railway and in Redoubt No. 1 ; the corner beyond was unoccupied ; the 12th Company was near the quarry, and the 3rd farther on in the trenches ; behind them the 8th and 4th Companies and the 1st Scout Detachment, and the 6th Company in Redoubt No. 8 ; farther behind the ravine were the 5th, 7th, and half the 10th Companies ; and towards the shores of Chin-chou Bay two Scout Detachments of the 13th

---

* A footnote in the Official History states that half the 10th Company was cut off by the Japanese, but evidently this was not so.

MAJOR STEMPNEVSKI (SEN.), COMMANDING 2ND COMPANY,
5TH REGIMENT.

[p. 43

and 14th Regiments were in trenches. Near No. 15
Battery were the 3rd Company 14th Regiment, and a
section of our 7th Company; the ground between
the scout detachments and No. 15 Battery was
absolutely undefended. Four machine guns under
Second-Lieutenant Lobyrev were at the disposal of
the 7th Company on the cliffs near the shore, and
four naval machine guns, under Midshipman Shimanski, were placed behind our 1st Scout Detachment.
The forts inside the position, which could have been
fought individually, and so have increased the ob-
stinacy of the defence, were without defenders : the
central redoubt, Battery No. 13, and many trenches
were absolutely unoccupied for want of men. I had
in the reserve the 11th Company 5th Regiment, and
two companies of the 13th Regiment, while I had
detached the following officers to command sections
of the position : right flank up to No. 1 Battery,
Major Stempnevski ; the centre—12th, 3rd, 8th,
and 4th Companies;—Lieutenant-Colonel Bielozor ;
left flank—6th Company, 1st Scout Detachment,
5th and 7th Companies, and the whole of the left
flank—Lieutenant-Colonel Saifoolin. The artillery
consisted of guns placed in fifteen batteries, as on
Map I. ; No. 1 Battery being armed with eight
8·7-cm. field guns.

From daybreak on the 26th the enemy began to
bombard the position ; and shells flew thick and
fast, more especially on No. 13. When it was light
enough, I looked at the enemy through my glasses.
His batteries extended in an unbroken line from
Chin-chou Bay to Hand Bay, and some batteries—
apparently of heavy guns—stood on the slopes of the

hills behind the town. The enemy did not husband his ammunition. Four gunboats, and perhaps destroyers with them, came close inshore in Chinchou Bay, and two large ships lay near the entrance to the bay in the rear of our position. These ships fired very heavy shell. There was no sign yet of the enemy's infantry, but the gun fire was so terrific as to compel us to retire into our bomb-proofs. Near by stood a bucket of water; being afraid of its being blown to bits, I ordered it to be placed under cover, and one of the men had just reached it, when a shrapnel burst close to him, and the water poured out over the floor, Bombardier Ptooski being wounded in the head, and I myself getting a scratch on my leg. As the shelter was filled with smoke, we found some difficulty in breathing in it, and the majority of us therefore went out into the redoubt. From there I saw the lines of the enemy's skirmishers round our right flank; our 4th and 8th Companies had opened fire, but the lines nevertheless advanced slowly on us, leaving on the ground behind them small black dots. Our fire was apparently very effective; we had not measured all our ranges in vain. At eight o'clock a large ship appeared in the bay on our own right flank; "Well," I thought, "the 2nd Company will be able to reach her." Imagine my joy when I saw that she was firing on the enemy and I recognized our *Bobr*, though, unfortunately, she did not keep up firing for long, but put out to sea again. It was about 9 a.m. when the enemy's skirmishing line was seen near Nan Shan station and behind the mounds close to the nearest villages, right in front of all the companies from the 2nd to the 8th. The rifle fire

resolved itself into one continual rattle and roar. An
orderly from Lieutenant-Colonel Bielozor came to me
with a report, in which he had written as follows :
" The enemy is in front of us and is attacking,
but do you know that there are 700 yards of trenches
near us absolutely unoccupied ? We must have help."
I myself saw that the Japanese were directing
their attack on our 8th Company. The line had
come to a standstill before all the other companies,
so I sent half of the 11th Company to the threatened
point. At this time I had three companies in reserve,
the 11th of my own regiment, and two companies of
the 13th. The enemy's companies got up to the
wire entanglements in front of the 8th and 4th Companies, but, finding their advance barred, they retired
in disorder, taking cover in the folds of the ground and
thence opening a tremendous fire. I was now certain
that we had nothing to fear from the Japanese infantry.
Just then another orderly arrived from Lieutenant-
Colonel Bielozor, asking for immediate reinforcements, but, having already sent him half the 11th
Company, I felt sure that that was sufficient. At
this moment the enemy's skirmishing line in front
of the 2nd Company occupied the southern extremities
of a small village, and as this place afforded excellent
cover, I saw that there was a danger of the enemy
collecting considerable forces behind it and overwhelming the 2nd Company, the more so, as it
was only 400 paces from the village to the
position. On seeing, however, that such an attack
would be taken in flank by the fire of the 2nd Company, I felt somewhat easier. The enemy's infantry
was now spread out round the whole position in a

semicircle, like his artillery, and the crackle of rifle fire was absolutely incessant. Besides this, we saw that the troops composing his right flank had gone down into the water in the Bay of Chin-chou and were effecting a turning movement through the water; but this advance was checked after the lapse of a few moments by our gun and rifle fire (at very long ranges, however). In all probability the men of this column were nearly all killed, as no movement could be detected among the Japanese bodies lying in the water—all were still.* The enemy's skirmishers kept closing in and then again retiring; but meanwhile our men, after beating back the infantry attack, suffered severely from artillery fire. I received word that Lieutenant-Colonel Radetski had been killed.

About eleven o'clock the commander of the 6th Company reported to me that his advanced trench was completely wrecked by artillery fire from the sea and from the front, and that it was impossible to obtain any cover in it. This was grave news. I noticed considerable movement among the enemy's troops before our left flank, and a mass of men began to move from the centre to the left flank. The troops of the enemy's right flank, which had been sitting in the water of Chin-chou Bay for some time, began to move forward. To defend this (left) flank I had: the 7th Company, half of the 10th Company, the larger half of the 3rd Scout Detachment of our regiment (the remainder had retreated into the trenches near No. 8 Redoubt), two Scout Detachments of the 13th and 14th Regiments, under the command of Lieutenants Bandaletov and Roosoi, and near No. 15

* See Note No. 4 at end of book.

Battery the 3rd Company of the 14th Regiment, under Captain Ushakov, with one section of the 7th Company. We had sufficient men to beat back an attack, but the losses of the 5th Company had caused me some anxiety. In order, therefore, to reinforce the 5th Company, I sent the remaining half of the 11th Company into the trenches to the left of No. 8 Redoubt, so as to enfilade the troops of the enemy attacking the 5th Company, and earlier still I had sent Captain Rotaiski's company into a so-called deep trench near by. These measures were sufficient to prevent the enemy from breaking through at the point held by the 5th Company. I built great hopes on our four machine guns, posted behind the 7th Company's left flank (see page 43). They constituted a tremendous power, practically equalling a whole company, and they were, moreover, cleverly concealed in some small pits. I immediately sent in a report. (I had forwarded reports of everything that had taken place on the field and also the reports of the different commanders.)

About twelve o'clock the enemy's rifle fire suddenly ceased, and his artillery also grew silent. Taking advantage of this, I went down to the road from No. 13 Battery to meet two gunners coming from the position. We noticed General Fock and his adjutant on the road. Major Visoki reported that the gunners had suffered severely, and that the ammunition supply was exhausted. As they had no rifles, I sent them away from the position, and thus, from twelve o'clock, we were left without artillery. Just before this sudden temporary cessation of fire I had already noticed from the hill how

our artillery fire was dying down and how cruelly the
enemy's shells blew our gunners to pieces; indeed,
the helplessness of our guns became apparent as
soon as the enemy's cannonade commenced.

It is impossible to imagine what such a fire is like.
An unceasing stream of shells burst over each battery
and over No. 13 Battery, where it was only possible
to sit right up against the earth-work, now and then
venturing to glance over it to observe what was
going on. When the fire had become positively
fiendish we took cover in the upper bomb-proof, a
relic of the Chinese war. It gave us sufficient cover
from small shell, and it was possible to write there,
send reports, and receive reports from orderlies, but
the fire from the ships made us fear for our safety.
A single shell would have been sufficient to bury us all
under the ruins of our shelter. All the ravines were
literally pitted with shell splinters. Our unfortunate
artillery was so occupied in its struggle with the
enemy's guns that it paid no attention to the ships
threatening the fortifications on our left flank. However, this was not surprising, as the batteries did not
themselves feel the fire of the enemy's ships.
From their front guns roared also, so from a feeling
of self-preservation they returned that fire at first as
energetically as they could. The order I had sent
to No. 4 Battery to direct its fire on the enemy's ships
had evidently not got through to the battery commander. Our fire began to slacken, and finally ceased,
owing to losses and, in many batteries, for want of
ammunition. In No. 9 Battery every man was
killed but one, and he continued to fire by himself
from each gun in rotation. He loaded the guns in

turn and fired them until a shell put an end to this hero. In spite of all my efforts I have been unable to learn his name. " Peace to your ashes, unknown hero, the pride and glory of your regiment ! " *

The greater number of our guns was unharmed, though two pieces in the centre of the position were dismounted, as were also all the guns of No. 15 Battery, against which the enemy's ships were firing.

A deathlike stillness now reigned along the whole position for an hour. Going down to the lower line of trenches, I tried to get to General Fock, who had been seen, as I have said, on the road to No. 10 Battery, but he had gone off somewhere, and I did not see him again ; possibly he went along the ravines to Ta-fang-shen station.

Soldiers of the 5th Company who had fallen to the rear said that it had gone badly with that company, and that it had vacated the advanced trench and occupied No. 9 Redoubt and the ravines near it. The men in all the other trenches and forts gallantly stuck to their posts. After an hour of silence, firing began again, rifles cracked, and guns roared. I went to my observing station. The enemy literally swept us with a hail of shrapnel. One shell burst right over the heads of two of my orderlies standing behind me, killing one outright and wounding the other in the head. A short time after, our small-arm ammunition magazine near No. 10 Battery caught fire.

Soon after there were some distressing signs of disorder on the left flank (the section defended by the 5th Company)—men were retiring and going back, without stopping, to the rear of the position;

* Usual form of address to the dead.

4

but I received no report from the commander of the 5th Company. I then noticed that the enemy's fire was concentrated on the 5th and 7th Companies. Though I had foreseen an attack on these points I was not afraid that the enemy would break through there, as Rotaiski's company and Redoubt No. 8, with its trenches, made it impracticable. Nevertheless, I felt the need of a larger reserve, and I reported to General Fock that I should have no men with which to renew the battle if the enemy should beat us back out of our advanced positions. I earnestly asked for reinforcements; but General Fock, guided, I suppose, by the general supposition that reinforcements are always asked for before they are needed, and thinking, perhaps, that I was making mountains out of molehills, did not pay any attention to my request, or else did not wish to satisfy it, and our position became critical. Our scouts on the left flank, as also the 5th and 7th Companies, were demoralized, especially the 5th.

Captain Lubeemov's company of the 13th Regiment, which was with me in the reserve, had disappeared somewhere, so that Captain Teemoshenko, who was sent by me to take it to the place where I had decided it should go (on the left flank, in the interval between our 7th Company and Captain Ushakov's company, near No. 15), could not find it, and came back. Thus I now had not a single company under my hand.* Afterwards it became known that Lubeemov's com-

---

* It is not stated what happened to the other company of the 13th Regiment, which was in reserve. A reference to the Official History will show that only one company out of these two is mentioned there also.

pany had received by an orderly an order purporting to come from me, and had taken up a position near our 5th and 7th Companies on the left flank. It had failed to reach its *correct* position (see last page), as no one was there to direct it. I do not, however, blame Captain Lubeemov; he had obeyed his orders, but went to the right, instead of the left, flank of Captain Ushakov. Captain Teemoshenko should have pointed out the right place, but he failed to find the company. Where Captain Lubeemov was wrong, was in altering his position without my orders.

Shortly after, about four o'clock, an officer came up and reported that the 6th and 7th Companies of the 14th Regiment were coming to my assistance. I received a note from General Fock, in which he ordered me to use these companies only to cover a retreat, and not to employ them in the trenches. Then I understood that General Fock was not going to help me to hold the position, which he might have done without much difficulty, since I only required one additional battalion in reserve.

Lieutenant-Colonel Bielozor now sent to ask for reinforcements. Although I could see no attack on his side, in view of the urgency of the request, and so as to be quite safe on our right flank (where an adjoining village was strongly held by the Japanese, and the railway embankment could screen large numbers of the enemy), I decided to send half a company of the 14th Regiment under Captain Kousmin, an excellent officer, well known to me.

About six o'clock bullets began to whistle over our heads in No. 13, and, my trumpeter being wounded, I took him myself into the bomb-proof to be attended to. On the left flank men in yellow jackets * were moving about in groups, and five minutes had not passed before Second-Lieutenant Sadykov came into the shelter and reported that the left flank was retreating. I rushed out and saw that the yellow-coats were streaming up, and shrapnel bursting over the 7th and 5th Companies, while a heavy cross fire was being kept up. The Japanese skirmishers had lain down in their places and there was no warning of their sudden advance. Seeing that our scouts were retreating, and that all the others might retreat with them, I, not having any orders to retreat from the position, galloped off to the reserve and ordered the one-and-a-half companies of the 14th Regiment, sent by General Fock, to move against the Japanese appearing near Work No. 10. As we rode down, we came into a hot fire from the neighbouring hills.

I thought that I could arrest the retreat and deliver a counter-attack from behind the reserve, and then, having taken No. 10 Battery, re-organize the left flank.

At the subsequent court-martial General Fock declared that I could not have ordered the reserve to meet the Japanese; but he was mistaken, being misled by Captain Rotaiski, who, giving evidence, declared that he saw the Japanese pursuing me and saw me escape from them through the window of a shed. I never got through any window, but I mounted my horse and galloped off to stop those retreating. The Japanese then fired on me from the hills above the shed. It was not I, but a Japanese officer, who jumped through the window, and was

* At this stage the Japanese were clothed in khaki.

overtaken by four men from the reserve and killed in the shed, as a proof of which his sword was presented to the commander of the 14th Regiment.

The order to attack *was* given by me, for the commander of the reserve rushed up to me and asked: " What are we to do ? " " Attack," I answered, and pointed out to him whom to attack and where. After that I galloped after the retreating soldiers and made myself hoarse shouting " Stop, stop, my men ! " But they in their turn shouted out to me: " Your Excellency, we have been ordered to retreat." I could not imagine who had given this order. As, however, at this moment the Japanese saw us retreating from behind the Nan Shan hills, and opened a terrific shrapnel fire, it was absolutely impossible to stop the men. A shrapnel bullet struck my mare's ear and wellnigh maddened her. I managed to rally my men in a position in rear, chosen earlier by me, about a verst from the Nan Shan hills, and when they had halted, I looked back towards the hills and saw two bodies of men running down into the valley ; they were probably the 5th and 7th Companies.

No. 13 was in the hands of the Japanese, who were to be seen on the heights above, firing down on the retreating men, who quickly hid themselves in the deep ravines. I now occupied the above-mentioned position in rear, brought up a battalion of the 14th Regiment, and lengthened the line as far as Ta-fang-shen station. I found the battalion in question in a ravine behind the position. Of the rest of the 14th Regiment I saw no signs ; probably they were somewhere in rear under cover. The commander of our scouts came in to me here with our colours.

Awaiting on this spot the enemy's attack, we heard heavy firing on the right of the Nan Shan position, and the enemy's guns ranged on us and on the right flank. Our companies on that flank passed across towards Ta-fang-shen, and I ordered them to concentrate 1 verst in rear of Ta-fang-shen on the road. For some reason the Japanese decided not to attack us. It was already quite dark when I went to the burning station of Ta-fang-shen to see to the dispositions of our troops there. Suddenly there was a terrific explosion, and I was covered with fragments of burning planks, beams, and hot bricks. How I and my comrades escaped death passes my understanding. The station was blown up at the instance of General Fock's staff—probably by his orders. One officer —Major Saliarski—and twenty men were killed by this senseless explosion.

Night had set in, when the 14th and 5th Regiments received the order to retire, and I, leaving some mounted patrols to watch the enemy's movements, went with the Mounted Scouts to Nan-kuan-ling. While moving along the road, I met our 7th Company and saw the whole of the 4th Division encamped in the wide valley. There I found the companies of the 5th Regiment which had retreated, and ordered them to report their losses. Very many of our comrades did not answer the roll-call, the first return showing a loss in killed and wounded of 75 officers and 1,500 men. It was awful to see the thinned ranks of my gallant regiment; my heart bled for my officers, who had brought up the rear in the retreat, but the spirit of those left seemed to be as fine as ever. I feel bound to pay tribute to our comrades who fell in the battle and mention some of their heroic deeds.

Lieutenant Kragelski refused to retreat, and bade each one of his men farewell as they passed him. Captain Makoveiev, commanding the 8th Company, had declared that he would never retreat, and he was true to his word, for he remained in the trenches, and was killed only when he had expended all the cartridges in his revolver. Major Sokolov, commanding the 9th Company, also refused to retreat, and sabred several Japanese before being bayoneted to death.

The whole of the left flank attributed the retirement to the receipt of an order, and consequently I set to work to sift the matter to the bottom. About six o'clock General Fock sent an officer with the order to retire. Though he did not come to me personally, this officer probably sent an orderly—who failed to reach me—and himself went to the left flank and conveyed the order to retire to the scout detachments of the 13th and 14th Regiments. This order reached the commander of the 7th Company through Second-Lieutenant Merkoulev, besides which the former saw the orderly on a black horse shouting and waving his sword towards the rear, and only then ordered his company to retire. The fact that this order to retreat was given, was confirmed by all the officers and men, and also by Ensign Kaminar (5th Regiment).

I placed the letter sent to me by Lieutenant Sadykov relating to this point before the commission which assembled to investigate General Stessel's conduct. It was there shown that Second-Lieutenant Moosalevski was present and heard General Fock give the order to retreat to my orderly officer, Lieutenant Glieb-Koshanski, who galloped back with the orderly on the black horse to see the general's order carried out. When I stopped the retreating scouts, Lieutenant Glieb-Koshanski and his orderly galloped as far as the Nan Shan hills, and the latter reached No. 10 Battery by a ravine when the Japanese were already in the position (this hero never returned). Our 7th Company and Captain Rotaiski's company were still at their posts, and began to retire only after the receipt of the order.

When those who had been in Port Arthur were assembled in St. Petersburg from all over the Empire to give evidence at General Stessel's trial, I only gave details of the Nan Shan fight in answering the questions put to me. The conclusion arrived at was this : the scout detachments of the 14th Regiment, shaken by the hasty retirement of those of the 13th Regiment at that moment, began to abandon their trenches about four o'clock, the time when I saw them retreating in a body. Lieutenant Roosoi had only ten men left in the trench, but the other companies—i.e., the 7th and 5th of our regiment, and Captain Rotaiski's company—remained on the position. Lieutenant Glieb-Koshanski and the orderly galloped up with a report to General Fock just as I was leaving No. 13 and had mounted my horse, and it was thus quite possible for the orderly on the black horse to have really galloped up to the position and given the order to retire before I had stopped the retreating scouts. Anyway, it was proved conclusively that the Japanese appeared in No. 10 Battery, and the other inner works of the position before the 7th and 5th Companies began their retreat.

And it was in this way. When the Scout Detachment of the 13th Regiment, under Second-Lieutenant Bandaletov, and part of the Scouts of the 14th Regiment began to retire (in consequence of the flanking fire from the gunboats, and *not* because of the rifle fire of the Japanese, whose skirmishers did not come closer than 600 yards), the enemy, taking advantage of natural cover, pursued them and, passing along the ravines and watercourses, occupied the trenches we had vacated, together with No. 10 Battery and farther points. As, however, the Japanese were not in great numbers, they could not break through the centre, the 5th Company being in the deep ravine, the 6th in No. 8 Redoubt, and Rotaiski's company in a deep valley. These companies could not have let the Japanese pass, and I repeat that the Japanese lines were in full view from where I was and did not move until the scouts appeared in our rear.

From accounts given by officers, this is what happened on the right flank. After the attack on the 8th and 4th Companies had failed, the enemy kept up a furious gun and rifle fire, but did not approach our trenches. This continued until the retreat of the 5th and 7th Companies had actually begun. When the retreat of the left flank was noticed from No. 8 Redoubt, and the Japanese began to sweep our right flank from No. 5, Major Goosov assembled all the officers there for a consultation as to what should be done. After some hesitation it was decided to retreat; and word of that decision was sent to other companies. However, the 4th and 8th Companies, remembering the order that there would be no retreat, refused to act on the decision. Our gallant Colonel Bielozor was in command, the company commanders being Captain Shastin of the 4th Company, and Captain Makoveiev of the 8th. On the retirement of the 6th Company from No. 8 Redoubt, the 3rd, 4th, 8th, and part of the 12th Companies, found themselves in a hopeless position. There were Japanese in their rear, Japanese machine guns on No. 5, and a large body of Japanese in front, ready to attack, which they soon did. Seeing their comrades on the heights, where our batteries had been, and also in No. 8 Redoubt, the enemy in front advanced to the attack, but our gallant companies momentarily stopped their desperate rush by a volley, which covered the ground with hundreds of the enemy's killed and wounded. Then, facing round on the enemy who was attacking their rear, they compelled him to take cover behind the hills. The Japanese on the hill signalled with white handkerchiefs to the companies to surrender, but they only received volleys in reply. Taking advantage of the indecisive action of the Japanese in their rear, Lieutenant-Colonel Bielozor decided to try and extricate his men from this unequal fight, and gave the order to retire. Under a heavy fire the men moved along the trenches to the rear of the position, suffering severely from the marksmen on the hills. In some places the men had to come up out of the trenches, which were filled with dead and dying, but eventually the companies succeeded in reaching No. 1 Battery. From that point, too, Lieutenant-Colonel Bielozor and Captain Shastin saw some Japanese columns trying to cut off our companies retreating from the centre of the position.

The enemy was advancing from the shores of Hand Bay. Our brave officers at once thought of covering our men by preventing this turning movement, in spite of the enemy posted on the hills, and to this end they collected their men, stopped them, and opened volley fire on the Japanese. The latter retaliated, and in their turn poured in a hot fire from rifles and machine guns. This fearful struggle continued for some time until not a single one of our men was left alive. They all fell in this unequal fight, defending themselves finally not only with their bayonets, but even with their fists. Lieutenant-Colonel Bielozor lost consciousness from loss of blood, and fell; while Captain Shastin also fell, dangerously wounded in the chest. Both were picked up by the Japanese Red-Cross men, and saved, thanks to a Japanese officer, who gave orders that they were not to be killed.* Our right flank retreated simultaneously with our left at the moment when the Japanese began to enfilade them from the hills.

Having received the order to follow the regiment to Nan-kuan-ling, I bivouacked with the 4th Rifle Division, leaving my mounted scout detachment there. This was at 10 or 11 p.m.

On my way I learnt from certain artillery officers

* General Tretyakov appears to have been under the impression that the Japanese were giving no quarter.

that General Nadyein had, at the critical moment, sent me two battalions (if only they had reached me !), but that General Fock had ordered them to return. At the court-martial this fact was not proved.

If, however, General Fock had decided to attack the left flank of the enemy, where they were already running out of shell and were engaged with our companies, with even his two regiments, and had brought up the whole of his artillery against this flank, the enemy would, without doubt, have been checked and the victory might have been on our side.

It is said that at the court-martial General Fock stated that he wished to attack. What a pity that this wish came too late !

One must watch for the first sign of wavering in the soldier in order to be able to judge the proper moment for throwing in the reserves, instead of keeping them miles behind the firing line, as seems necessary according to General Fock's principle— " Keep back your reserves as long as you possibly can, as they are always asked for and sent up too early." That is all right as far as it goes, but at the same time reserves must be used exactly at the right moment. I understand the meaning of this principle, but in order not to be misled in adopting it, it is essential to follow the course of the action very closely.

It was stated at the court-martial that the whole of Lieutenant-Colonel Golitsinski's battalion of the 14th Regiment was sent to the position, by General Nadyein, but never reached it, occupying instead the trenches made by me beyond Ta-fang-shen on the seashore, in case the enemy tried to make

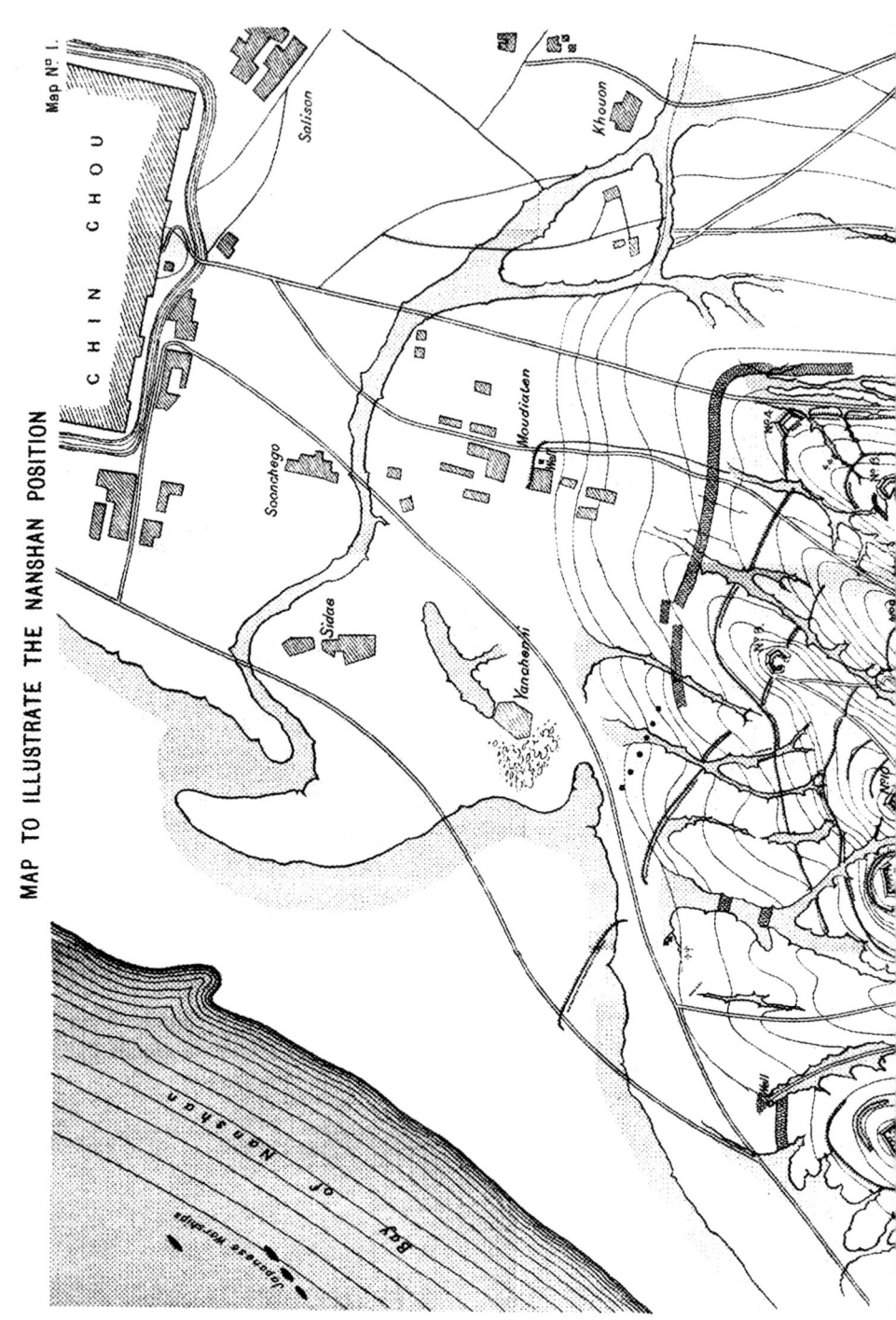

MAP TO ILLUSTRATE THE NANSHAN POSITION

Map Nº 1.

CHIN CHOU

Salison

Khouon

Moudiaden

Soonchego

Sidae

Vanchephi

Bay of Nanshan

Japanese warships

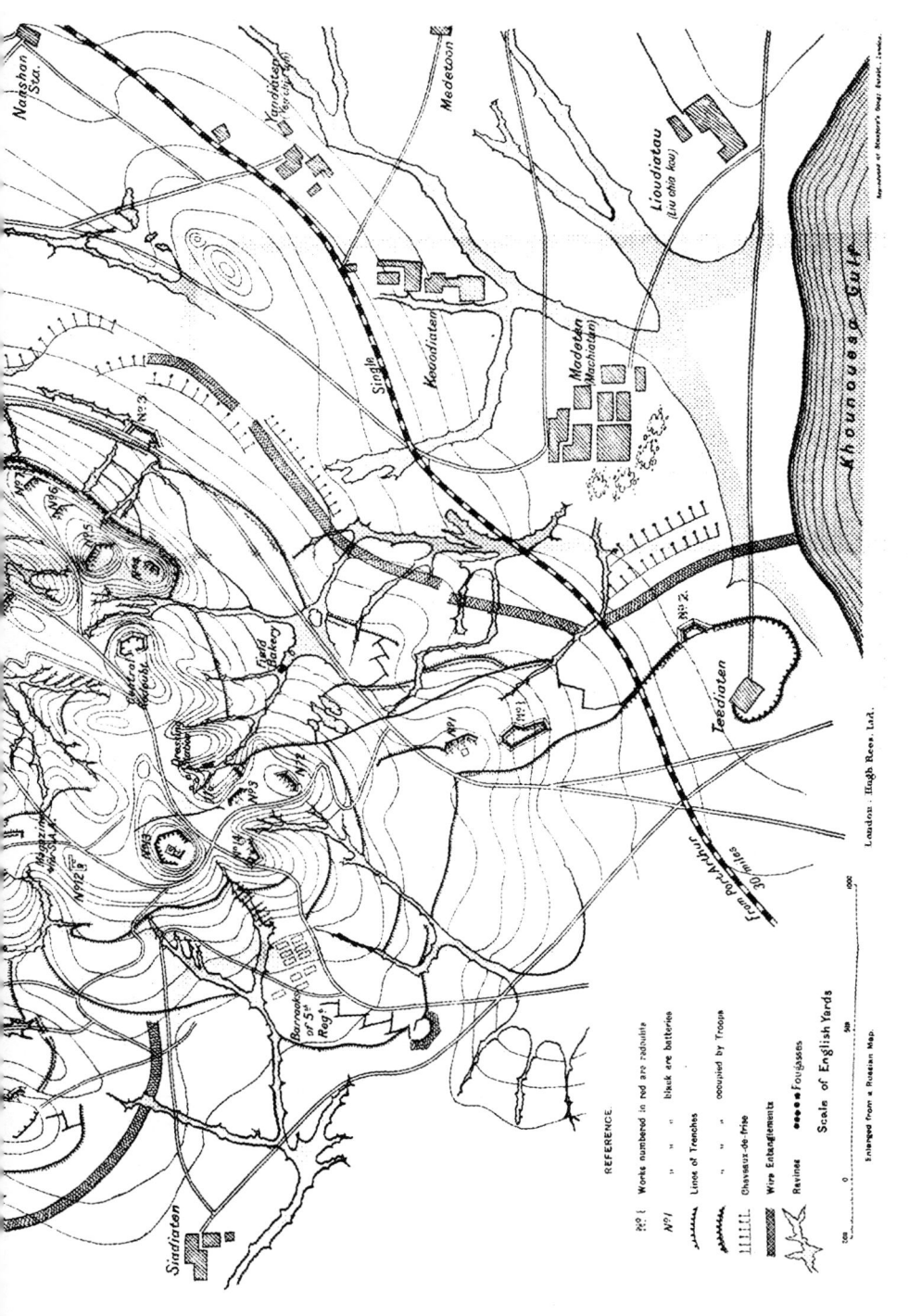

Nanshan Sea

Siadiaten

Yandiatesy (Tang chia tsun)

Medetoon

Lioudiatau
(Liu chia kou)

Siogle

Kevodiaten

Medeten (Machiaten)

Teédiaten

No. 2.

To Port Arthur
For 30 miles

Khounousa Gulf

Barracks
of 5th Regt.

Magazine
No. 12

Field
Bakery

No. 1

No. 2

No. 3

REFERENCE.

No. 1   Works numbered in red are redoubts
No. 1   ,,   ,,   ,,   black are batteries
        ,,   ,,   ,,   occupied by Troops
        Lines of Trenches
        Chevaux-de-frise
        Wire Entanglements
        Ravines   ●●●●● Fougasses

Scale of English Yards

Enlarged from a Russian Map.

London : Hugh Rees, Ltd.

a turning movement through the water of Hand
Bay.   This was more than a verst from the position,
in rear of its right flank.   What they wanted a
battalion there for, I really do not understand.   I
know nothing about this strange manœuvre, and I
never saw the battalion, but it would have played
a great part if I had had it with me in the centre.

There cannot be two commanders in one part of
a field of battle, and we had three—General Fock,
General Nadyein, and myself.

CHAPTER III

Night alarm during the march to Nan-kuan-ling—Disappearance of the baggage train—Continuation of the retreat towards Port Arthur—Occupation and fortification of the "Position of the Passes"—Japanese attacks on the position on July 26, 27, and 28—Capture of Yu-pi-la-tzu and Lao-tso Shan—General retirement to new positions, July 29.

I HAD hardly gone two versts from the bivouac, when we heard firing behind us. A moment afterwards a vague noise reached us, soon distinctly recognized as the rumbling of a baggage wagon. In another minute it had rattled past us at full speed. Behind it galloped a field battery scattering or destroying all that came in its way, and after the battery came a hurtling mass of wagons, mounted men, riderless horses, and unarmed men, and, to make matters worse, somebody raised the alarming cry of "Japanese cavalry! Japanese cavalry!"

The din and confusion were awful, and from the bivouacs behind us shots and volleys were heard. Together with the other officers near me I rushed to the rear of the column to restore order. I also ordered our band to strike up a march, and, thank God, its martial strains restored confidence among the fugitives—the noise ceased, and the men became quite calm and collected.

The band played all the way to Nan-kuan-ling,* and we were saved further panics in consequence.

* See Maps II. and VI.

62

Having been shown where to bivouac, I sent to
the baggage train for bread, tea, and sugar, but alas!
the baggage was not to be found. What was to be
done? Our men had had neither food nor drink
all day. Tents and great-coats had been left on the
field of battle, so that the men had nothing but their
rifles and cartridges with them. We started to hunt
for food.

I sent, of course, to the railway station. We saw
through the window that all the rooms were packed
with officers of every regiment, and the staff of
the 4th Division was there too. Having forced my
way into the buffet, I approached Lieutenant-Colonel
Dmetrevski, the chief of staff of the 4th Division,
who, in answer to my question, "Where has our
baggage train been sent?" told me that it had been
sent straight into Port Arthur by General Fock's
order, and he could not say where it was now. The
commanders of the 13th, 14th, and 15th Regiments
were there too. I asked the first of these for
200 poods * of bread, a quantity of which I saw
loaded up on some wagons standing close at
hand. In an hour we had unloaded them and distributed the bread, each man getting about 4 lb.
I had a piece about that weight, as had also all the
other officers; of meat, there was absolutely none
to be had.

All available articles of food in the buffet had been
eaten before our arrival, but I succeeded in getting
some salt wherewith to flavour my bread.

Having slept for three hours on the bare ground,
we got up to resume our march. No one molested

* 1 pood = 38 lb.

us during the night; the morning broke cold and foggy.

According to the " order of march " we should have been at the head of the column, but some regiment forestalled us, and we had to wait nearly an hour before making a start.

At about midday we reached a pass in the hills, well lined with trenches, and, after making a short halt in the pass itself, we pushed on, marching at a good pace.

At the instance of General Fock the mountain road had been repaired at an earlier date, and now did us sterling service, but, hard as we went, we did not overtake our baggage, and the whole of that day we had nothing but the bread procured at Nan-kuan-ling from the 14th Regiment. We spent the night in a picturesque defile, and perforce lay down to sleep on empty stomachs.

On May 28 we overtook an enormous train of baggage from Dalny,* accompanied by the male inhabitants of the town, with their women, children, and household goods. As the horses in the wagons were wretchedly small, the train had to come to a standstill, blocking the road from end to end.

We went round by a narrow side road, and in the evening reached the great Shipinsin Pass,† where at last we overtook our baggage.

Now in high spirits, we bivouacked, cooked our suppers, ate them ravenously, and slept the sleep of the just.

* The inhabitants of Dalny received the news of the battle of Nan Shan on the evening of the 26th, and were ordered to proceed to Port Arthur at eleven that night (see Official History, Part III., p. 12).

† That between Triple Peak and An-tzu Ling (see Map VI.).

On the following day, May 29, we began to ascend the pass, which, thanks to our excellent horses, our baggage train speedily traversed, and although at midnight we lost our way, owing to bad maps, we eventually reached the outskirts of Port Arthur and halted at the village of Pa-li-chuang, where we had been ordered to rest for three days.

General Stessel visited the regiment the following day. The companies quickly formed up near the bivouacs, and the general rode round them all and thanked them for their splendid behaviour. The men felt tremendously encouraged, many of them having laboured under the dire impression that we had committed a crime by surrendering Nan Shan to the enemy.

General Stessel called to the front all those wounded who had remained in the ranks, in order to address them, and to bestow praise and rewards in the shape of the Cross of St. George. There were, however, so many of them (more than 300) that the general thought it was impossible to get so many crosses; he therefore ordered the doctor to inspect them and separate the badly from the slightly wounded. There were sixty of the former category, and they were given St. George's crosses accordingly. These were the sole recipients of rewards for the Nan Shan battle, those slightly wounded receiving nothing for their bravery—and the number of such was great.

I have already mentioned the fact that our men came away with only their rifles, most of the tents and great-coats having been left on the field of battle. It was fortunate that just before the battle we had transported the bulk of our stores into Port

5

Arthur, where they had been deposited in Captain Preegorovski's house, which had been hired for the purpose. We brought all we wanted out of Port Arthur without delay, and distributed the necessaries among the men. At the same time we drove out with us a large herd of cattle, amounting to about 200 head.

I forgot to mention that our ordinary military anxieties on the Nan Shan position had been augmented by the worry due to an order to collect all the cattle belonging to the inhabitants and to drive them to the rear of the position. Some officials, supplied with money, were sent out for this purpose, but as they could not effect their object without the assistance of the regiment, the whole burden of the work fell upon us.

Unfortunately, the order was given when the enemy was already in touch with us, but we managed to collect about 1,000 head and drove them to the rear of the army, almost into Port Arthur.

After three days' rest we moved into Port Arthur and stopped in a village near Serotka Hill, * forming the reserve of the 4th Division, which took up the position Shuang-tai-kou, Yu-pi-la-tzu, Chien Shan, and Lao-tso Shan.†

The 4th Division had been reinforced by a detachment of mixed companies of the 7th Division, under the command of Colonel Semenov, and it was this detachment that occupied Lao-tso Shan. I do not know exactly what they had done amiss, but I re-

* Better known as Orphan Hill ; shown on British official maps as Kan-ta Shan, that being its Chinese name.

† Called by the Russians the Green Hills.

VIEW OF THE COUNTRY AT THE POSITION OF THE PASSES. IN THE DISTANCE ON THE LEFT ARE SEEN THE PEAKS OF CHIEN-SHAN.

member it was commonly said that the mixed companies were not to be depended upon, which is not to be wondered at, seeing that they had no stiffening of seasoned troops. The commanders of the companies did not know their own men, nor had the men any knowledge of their commanders. No one felt responsible for the actions of the different units. This organization was considered a huge mistake on General Kondratenko's part; but, however that may be, the position in question was held by us from the time of its occupation, on May 31, till July 28, in spite of the fact that it had not previously been fortified.

During this time the 5th Regiment was divided into two parts, and I was put in command of the left flank of the defence, and began to fortify the position on 174 Metre Hill and the country in front of it, as also the western side of Feng-huang Shan * from the Great Mandarin road to Eight Ships' Bay. Stationed along the shore of the latter was Captain Sakatski's detachment, and two other detachments were on the banks of Louisa Bay, both under my command, the former having with it four small naval guns under Midshipman Doudkin.

Our 6th and 7th Companies occupied and fortified Feng-huang Shan from the Great Mandarin road up to Major Sakatski's detachment. Our three scout detachments occupied and fortified the 174 Metre and Headquarter Hills, and also Height 426.† The 3rd and 9th Companies occupied 174 Metre Hill, while the 2nd and 4th held 203 Metre Hill. They all worked hard at their fortifications under the

* Known by the Russians as the Wolf Hills.
† The Russian name is Bokovi (Side) Hill.

supervision of their officers, in accordance with orders given by me.

174 Metre Hill had to be fortified as strongly as possible, as, having once captured that, the enemy could sweep our extremely weak western front, occupy the valley stretching in the direction of the New Town, and command the latter and the bay.

The other companies of the regiment were quartered in various positions near. At times when the advanced regiments behind Feng-huang Shan were threatened, the 5th Regiment served as the reserve for the different sections of the advanced line.

Our work advanced slowly, because we had very few tools.

Besides fortifying the position, I had to build shelters for the reserves and stores for small-arm ammunition in the fortress itself.

I detailed two companies of the 7th Division for this work, utilizing all the material we could find in the town. Having no sapper officer with me, I had personally to supervise everywhere—on the advanced positions as well as in the town. It was a great help that the officers of the 5th Regiment were, thanks to constant practice, excellent sappers.

We could only obtain tools with great difficulty and from various sources. Most of them we got from Colonel Grigorenko, commanding the Engineers in the fortress, and from the railway authorities.

The number of men given me to carry out the work which I had been ordered to do was insufficient, so I asked if I could employ the whole of my regiment. I received permission early in June, and moved the regimental staff to Division Hill, where we made ourselves very snug, pitching a huge marquee and getting our field kitchen into working order.

Generals Kondratenko, Smirnov, and Stessel came out to us fairly frequently. Our work progressed rapidly, as we had got over the tool difficulty, but we had very few barrows, etc., for transporting the earth.

A stubborn defence having been determined upon, it was necessary to construct a great number of splinter-proofs as well as shelters for ourselves and our kitchens ; and for this we needed an abundant supply of beams and planks.

Besides this activity we had constantly to send detachments to the advanced positions held by the regiments of the 4th Division.

Other regiments continually borrowed the tools I had collected, but did not return them.

I frequently went on long personal reconnoitring tours, during which I made myself acquainted with the advanced positions and their fortifications.

It seems that General Fock expected that the Japanese would most probably attack our position across the flat stretch of country between the hills and the sea. In any case, he paid most attention to fortifying this particular part of the position. To me, however, it was very clear how difficult it would be to attack a fortified position across the open under effective gun and rifle fire. Not even taking into account the Japanese love of hill-fighting, it was obvious that the hills were by far the best point of attack, and these General Fock wished to have defended only by the scout detachments.

Here the defenders were deprived of their strongest

weapon, viz. distant, and even close, rifle and artillery fire. As to the assailants, numerical superiority and the power of initiative gave the Japanese tremendous advantage in the hills, the more so, as our position was very much extended, covering about 8 versts for five regiments of three battalions each (about 10,000 men). The Japanese guns could, moreover, demolish our trenches, whereas our artillery could not find any targets.

When I inspected the position at the beginning of July, I noticed that the position at Shuang-tai-kou (between the hills and the sea) was splendidly fortified (the trenches were deep, with a magnificent field of fire), but the hills were left entirely without fortifications.

I rode down into Yu-pi-la-tzu, where there were two scout detachments—of what regiment, I do not remember. There were no trenches and, above all, no cover from gun fire. This was a great mistake, as the whole of the enemy's artillery fire might be directed on Yu-pi-la-tzu, and our men driven out of it, after which the Japanese could occupy the hill without loss.

Having ascended the hill, a magnificent panorama met the eye. The whole country as far as Dalny and the bay beyond lay before one as the lines on the palm of the hand, and in the daytime every single movement of the enemy could be noted.

Yu-pi-la-tzu Hill was a very important point. If we lost it, we should have to retreat to the Shipinsin Pass.* But the enemy did not hurry matters. Having come within long-range rifle fire from the hills (as was to have been expected, he paid no attention

* Near Lieh-shu-fang.

THE NEIGHBOURHOOD OF YU-PI-LA-TZU.

to the low-lying ground), he dug trenches and set to work to lay his plans with deliberation.

From the moment of his first coming into touch with us, at the beginning of May, till July 26, he pressed our right flank, and compelled us to change our position, and on the 26th commenced his attack on the entire hill section.

The 5th Regiment was moved up to act in support. Some time before this our 3rd Battalion had been sent to the right flank to Lao-tso Shan, where we lost two excellent officers, Captain Koudriavtsev and Lieutenant Popov.

The 3rd Battalion had to bear the brunt of the retreat from Lao-tso Shan, since, as had been expected, the mixed companies on the right flank did not distinguish themselves when it came to fighting.

On July 20 my 2nd Battalion was directed to go to 11th Verst station* to the headquarters of the 4th Division, and there it went accordingly, under the command of Major Stempnevski (jun.).

When the enemy began his decisive attack on the 26th, I was moved up with the 1st Battalion, which was then commanded by Major Stempnevski (sen.), a splendid all-round officer. I arrived with my battalion in the morning and found all our commanders with the divisional staff—Generals Stessel, Fock, and Kondratenko. The battle was raging along the whole line.

As all the positions were divided into sections, and each section had its commander, I was free to become a spectator of all that was going on. We went by train to 11th Verst, and had only just got

* As its name implies, the station 11 versts from Port Arthur.

down out of the carriages, when the 1st Scout Detachment, under Lieutenant Kostoushko, was ordered
to move on Yu-pi-la-tzu Hill, where the defenders
had been decimated by the ceaseless artillery fire.

The 1st Battalion was then moved to the Shipinsin
Pass, where, judging by the artillery fire, a determined attack was in preparation, and only our 7th
and 8th Companies were left with the regimental
staff.

General Fock directed the whole defence.

The fighting of July 26 and 27 did not cost us
very dearly, except for severe wounds received by
Lieutenant Kostoushko (a wound in the chest, and
a number of other wounds in the left shoulder and
side). This officer had thrown himself, with a part
of his scouts, on the enemy, who had already seized
some of our trenches on Yu-pi-la-tzu Hill. This was
on the night of July 27–28.

Towards evening on the 26th, General Stessel had
sent a telegram to the town saying that all the attacks
of the Japanese had been unsuccessful that day.

On the 27th the battle was again renewed along
the whole line. Lao-tso Shan was swept by the fire
of very heavy guns—probably 6-inch, judging from
the size of the shell bursts. It was very difficult
for our artillery to cope with these guns, as they were
not only very far off, but also well concealed.

Having nothing to do, I went to my 1st Battalion,
which was drawn up as a reserve on the declivity of
the Shipinsin Pass. Scarcely any shells burst near
us ; they all went " over," shattering the rocky
sides of a ravine lying behind.

Our battery on the pass itself was literally swept

TRIPLE PEAK, WHERE THE MEN ARE STANDING.   IN THE DISTANCE ON THE LEFT IS YU-PI-LA-TZU HILL.

p. 73]

with Japanese shell, and there was a continuous roar of musketry fire, under which our men were, however, perfectly calm, and even joked about the bad shooting of the Japanese gunners. Though this went on all day, the defence stood firm the whole time.

However, things went badly for us on Yu-pi-la-tzu Hill. The Japanese crawled up its abnormally steep sides on to the hill-top itself. All shelter had been destroyed by artillery fire, and a corner of a casemate had fallen in and crushed the officer commanding, Lieutenant-Colonel Goosakov, whose loss every one felt keenly. (It is opportune to mention here that he was the only staff officer who helped me to organize the defence of the rearward position which covered our retreat from Nan Shan.) At this period of the conflict the defenders concentrated behind stones and ruined trenches, with the enemy only a few paces from them.

The staff officers shouted out that Yu-pi-la-tzu had to be abandoned, as its further defence would only cause us enormous losses, because the trenches no longer gave cover from the effects of Shimose and shrapnel. Since, however, the majority were against giving up this important hill, which was such an excellent observation point, the commanders decided to rebuild the trenches during the night and continue the defence.

At four o'clock in the afternoon our 8th Company was sent to Yu-pi-la-tzu Hill with as many tools as could be found, to reconstruct the old, and make new, trenches. Captain Sakarov, late commandant of Dalny, who built the railway and port there, was put in command. (After leaving Dalny, this excellent officer decided to leave the Port Arthur Fortress Sapper Company, which was commanded by Lieutenant-Colonel Jerebtsov.) The Japanese met with practically no success on this day, and we held on to all our positions.

Very early on the morning of the 28th, being awakened by a terrific cannonade, I got up and went to headquarters, where I found all the staff officers already up. In order the better to watch the course of the action, General Stessel, with some of his staff, had gone to the top of the nearest hill, and thither I repaired also. General Fock remained with the telephones, keeping all his staff with him (he had new adjutants; the old ones, Captain Kvitkin and, subsequently, Captain Yarsevitch, had rejoined their units).

On reaching the top of the hill, a magnificent panorama of the hill country lay before us. The crest nearest us, which was occupied by our troops, was completely wreathed with puffs of white smoke. In some places the smoke spread over an enormous extent and curled high up into the air. It lay thickest over Lao-tso Shan, for the heaviest types of shell were constantly bursting there, and the sky was dotted with little round white clouds from bursting shrapnel. At the same time the attentive and well-trained ear could distinguish the ceaseless far-distant roll of rifle fire, due to the rattle of musketry along the line occupied by us.

Our 1st Battalion had not yet come into action, but was to be seen as a black spot near a zigzag in the road leading to the Shipinsin Pass.

We stayed about a quarter of an hour on the hill, and then went down to the telephones (one can follow an action better from near the telephones, even though they are placed lower down, as in this case). It is a pity that they did not think of putting them in a place where it was possible to see the battle with one's own eyes as well as hear reports, as, for example, on the top of the hill we had just left.

General Fock met us below, and at once gave General Stessel full details of all that had taken place. Our men had stood firm everywhere, except on Yu-pi-la-tzu Hill, where things were going badly with us. It was a physical impossibility to hold on there, in spite of the new trenches, on account of the artillery fire concentrated on the hill. Hence it was decided to abandon Yu-pi-la-tzu, and orders were sent there accordingly.

When this decision had been arrived at, General Fock said, in his short, sharp way of speaking: "Well, it is impossible to hold on to Yu-pi-la-tzu. It would entail too heavy losses. Even if the companies there left it of their own accord, it would be nothing serious; but to give up Lao-tso Shan, that would be a disgrace, almost amounting to treachery." He had only just said this, when news came that Lao-tso Shan had been evacuated by the troops holding it. " Now we shall have to make a general retreat," said General Fock, and he gave orders to retire and to take up a new position with the right flank at Ta-ku Shan—the centre near 11th Verst, and the left on Feng-huang Shan.

In order to give the line cohesion, my left flank (Captain Sakatski's detachment) was put at the disposal of the officer commanding the 15th Regiment. I had to occupy without delay the spur of 174 Metre Hill, as well as that hill itself and 203 Metre Hill, and also Division Hill and the crest of Pan-lung Shan lying in front of it. The 5th Regiment thus filled up the gap between Forts Yi-tzu Shan and Ta-yang-kou North, which had long ago been prepared by us. The staff, with General Stessel at its head, collected in the building occupied by the staff of the 4th Division (a station at 11th Verst) and quietly waited there until the regiments had taken up their allotted positions.

Notwithstanding the statements of certain war-correspondents, I saw no signs of any panic or disorder during this retirement. Every one was perfectly calm, and the army withdrew to its new positions correctly and without any confusion.

Suddenly there appeared in the valley to our right a Red-Cross train full of wounded, a sight which always impresses one ; there was a long stream of wagons, accompanied by bearer-company men, doctors, and those of the wounded who were able to walk. Behind this train appeared a reserve column. At that depressing moment I remembered how our band had put new spirit into us during the night alarm near the Nan-kuan-ling Hills, and felt a desire to repeat the experiment.

So, having obtained permission from General Stessel, I sent for the band, which was bivouacked near the railway station, and soon the strains of a stirring march crashed out over those hills, dark with death and blood. The retreating army formed into columns, and, picking up the step by the band, swung past General Stessel. This march-past continued for nearly an hour under the very eyes of the enemy. Our splendid 3rd Battalion was the last to go past, bearing with it the body of Captain Kvitkin, General Fock's former A.D.C. The 5th Regiment had lost altogether 2 officers and 60 men. They had borne the whole brunt of the Japanese final attacks, and had covered the retreat of the other regiments, presenting an impregnable front throughout every attack.

It is obvious from the foregoing details that the retreat from Lao-tso Shan was made in perfect order.

The following is a description of the action of our companies on Lao-tso Shan :

The positions occupied * by the regiment were as follows :

The detachment of Colonel Dounin, commanding the 3rd Battalion 5th Regiment, consisting of the 5th, 6th, 9th, 11th, and 12th Companies, and the 2nd and 3rd Scout Detachments of the 5th Regiment and the 1st Company of the 27th, was posted before the battle on Lao-tso Shan, and occupied the section from the valley (near the small hill occupied by the 11th Company of the 27th Regiment) to a spur $\frac{3}{4}$ verst from the village of Vodymin † and touching the foot of Chien Shan.

The various companies occupied the following sections :

1. The 9th Company and 3rd Scout Detachment 5th Regiment, on the right flank in the valley.

---

* Our Official History states that only three companies of the 5th Regiment were allotted to this section, but adds later that the 5th and 6th Companies were brought up and absorbed in the fighting line. They are here given as being in reserve.

† A village 1½ miles north-east of Hou-chia-tun.

2. Next to these the 2nd Scout Detachment, to the left of the valley and covering Lieutenant Naoomov's battery.

3. Farther to the left, the 12th Company 5th Regiment.

4. On the extreme left flank, near Vodymin, the 11th Company 5th Regiment and, as a reserve, the 1st Company 27th Regiment.

5. The 5th and 6th Companies 5th Regiment formed the general reserve.

On the morning of the 26th the Japanese opened a heavy gun fire on our positions, followed by a vigorous attack, but they obtained no hold anywhere that day, as our men held on to their positions and beat them back at every point.

On the 27th the Japanese repeated their attacks, but had no more success than on the preceding day, whereupon they proceeded to make a night attack.

Some companies to the right of Colonel Dounin retreated without firing a shot, and so hurriedly, that they failed to inform the companies on either side of them.

The Japanese rushed into the gap thus created, and, working round to the rear, began to pour a flanking fire into the other companies, who were ignorant of what had happened, and had remained in their positions. Taken by surprise, these companies lost their heads in turn and retreated, also without informing their neighbours. In this manner the gap grew rapidly until it extended to Colonel Dounin's troops, when the following became the position of affairs :

The 9th Company and 3rd Scout Detachment of

the 5th Regiment occupied the valley, being in touch on the right with the 11th Company 27th Regiment. The 3rd Scout Detachment formed the outpost line, with the 9th in reserve behind it.

About three o'clock * on the morning of the 28th the piquet on the right, which was keeping touch with the 11th Company, reported that a retreat was in progress on that side.

Captain Koudriavtsev, commanding the 9th Company, sent an orderly to the hill occupied by the 11th Company to find out what was going on there. The orderly returned immediately and reported that the 11th Company had gone, that a small body of Japanese was occupying the hill, and that reinforcements were coming up to them. At first Captain Koudriavtsev did not believe this, and wanted to send a more reliable man, but just at that moment shots rang out from the hill in the direction of the 9th Company and 3rd Scout Detachment, and Captain Koudriavtsev's doubts were dispelled. He consulted with Lieutenant Choulkov, commanding the 3rd Scout Detachment, and they came to the conclusion that it would be unreasonable to try and hold the position and defend the valley with the Japanese on the hill above. They therefore determined to go up with the 9th Company before daybreak, while there were not many Japanese on the hill, retake it, and, having got possession of it, re-establish communication with the troops on the right, and thus fill in the gap that had been left in the line. Arrived at

* Ta-po Shan had actually been captured by the Japanese the previous evening about ten o'clock, two counter-attacks afterwards failing.

this decision, Captain Koudriavtsev arranged with
Lieutenant Choulkov that they should support each
other, and if either had to retreat, he would immediately inform the other, and, in order to avoid mis-
understandings, written messages only were to be
accepted.   Captain Koudriavtsev then told Lieutenant Choulkov to remain in his present position
with the 3rd Scout Detachment and await his
orders, while he himself, with half the 9th Company,
started to make the attack, the other half of the
9th Company being left meanwhile under Acting
Ensign Shishkin with orders to follow him as a
reserve.

In spite of the terrible fire with which the Japanese
met the attackers Captain Koudriavtsev with his half-
company reached the trenches, and with a wild
"hurrah" rushed in with the bayonet.   The blow
fell partly on the Japanese flank.   A hand-to-hand
fight ensued.   Unfortunately, Captain Koudriavtsev
was killed, and Serjeant-Major Evlanov wounded as
he was mounting the hill; many of the men also
were placed *hors de combat*, and the remainder, not
feeling themselves strong enough to overpower the
enemy, began to retreat, carrying with them the body
of their dead captain.   In the darkness our men did
not retreat back along the line of their advance, nor
towards the 3rd Scout Detachment and the reserve,
but in the direction in which the other companies had
retreated previously.   The reserve half of the 9th
Company, not knowing what had happened, but
guessing from the direction of the firing and the
noise of moving men that the 1st half-company had
retired, and being met, moreover, by a heavy rifle fire

themselves, began to retreat in the same direction. Acting Ensign Shishkin, unfortunately, did not think of telling Lieutenant Choulkov what had happened, and the latter awaited word from Captain Koudriavtsev, as had been arranged. In this way twenty minutes or half an hour passed. Then, as day broke, the Japanese fire from the hill became still heavier and more vicious.

Lieutenant Choulkov learnt of the failure of the 9th Company from some of the rank and file who had got left behind in the retreat, and who stumbled upon the 3rd Scout Detachment in the darkness. Fully alive to the danger of being surrounded, he ordered the outposts to come in, and sent word of the position of affairs to a company extended to his left. Fearing for the fate of the machine guns, which were behind him, Lieutenant Choulkov sent one section to them as escort, but the guns were gone. As soon as the outpost line had come in, Lieutenant Choulkov began to retreat with his command in a compact body, and soon joined up with the reserve, behind which Colonel Dounin concentrated the retreating troops and brought them into a state of order.

The reserve was in the valley, and, hearing of the retreat of the companies to his right, Colonel Dounin ordered what reserves he had to occupy a neighbouring hill on the right, in order to hold up the enemy's advance while he formed a new defensive line from the village of Vodymin across Riji Hill,* through Lieutenant Naoomov's battery of 57-mm. guns, and farther on to some unnamed hills. Thanks to Colonel

* Not to be confused with a hill of the same name on the Western Front of the Port Arthur defences.

6

Dounin's dispositions, and to the courage of the officers of the detachment, they succeeded in forming the new defensive line at the point mentioned, and in cooling the ardour of the Japanese in their fiery advance.

A short time afterwards the order to retreat was received from General Fock.

While Colonel Dounin was giving the necessary orders, another order came in from General Fock to retire on Height No. 86.*

Colonel Dounin retreated in splendid order, in some cases personally conducting the skirmishing line, and, covering one company with another, occupied the positions ordered by General Fock— namely, Height No. 86, next a position near the village of Hou-chia-tun, then Saidjashalin,† and finally 11th Verst. Having covered the retreat of parts of the 13th, 14th, and other regiments, the companies themselves passed behind Feng-huang Shan.

The whole of the force, and especially the officers, acted in a manner worthy of the highest praise. In holding back the victorious Japanese, all the companies displayed remarkable bravery; for instance, the 11th Company of the 5th Regiment with the 1st Company of the 27th Regiment held Vodymin for two-and-a-half hours, though surrounded on three sides. Nevertheless, they broke their way through, taking with them a machine gun that had been left on the road and three wounded men of the 26th Regiment. The 6th Company, which held back the Japanese

* Probably a hill between Vodymin and Hou-chia-tun.
† A village midway between Vodymin and 11th Verst station.

with rapid fire in order to allow its comrades to get away, continued to hold its ground under a heavy cross-fire from rifles and guns, and, amongst others, lost its gallant commander, Lieutenant Popov, who set an example of unparalleled bravery to the whole of his company.

After the evacuation of Lao-tso Shan the army took up the new positions assigned to it, and we remained near the station (11th Verst—the headquarters of the 4th Division) and prepared to cook our breakfasts.

But suddenly a bullet whistled past, followed by another, and this reminded us that no one was covering our rear. The staff got into some confusion, wagons were hastily horsed, and two companies (I do not remember which regiment they belonged to) were ordered to move in the direction of the enemy and hold him back. These companies quickly occupied a height close by, covering the staff from the enemy, and the firing became general. The whistling of bullets became more frequent, and the horsing of the wagons of the staff was hurried on. We saw that it was useless to try to breakfast in such an unpleasant place, and the staff, with fifty Cossacks and accompanied by General Stessel, began to move into the fortress, stopping every now and then to see what was going on in front. I rode off to 174 Metre Hill, and on the way climbed a fairly high eminence to see what was happening in rear. I found our own battery there placed in some well-constructed trenches, and the guns directing their fire on the station at 11th Verst. Everything was soon put in order, and nothing further happened to prevent our men occupying their new positions, on which could already be seen the rising smoke of the field kitchens.

Towards the evening of July 29 the 5th Regiment had settled down in its new positions, had supper, and turned in for the night, except the outposts, whom I had sent out far in front in the direction of the enemy. (I always did this, even when our own troops were in front of us, as on this occasion.) I placed my staff on Division Hill, and built an office, and a mess-room for the officers.

The situation was a very picturesque one. In front were the ridges of Division Hill, with two neighbouring eminences, all crowned with our trenches, to the left wooded slopes, and towards Fort Yi-tzu Shan a small but glistening stream, with banks covered with slender, waving grasses. (See Map IV.)

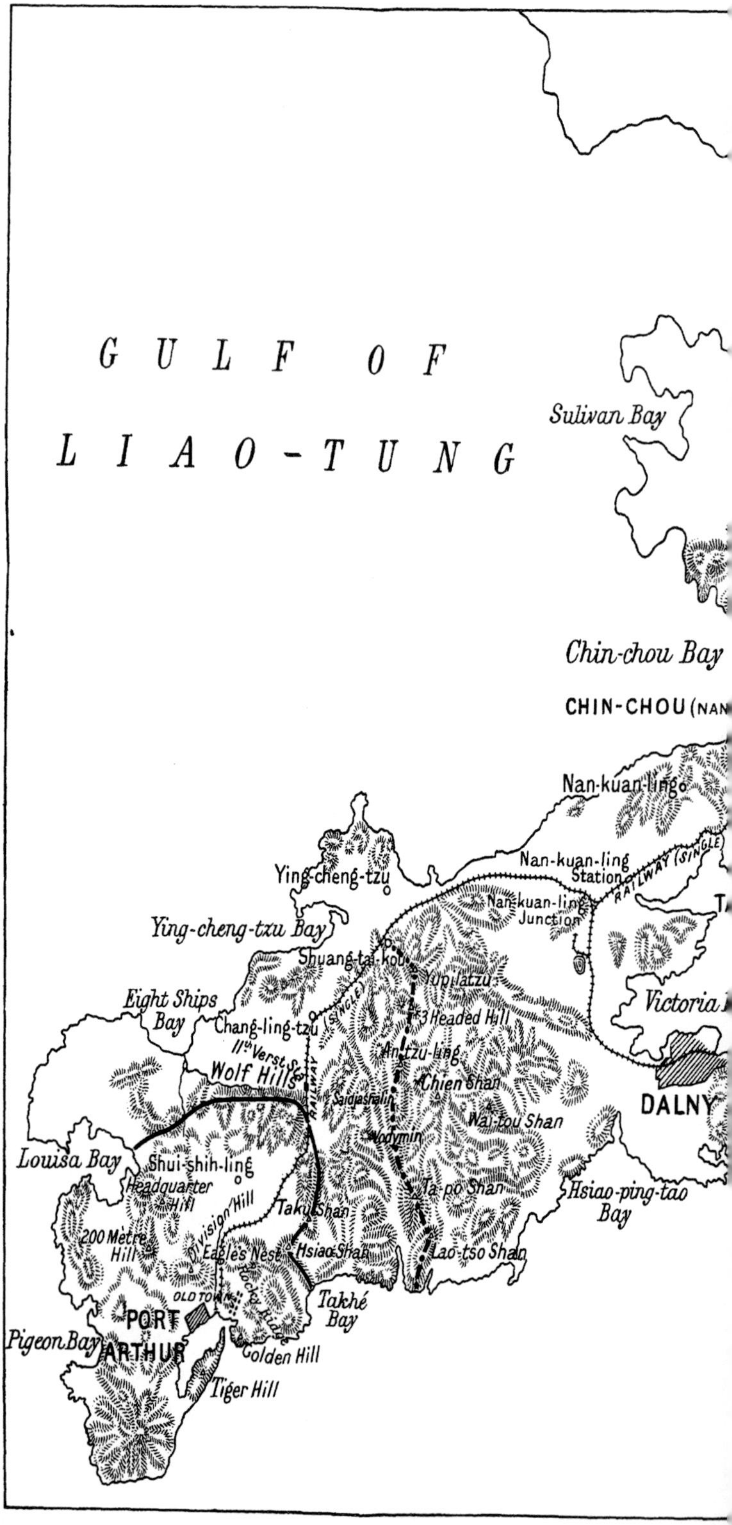

GULF OF LIAO-TUNG
Sulivan Bay
Chin-chou Bay
CHIN-CHOU (NAN
Nan-kuan-ling
Nan-kuan-ling Station
RAILWAY (SINGLE)
Nan-kuan-ling Junction
Ying-cheng-tzu
Ying-cheng-tzu Bay
Shuang-tai-kou
Yupilatzu
Victoria
Eight Ships Bay
Chang-ling-tzu
11th Verst St.
3 Headed Hill
An-tzu-ling
Wolf Hills
RAILWAY
Chien Shan
Saidjashalin
DALNY
Wai-tou Shan
Vodymin
Louisa Bay
Shui-shih-ling
Headquarter Hill
Ta-po Shan
Hsiao-ping-tao Bay
Division Hill
Taku Shan
200 Metre Hill
Eagle's Nest
Hsiao Shan
Lao-tso Shan
OLD TOWN
Rocky Ridge
Takhé Bay
PORT ARTHUR
Pigeon Bay
Golden Hill
Tiger Hill

Lo

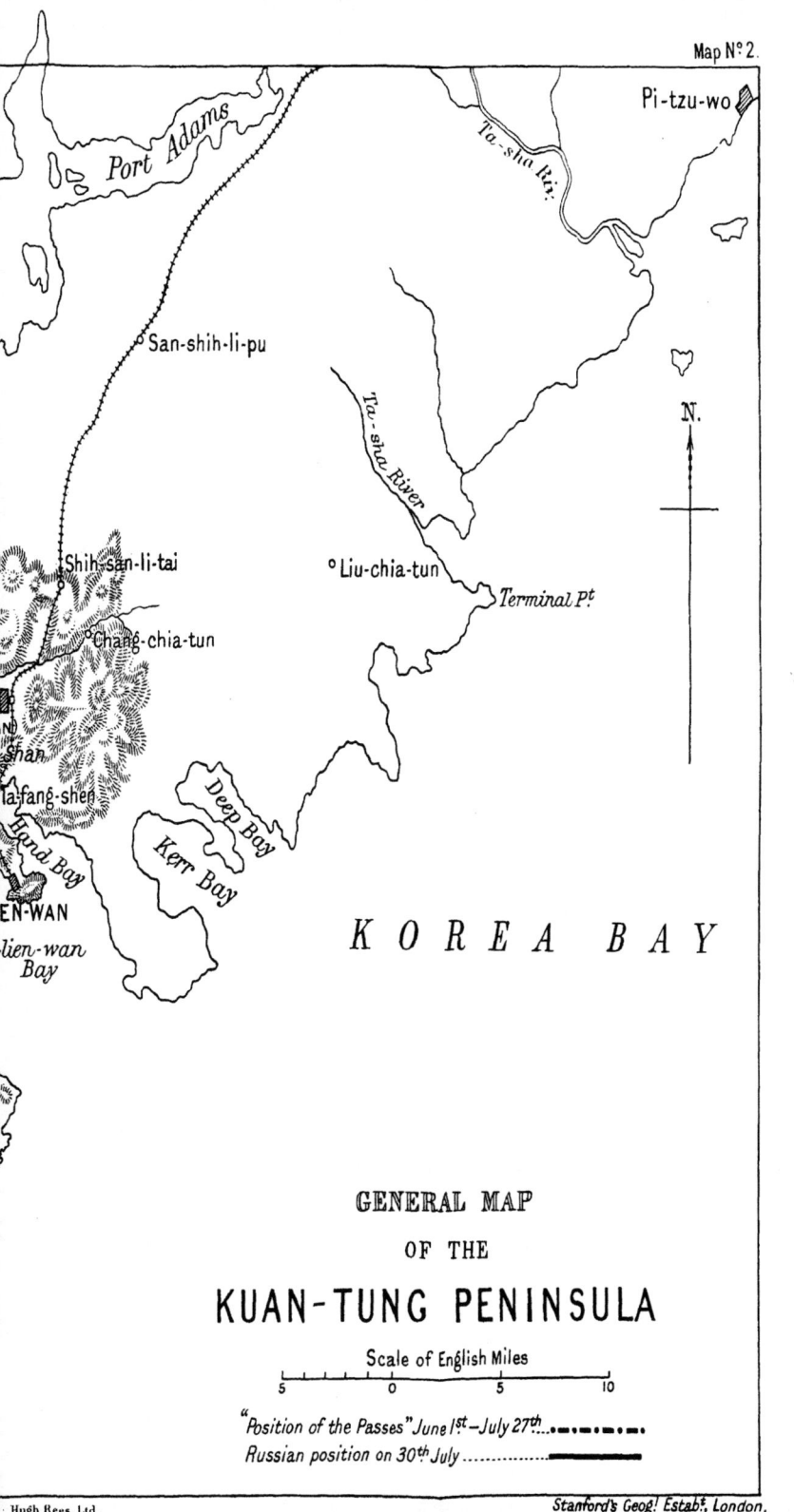

Pi-tzu-wo

Ta-sha Ho.

Port Adams

San-shih-li-pu

Ta-sha River

N.

Shih-san-li-tai

Liu-chia-tun

Terminal Pt.

Chang-chia-tun

Ni Shan

Ta-fang-shen

Deep Bay

Hand Bay

Kerr Bay

EN-WAN

lien-wan Bay

KOREA BAY

GENERAL MAP

OF THE

KUAN-TUNG PENINSULA

Scale of English Miles

5   0   5   10

"Position of the Passes" June 1st — July 27th ......

Russian position on 30th July ....

Hugh Rees. Ltd.

Stanford's Geogl. Estabt., London.

CHAPTER IV

Retreat from Feng-huang Shan, July 30—Fortifying 174 Metre Hill—
Capture of Kan-ta Shan—Attacks on the advanced hills, Au-
gust 13, 14, and 15—Retreat to Namako Yama and Division Hills—
Losses.

EARLY on the morning of July 31, I learnt that our
men on Feng-huang 'Shan had hurriedly retreated
into the fortress without offering any serious
resistance to the enemy. This was extremely un-
welcome news, for now we should have to come
into direct touch with the enemy round the
fortress itself.

Major Saratski's force had to occupy the crest
of Pan-lung Shan from Headquarter Hill to the redoubts of the 26th Regiment near Fort Yi-tzu Shan.
As this detachment proved insufficient for the defence
of this section, I sent up our 11th and 12th Companies,
with some volunteers from our non-combatant company under Sergeant-Major Bashchenko.* I posted
Midshipman Doudkin's four small naval guns there,
and disposed the remainder of the regiment as follows:
on 203 Metre Hill the 2nd and 4th Companies, on
174 Metre Hill the 5th and 9th Companies, and on
Height 426 the 2nd Scout Detachment, with the
3rd Detachment in an advanced position; on Division Hill the two Q.F. batteries of Colonels Petrov

* See footnote, page 232.

and Romanovski (which had arrived from Kiev) were posted with our 5th, 6th, and 7th Companies; on Headquarter Hill the 1st Scout Detachment. The remaining companies were in reserve.

Since, however, the line occupied exceeded 6 versts in length, we had all too few men for such a wide extent of front.

I now return to our retreat from Feng-huang Shan.

The hill and the position near 11th Verst, like that on Ta-ku Shan, had been very weakly fortified by us. I was well acquainted with the works on Feng-huang Shan and those in continuation towards the right flank, having gained this knowledge during, and before, the fighting on the "Position of the Passes."

These fortifications consisted of deep trenches with hardly any parapet, placed at the very foot of the hills which lay behind them, in accordance with General Fock's system. Right close up to the trenches grew high *kao-liang*,* which completely blocked the field of view from the trenches, and, like the plan of the trenches themselves, the positions selected for them afforded an example of the blind application of a principle † in itself sound enough. The man responsible for the defence of the right flank of Feng-huang Shan unhappily failed to apply this principle correctly.

In his anxiety to adhere to the principle of a flat trajectory he entirely lost sight of the fact that every small mound, if only two or three feet high, presents an impenetrable barrier to a low-flying

* Millet. † "The flatter the trajectory, the better."

bullet. He also quite forgot that the slope of the hill of itself affords an obstacle difficult to surmount; and he, moreover, ignored the difficulties of an eventual retreat from the trenches up the side of the hill, sometimes a very steep one, as was the case at Feng-huang Shan.

So the trenches on the right flank of Feng-huang Shan were placed at the foot of its northern side. In front of them grew *kao-liang* to the height of 5 feet. The regiments occupying this position were disposed throughout the trenches in question.

One of the officers of the 13th Regiment described what happened thus :

" Having retreated from the Shipinsin Pass, the regiment occupied part of the trenches on Feng-huang Shan, and began to cut down the *kao-liang*, but only had time to destroy a belt of about 50 yards of it in front of the trenches. They had supper and spent the night comparatively quietly. Very early in the morning there was a stir among the *kao-liang*, and before the men had time to seize their rifles, the Japanese were 20 paces from the trenches. Our troops, spread out over a wide front, were unable to withstand the rush of the Japanese columns and retreated up the hill and beyond. There were no trenches on the top of the hill. Seeing the retreat of the troops in the centre and the Japanese in possession of their trenches, the other regiments also began to retire on thus finding their flanks exposed. Thanks to our artillery, the Japanese were prevented from advancing any farther and stopped behind the hills which they had occupied. Only Ta-ku Shan and Hsiao-ku Shan * were left in our hands."

Another officer of the 13th Regiment gave the following description of the fight:

" After the battle round Lao-tso Shan our men had to occupy another position, of which the left flank was Feng-huang Shan. The 13th Regiment occupied the section from the Great Mandarin road to 11th Verst on the railway. We had the 1st, 2nd, 3rd, 4th, 5th, 6th, 7th, and 8th Companies in the first line, and the 9th, 11th, and 12th in the reserve, the 10th Company forming the artillery escort. The whole of the 14th Regiment was in reserve behind the 13th. The position occupied by us was fortified according to General Fock's system, *i.e.* the trenches were dug at the very foot of the hill, so that they afforded but a very poor field of fire, and the Japanese could take advantage of cover behind every clump or mound on the ground in front. Besides this, in front of the trenches was *kao-liang* of such a height that the whole of the foreground was completely hidden from our men sitting in the trenches. We did all we could to destroy this vile stuff, but we had no time to cut it down for more than 50 paces from the trenches, and in some places to even a less extent.

" Colonel Prince Machabeli, commanding the left, considering that his reserve was too weak, decided to strengthen it by one company, and despatched accordingly the following order to the firing line :

* These two forts were on the *Eastern Front.* The author probably refers to these here as being the only two points in *advance* of the main defensive line now left in Russian hands.

' Send back one of the companies from the position to the reserve.' * Captain R—— received this order. On either side of him was Major G——, commanding the 2nd Company, and Lieutenant L——, commanding the 3rd Company. Captain R—— decided that he would join the reserve. Unfortunately, Lieutenant L—— came to the same conclusion, so they both went back to the reserve. It is not known what Major G—— decided to do, but he also disappeared somewhere.

"The Japanese saw these companies going away, and, springing up to the attack, hurled themselves into the gap without firing a shot, the high *kao-liang* allowing them to come right up to our trenches unobserved. Having gained this unoccupied point, they worked round to the flank, and even the rear, of the other companies, and poured in a murderous fire. The 4th Company hurriedly evacuated its position, but the 1st and 5th held on for some time. At last, the 1st Company having lost 101 men and the 5th 105, they began to retire, and, following them, all the other companies climbed up the hill under a hail of bullets from the Japanese now occupying our trenches. There were no trenches at the top of the hill, so our men went on into the town. Colonel Machabeli was held responsible, and was removed from the command of the regiment in consequence."

This gallant field officer was afterwards killed on the West Pan-lung Redoubt under the following circumstances. The Japanese attacked the redoubt and took the front glacis. Our men were lodged in the rear. Colonel Machabeli stopped those who

* A forceful example of the consequences of a badly worded order.

were retreating and, having inspired them with a
fiery speech, rushed forward, calling on his men to
follow him. Another moment and the Japanese
were driven out of the redoubt.

After this exploit Colonel Machabeli went back
to the rear face of the redoubt, and had only just
sat down to get his breath, when one of the men ran
up and reported that the Japanese had again captured the front glacis. Once again Colonel Machabeli collected his men round him and threw himself
on the Japanese, but just as he was jumping across
the inner ditch a bullet struck him. Our men hesi-
tated, wavered, and then evacuated the whole redoubt, which remained from that time, together
with the body of the gallant colonel, in the hands of
the Japanese.

After the capture of Feng-huang Shan the Japanese
took a rest, being contented with reconnaissance
work only ; while, in the meantime, we strengthened
our positions, built kitchens, and made communication trenches between the fortifications.

The companies bivouacked in places screened from
the enemy's view. Luckily we had a good deal of
rain, which gave us water in abundance. The
soldiers dug out ponds near their bivouacs, and not
only washed their clothes, but even indulged in the
luxury of bathing.

Our scout detachments fared worst of all in this
respect, for they were far out in front, and had no
water.

We were much delayed in our work by the rocky
nature of the soil and the want of tools, especially

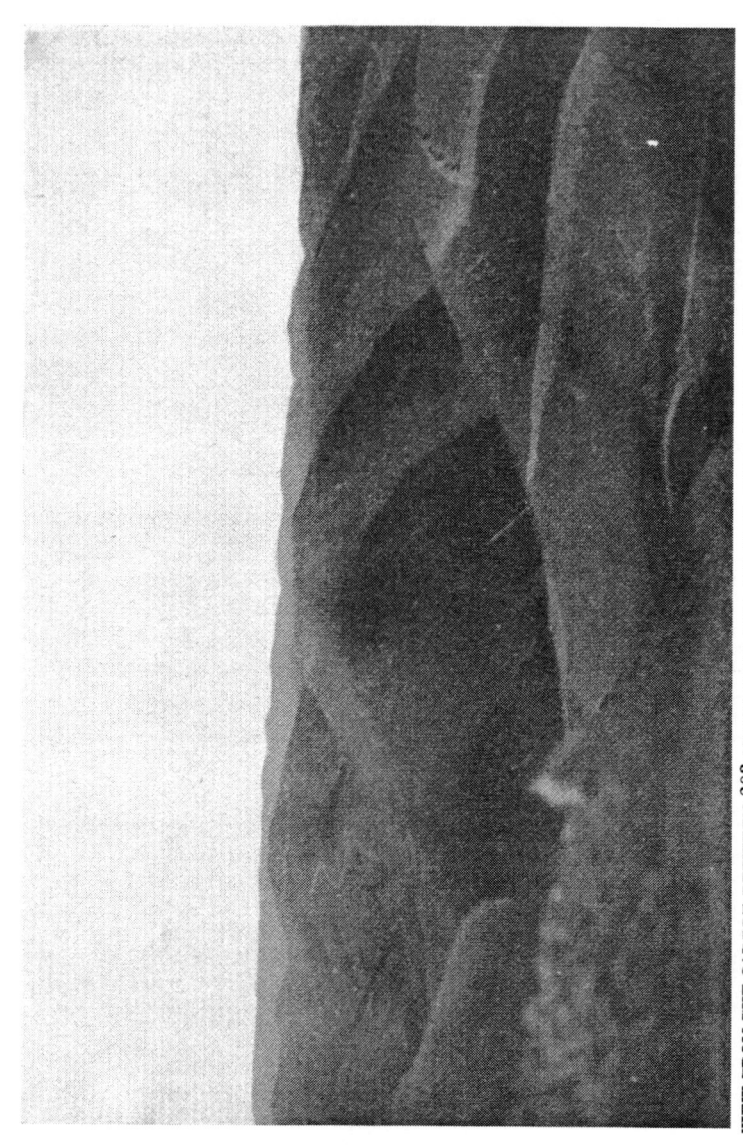

VIEW FROM THE SADDLE BETWEEN 203 METRE HILL AND AKASAKA YAMA TOWARDS 174 METRE HILL, UP WHICH A ZIGZAG ROAD IS SEEN. ON THE RIGHT IS SHOWN NAMAKO YAMA. THE TRENCHES ON THE EXTREME RIGHT OF THE PHOTO ARE ON THE RIGHT FLANK OF AKASAKA YAMA.

picks, good axes, and shovels, of which implements we needed a very large number. There was a sufficient quantity of wood in the town, but we required an enormous amount of it on the position itself.

We had to make provision for dug-outs at the rate of 50 per cent. for each company for the winter, besides kitchens and baths for the battalions, and shelters for the officers. Supplies of wood were brought up on our baggage animals to all points on the position, but there was scarcely a sufficiency for all the needs of the companies. We worked day and night for a long time, dividing our men into three reliefs ; nevertheless, our trenches were far from being completed.

Besides the enormous amount of spade work we had to do, we were handicapped by having to furnish a very strong outpost line.

We had no fortifications on 174 Metre Hill capable of resisting a direct attack, and a night attack might always be crowned with success, so that our men did not get much sleep. I very much feared night attacks, and so determined to strengthen our trenches by building redoubts. We had, however, as already stated, but few tools and little time, and there was so much work to be done, that it was absolutely impossible to prepare for every contingency.

The enemy was at close quarters and could attack at any moment. We had thus to watch his every movement, the more so, as we had no definite line of obstacles barring the way to the fortress, and even a slight advantage gained at night might give the enemy an open road into the New Town and, perhaps, even farther. For this reason I felt extremely uneasy.

Throughout the siege a third of the regiment was always on the alert.

This would not have been necessary if we had had a better line of defences and obstacles, or at least twice as many forts as we actually did have. There would have been no moral and physical wastage, and scurvy would not have hampered the defence of Port Arthur.

Although our own primary object was the fortification of 174 Metre Hill, we could not do very much work on the positions during our stay in Port Arthur, being constantly sent to the reserves stationed at Ying-cheng-tzu, * or to the right flank, or to the centre near the pass.

We began to work seriously at the fortifications only from the moment of the general retreat into Port Arthur, but even then we were sadly handicapped by the want of tools. It was lucky that the enemy did not worry us much, but turned his attention mainly to the right and centre.

The first shell fell into the town on Sunday, August 7.

On the 8th, the Japanese captured Ta-ku Shan and Hsiao-ku Shan. A number of the assaults were beaten back by the troops holding the hills, who fought day and night several days running. But there is a limit to human strength. On the third night the Japanese captured the hills, finding most of the defenders asleep. I was told this afterwards by men who had taken part in the defence.†

---

* Situated at the extreme left flank of the " Position of the Passes."

† This plea of utter prostration from constant fighting seems to be a poor excuse for the capture of the forts by the Japanese. The resistance was, in reality, *most* stubborn.

After the capture of Ta-ku Shan we noticed (from the observing stations we had organized) signs of a Japanese concentration near Louisa Bay. With a view to obtaining better observations, I was ordered to occupy Kan-ta Shan with a section under an officer. A ring trench had been made on this hill (I do not know who constructed it), but *kao-liang* surrounded the hill, and its defence was therefore a very difficult matter, as it was possible to get close up to the top under cover of the millet. Besides this, Kan-ta Shan was nearer to the enemy than to us, and was, moreover, in front of Colonel Semenov's section, and not mine. Steeling my heart, however, I sent a section there under Acting Ensign Shishkin. This section could easily be cut off and destroyed, for which reason I posted at night a strong piquet behind Kan-ta Shan for its support. From the moment we occupied this hill we had nightly skirmishes with the Japanese.

The enemy began to press us on all sides until, on August 10, they captured Kan-ta Shan by a night attack, but abandoned it in the day, when we again took possession—only for a day, however, for the Japanese recaptured the hill on the following night, and this time fortified themselves strongly on it.

However much we longed to see our fleet cruising on the flanks of the enemy's line of investment, our desire remained unsatisfied, for the ships did not dare to leave the harbour,* the enemy's fleet being

* It may be noticed that General Tretyakov makes no mention of the disastrous sortie made by the Russian fleet on August 10.

vastly superior, both in the number of ships, and in their quality.

We now had the pleasure of seeing five large Japanese battleships appearing every day on the horizon before Port Arthur.

On August 11, 12, and 13 we saw considerable signs of movement on the enemy's part in the direction of our left flank. Trains of baggage and bodies of troops were on the move. They carried out their manœuvre very cleverly, making full use of all the cover afforded by the unevenness of the ground. However, they showed themselves occasionally to our observers posted on the hills, and at night our sentries, who were posted far out in front, could plainly detect the sounds of moving wagons and marching men.

It was evident that the enemy was preparing to attack 174 Metre Hill. In view of this contingency we were reinforced by two companies of young sailors under the command of two of our officers, Lieutenants Afanaisev and Siedelnitski.

In order to prevent the enemy from breaking through between Height 426 and Headquarter Hill, I ordered the sailors to make a trench connecting Height 426 with the fortifications on Headquarter Hill.

Two companies of the 14th Reserve Battalion were sent up to strengthen our reserve. I placed Major Ivanov in command of the firing line. The reserve was posted near the bivouacs of the regimental staff of the 5th Regiment, behind Division Hill.

In view of the fact that Peredovaya (Advanced)

Hill * was very far in front, and held only as an observation post by the 3rd Scout Detachment, this detachment had orders, in case of a very determined attack, or a turning of its flanks, to retire to Headquarter Hill, where a position had been prepared for it.

I was very much afraid that the Japanese would take advantage of their superiority in numbers, make a night attack, and capture our weak trenches, the more so, as we had prepared practically no obstacles, not having had time to do so. We had only succeeded in putting up wire entanglements across the front of the trenches on Height 426 and Headquarter Hill.

We had been supplied with some star-rockets for use at night, and batteries for these had been stationed on Division, 203 Metre, and 174 Metre Hills.

Events turned out as I had expected. On the night of August 13–14 (I do not remember at what time exactly) a mounted orderly reported that large bodies of the enemy were moving up the road to Headquarter Hill, and a few minutes afterwards I heard heavy firing near Advanced Hill.

I got up and went with my orderlies to Division Hill, to the reserve, finding every one at his post.

A report was now brought in that all our scout detachments had been driven back on to 174 Metre Hill and had occupied a line extending from that hill in the direction of Pigeon Bay.

A terrific fire broke out and spread along the

* The Russian name for a knoll at the northern end of Headquarter Hill. Subsequent reference will be by the name of Advanced Hill.

whole front. Our star-rockets hissed, speeding high into the air, and their brilliant light showed the whole ground in front.

Another orderly galloped up with a report from the commander of the 1st Scout Detachment to the effect that the 3rd Scout Detachment had evacuated Advanced Hill and joined him, and that in conjunction, thanks to the star-rockets, they had beaten back the Japanese, who had fallen foul of the wire entanglement on the right flank of Headquarter Hill. The enemy's losses had been very heavy.

I at once sent a report of what had occurred to Colonel Irman,* but he himself came up to Division Hill shortly afterwards.

Rain began to fall and soaked us to the skin. At daybreak the firing somewhat slackened, but shortly afterwards the enemy's artillery re-opened, causing heavy losses to our companies.

Rifle and gun fire continued all day from both sides. The enemy swept 174 Metre and Division Hills with his guns, while our own artillery in turn swept the plains below, as the enemy offered no good target anywhere.

Having suffered considerably from our rifle fire, the enemy lay low and did not attempt to make a general assault. A Japanese column had worked round our left flank and essayed to attack Height 426, but the hostile troops were held up by the wire entanglements and were entirely annihilated by our 2nd Scout Detachment, which had been strengthened by two sections of the 3rd Company from 174 Metre Hill.

* General Tretyakov's immediate superior.

We suffered severely from the enemy's artillery fire.

Thus passed the whole of that day (August 14). The two batteries of Colonel Petrov and Colonel Romanovski, posted on Division Hill, sought in vain for targets, but the enemy kept under cover with remarkable skill.

There were constant alarms during the following night, and firing continued without ceasing. The enemy again attacked our trenches, but retreated after losing heavily. In order to be ready to beat back a night attack, we had moved the reserve nearer to the firing line. Knowing every inch of the ground, at about 10 p.m. I started off with Colonel Irman and two companies towards Headquarter Hill. There was fairly heavy firing in front of us.

We went on full of assurance, but in the darkness we lost the road. We took our bearings by the features of well-known hills, yet these same hills seemed now to be quite different from those we knew so well by day, and the sound of shots rang out from all sides more loudly the farther we advanced.

Now we must have reached Headquarter Hill—but no ! it was not there. The firing was soon heard, not only in front and from the flanks, but also far in rear. We found ourselves in a very unpleasant position. " Do you think we have gone beyond our firing line ? " I said to Colonel Irman. He answered that he had not the faintest idea where he was. Then I proposed that we should halt and send out scouts.

What if we were taken for Japanese by our own people and met by a volley ! That would be awkward indeed. So we halted and had a good look round,

7

but the place was absolutely unfamiliar. Still, firing was going on all around. It was the most stupid position I have ever been in. "Let us turn back, Vladimir Nicholaievitch," I said to Colonel Irman; "we shall certainly reach some place that we can recognize, and then we shall be all right."

Colonel Irman agreed, and we turned "right-about." Some time passed, and at last we made out the silhouette of Namako Yama, and once more breathed freely.

We decided to leave the reserve behind the slopes of 174 Metre Hill, where the men lay down under arms on a ploughed field. Major Ivanov came up to us, and we gave the reserve into his charge, we ourselves starting off for Division Hill to try to get a little sleep.

It had only just begun to grow light, when I was inundated with reports from the hills attacked, the Japanese having continued their various attacks all night. They had come up to the wire entanglements, but, failing everywhere to get through, they slipped away again in the darkness. Our star-rockets did sterling service throughout.

The dawn had not fully broken before the enemy's artillery thundered forth. I came out of the dug-out of the commander of the 6th Company, and began to observe over the top of the breastwork. Our three hills were wreathed in smoke from the enemy's high-explosive and shrapnel shells, and looked like veritable volcanoes in eruption. Though our men had sufficient cover from shrapnel, the high-explosive shells, filled with Shimose, caused fearful havoc.

A stream of wounded, on foot and in stretchers,

was moving along the road from the hills. It was evident that the enemy was determined to drive us off Advanced Hill, and our position was a serious one. I consequently sent a report to that effect.

A message came in from Headquarter Hill asking for reinforcements, and, pending the arrival of the reserves, I sent one section of the 6th Company out of the trenches. General Kondratenko saw that here was no child's play, and sent us two additional companies—the 2nd (Rotaiski's) and the 3rd (Levitski's) of the 13th Regiment.

It was a difficult thing to hold on to Advanced Hill, as it had been the last to be fortified. The depth of the trenches was normal, but their finish left much to be desired. We had made shrapnel-proof head-cover, but had had no time to trace traverses or make cover for the reserves, so that our men suffered severely from the enemy's shell fire, which was very heavy.

Before seven o'clock on the morning of August 15 all three hills had sent in requests for reinforcements, in compliance with which I immediately sent forward the two companies of the 13th Regiment, as I saw companies of other regiments coming to our assistance. General Kondratenko arrived on the scene at about 8 a.m. Having explained how matters stood, I drew his attention to the dangerous position of our present observation post. Bullets were whistling around us from all directions.

At this time Colonel Petrov's and Colonel Romanovski's batteries, stationed on Division Hill, prepared to open fire, although they had little hope of success, as the enemy's batteries were not visible and his infantry was attacking from points which were only within reach of the batteries far away behind Fort Yi-tzu Shan. The consequence was that our men had to fight the Japanese infantry under a murderous artillery fire without the support of their own guns.

The situation was an impossible one, as it had been at Nan Shan.

About 11 a.m. Colonel Irman rode up. Reinforcements arrived also. The enemy's gun fire was so terrific at this time, that I wondered how our men could continue to make any defence. But they were putting up a gallant fight, for we could see how they dashed out of their trenches, now to the right, now to the left, how the reserves posted in rear of the hills reinforced the men in the trenches, and how they again charged out of the trenches and then retired behind their scanty cover. The majority of our officers were wounded and officers of other units took command, but, judging from the enormous losses of the 5th Regiment, one could not help feeling that there were but few left in the trenches at all.

Major Ivanov had used all his reserves, and sent in asking for more. Reports were received from every quarter stating that the trenches had been absolutely wrecked by the enemy's shells, and that it was impossible to hold on under such artillery fire. The fire was indeed terrific, and General Kondratenko felt inclined to order a retreat; but I sent up two more companies to the left flank, one of them (a company of the Reserve Battalion) to the reserve behind the left flank, as the enemy was devoting his main energy towards that side. And now, at midday, it seemed as if the Japanese had concentrated the whole of their artillery, not only to utterly destroy the defenders, but to level the very hills themselves.

Our guns were still inactive, being unable to locate the positions of the enemy's batteries. As I have mentioned before, however, two batteries standing near us were preparing to open fire. This drew the enemy's attention, and he began to pour a stream of shell upon us as well as bullets. One of them burst close to Major Schiller, and killed him outright, and also wounded Colonel Petrov, the battery commander. The former was struck by a large splinter in the left breast and the latter in the left eye (he died the following day in hospital).

A little before this we saw unmistakable signs of a speedy retirement.

In order not to be taken at a disadvantage, I had arranged for a second line of defence (174 Metre Hill, Namako Yama, and Division Hill). When I had done this, and inspected our trenches with Captain Sichev, commanding the 6th Company, I noticed that the enemy's rifle fire was especially directed on our trenches on Division Hill. We had not long to wait for confirmation of this fact (if it were needed), for Captain Sichev was wounded in the leg—luckily, not seriously, as the bullet did not touch the bone.

Having completed my round, I returned to General Kondratenko, and saw that our men were streaming away from Headquarter Hill, like powder spilling out of a barrel, and shortly afterwards from Height 426 also. An exclamation of annoyance escaped the general. " See ! surely it is easier for them there than it is on Height 426. What are they running for ? They *must* be stopped ! " Colonel Irman, who was standing

near, took the general's words as an order and hurried
off to carry it out, taking Captain Iolshin of the
general staff with him.*

"And you, Nicholai Alexandrovitch," said General
Kondratenko, turning to me, "take a company, and
attack their left flank when they come down the hill
in pursuit." There was a company waiting not far
behind us, and I should very soon have carried out
the order given me, but I had scarcely gone half a
verst with the company, when a mounted orderly
galloped up and gave me an order to return immediately to General Kondratenko and hand over the command to Lieutenant-Colonel Naoomenko, who was
close to me at the time. When I again reached
Division Hill, I saw our army in full retreat from the
three advanced hills. On the crest of the hills that
had been occupied by us (Height 426, Headquarter Hill,
and Advanced Hill) appeared lines of the enemy's
skirmishers. Our men retreated without haste, returning the enemy's fire, but strewing the ground
they were passing over with bodies. Three mounted
men were seen galloping along the retreating line;
they were Colonel Irman, Captain Iolshin, and Colonel
Zoobov, the latter commanding the 4th Reserve
Battalion. But their efforts were in vain and the
retreat continued without check.

When Colonel Irman returned, he reported that
he had been unable to stop the retreating line, and the
only men who paid any attention to him were a few

---

* Our Official History (Part III.) states that Headquarter Hill was
captured on the 13th, and Height 426 (Bokovy) on the 15th. From
this account it is evident that the former also was not occupied until
the 15th.

scouts of the 5th Regiment and the 1st Company of the reserve battalion under Lieutenant Sadykov, whom he recommended for a St. George's Cross.

I consider it my duty to state here that Major Ivanov acted in the most heroic manner during the battle. When the 6th Company refused to go up Headquarter Hill to the help of their comrades, Major Ivanov said to the men : " If you don't come with me I shall lie down here to be shot " ; and, running out on to an open space that was swept by bullets, he lay down on the ground. Then the commander of the company rushed up with his men, lifted him up, and said that the company would follow him wherever he liked to lead them. However, on reaching the hill, they found that it had been evacuated and was now strongly held by the Japanese. Major Ivanov then took the company back to Division Hill.

General Kondratenko ordered me to stop the retreat and to form a reserve for our subsequent defensive line, and I set out to do my best. When the Japanese appeared on Height 426 and Headquarter Hill, our artillery swept these heights with shrapnel, and cleared the summits of yellow-peaked caps in a moment.

This was timely relief, as the Japanese began to bring a flanking fire to bear from the trenches on Headquarter Hill on the lines at Pan-lung Shan, and our 11th Company suffered severely from this fire. Things were already going badly at Pan-lung Shan, and it was of vital importance to know what was to be done next. To decide this, General Kondratenko summoned all the commanders to come to

Division Hill. I also went there the moment I had formed my reserves and posted them in a safe place.

Colonel Irman, Colonel Zoobov, and others were already there. The noise of battle had become less, and for the moment the Japanese showed no signs of advancing any farther.

Our artillery ceased firing, as its targets had disappeared over the top of the hills and taken cover in the *kao-liang*. This was about 2 p.m.

Before undertaking anything further it was decided to make an inspection of the positions behind us on Pan-lung Shan, which General Kondratenko ordered Colonel Naoomenko and myself to do. We immediately went to Pang-lung Shan, from which our 11th Company, under Second-Lieutenant Lobyrev, had already retreated. I asked: "Who ordered you to retreat?" and he answered: "Major Katishev [commanding the 11th Company; he had been wounded in the arm and had been taken to the field hospital]. He told us to retreat, as it was impossible to remain in the trenches, for Headquarter Hill was in the hands of the Japanese." On hearing this, I said: "You are never to retreat without orders from a senior commander. Go back again!"

Second-Lieutenant Lobyrev, a quiet, brave fellow, answered: "It is all the same to us—we will go back"; then, turning quickly to his men, he shouted out: "Company, about turn, to the old position—march!" and the company turned round and re-occupied its trenches.

Having made an inspection of these trenches, we came to the conclusion that it was, indeed, impossible to remain in them, as their left flank rested on Headquarter Hill and there was hardly any cover from fire from that side.

We informed General Kondratenko of the result of our inspection, and he decided to evacuate Pan-lung Shan entirely as far as the redoubts on the right flank of Division Hill. This was done at about 7 p.m.

Between Pan-lung Shan and Division Hill there was a position favourable for defence, and I had already had some work done on it and commenced the construction of a large lunette. We should have occupied this position with the companies which retreated from Pan-lung Shan, but as we had no tools for completing the works we had to abandon the idea of holding it, and all the companies were taken from Pan-lung Shan and placed in reserve behind Division Hill and Namako Yama. The three scout detachments were posted between 203 Metre Hill and Fort Ta-yang-kou North, where they could get some rest.

I will now give a detailed account of the fighting on each of the hills attacked.

ON TRIOK-GOLOVY HILL (THREE-HEADED HILL) *

About 10 p.m. on August 13 the outposts were driven back by the enemy on to their supports. The 1st Scout Detachment was surrounded, but fought its way through at the point of the bayonet, bringing along two badly wounded men and two Japanese rifles.

At eleven o'clock the Japanese attacked Advanced Hill, which was held by one section (the 3rd) of the

* The Russian name for Headquarter Hill.

3rd Infantry Scout Detachment, consisting of 36 men. Favoured by darkness, the enemy completely surrounded the hill on all sides. The non-commissioned officer in charge, Nazarov, seeing that there was no escape, attacked the enemy, and at this moment a star-rocket burst, and by its light the men on Headquarter Hill saw the Japanese, and at once poured a hail of bullets into them, thus enabling Nazarov to fight his way back to Headquarter Hill.

Having taken Advanced Hill, the Japanese climbed up Headquarter Hill, but were beaten back with heavy losses. Half an hour later they raised the cry of " Banzai! " and again stormed our trenches from the right flank, but in doing so they fell foul of the wire entanglements and were nearly all wiped out.

About 2 a.m. the enemy repeated the attack in great force ; but only a few reached the trenches, where they were bayoneted by our men. In this attack the darkness greatly assisted the enemy, as the supply of rockets being exhausted, no more could be sent up.

Towards morning on August 14, covered by fog and rain, the enemy tried to overwhelm our scouts, but without success. In this attack Acting Ensign Zakrejevski was wounded, the sergeant-major of the 1st Detachment killed, and several scouts wounded.

I must mention a very fine piece of work on the part of Corporal Vagin of the 3rd Scout Detachment. Entirely on his own initiative, he occupied with his section a hill that had been left unfortified, and by enfilade fire afforded great relief from pressure on Headquarter Hill and Height 426, whilst at the same time beating back the Japanese attacking his own party.

All the non-commissioned officers acted like true

heroes, and one of them, Lance-Corporal Khaidoulin
(a Tartar) of the 1st Scout Detachment, seeing that
the men of his section had expended all their ammunition during the third attack, jumped up out of the
trench and shouted out, " Let us die, lads, for the
Czar and our Faith ! " and prepared for a bayonet
charge. Just at that moment ammunition was brought
up, and the Japanese were driven off by rifle fire.

In the morning it was seen that the Japanese
had captured Advanced Hill, Kan-ta Shan, and a
small hill in front of the 12th Company at Pan-lung
Shan, from which they opened rifle fire, but the Baranovski guns on Height 426 drove them under cover.

On account of sickness (dysentery) Lieutenant
Choulkov had been sent to hospital, and Acting
Ensign Elechevski was sent to take his place.

On the night of August 14 the supply of ammunition began to run short and firing was stopped.
Thinking that we had abandoned the trenches, the
enemy tried to capture them. He was met at the
very edge of the trenches by some volleys which
almost annihilated him, only one officer and five
men, who had hidden behind some stones, being left.
At daybreak Sergeant Zmoushko, noticing that the
men behind the stones were not dead, began to watch,
and as soon as the officer showed his head, he shot
him. Seeing their officer killed, the soldiers ran
back, but were all shot down.

The ground in front of the trenches was strewn
with the bodies of the Japanese. In the morning
(August 15) the men of the 1st Scout Detachment
left the trenches in order to clean their rifles, which
had become choked from continual firing, and their

place was being taken by a company of the 4th Reserve Battalion ; at this moment, however, the trenches were swept by such a terrible fire that the new arrivals gave way and began to retreat. The men of the Scout Detachment rushed up towards the trenches, but, being unable to stem the retreat, they themselves retired behind the slopes of the hills lying in rear, and thence (when Headquarter Hill had been occupied by the Japanese) to Division Hill.

Colonel Irman galloped up to the retreating men and compelled them to turn back ; but the Japanese opened such a deadly fire from the machine guns and rifles, that again they turned their backs. At this time our field artillery swept the captured hills with shrapnel, upon which the Japanese took cover, and ceased firing on the retreating columns.

I consider it my duty here to mention the names of two of our heroes. When our men were stopped by Colonel Irman, they suffered such heavy losses that they again began to retreat, except two men of the 5th Regiment, Corporal Trusov and Private Molchanov, who got right into the Japanese trenches ; but finding that they were only two, while the enemy filled the trench, they beat a retreat—not, however, before Molchanov had killed a Japanese officer. They were both wounded slightly on their way back, but nevertheless remained in the ranks.

On Bokovy Hill (Side Hill) *

At 10 p.m. on August 13, the sentries on Height 426 reported that four columns, each two companies

* The Russian name for Height 426.

strong, were advancing on the hill. Second-Lieutenant Andreiev immediately sent some sentries out to the wire entanglement to give him warning when the enemy had descended the opposite slope and reached the wires.

At eleven o'clock the sentries reported that the Japanese were close at hand. Volley firing was immediately opened, and Midshipman Doudkin's small guns also commenced firing, upon which the Japanese, after suffering considerable losses, retreated behind the hill.

At midnight they again attacked the hill, but were again repulsed, and up to 5 a.m. they attacked seven times without any success whatever.

They left piles of bodies in front of and amongst the wire entanglements.

During the third attack it was seen that a column of two companies had got through the wire on the right flank. A section of the 2nd Scout Detachment was immediately sent against them under the command of Lance-Corporal Noskov, and this section, together with the Baranovski guns, posted on that flank, and two sections of the 9th Company sent from 174 Metre Hill, put them to flight.

When day broke, 432 Japanese bodies were counted round the wire entanglements.

By 7 a.m. half the trenches had been destroyed by the enemy's artillery, so that one section had to be withdrawn and posted on the opposite slope of the hill.

At 9.30 a.m. the Japanese broke through the wire entanglements and got half-way up the hill, but they were met by fire from the trenches—from the left flank by volleys from the section of the 2nd Infantry Scout Detachment, and from the right by volleys from the sailors under the command of Lieutenant Afanaisev; and, not being able to make any headway, they retired. At 11 a.m. Second-Lieutenant Andreiev was wounded, and the command devolved on Lance-Corporal Kobrintsev. Captain Rotaiski was sent to reinforce, but he did not occupy the trenches, remaining instead behind their left flank.

During the day the enemy began to increase his efforts against Height 426, and in consequence the reserve was sent for, but did not arrive, though two companies of the 4th Reserve Battalion were supposed to have been sent up.

About midday, when the 1st and 2nd sections of the 1st Detachment were annihilated by artillery fire, a half-company of the reserve battalion, under a second-lieutenant of the 27th Regiment, arrived and occupied the right trench, and in the night another half-company, with a sergeant-major, was sent up with orders to occupy the saddle between Headquarter Hill and a small hill to the left of it. Firing went on the whole day, and on the night of August 14–15 the enemy made two attacks, but only succeeded in one case in getting up to the wire entanglement, where more than two-thirds of the attacking party were lost.

The hill was captured at midday on August 15. We retreated from the advanced positions, but were in consequence considerably stronger on Division Hill, Namako Yama, and 174 Metre Hill, on account of the reserves concentrated there.

In view of the anticipated attack on these hills,

we had to work hard on them, the more so, as Namako Yama was very weakly fortified. The trenches were small and unfinished, and the ground solid rock.

If only these trenches had been prepared beforehand, it would have been quite a different matter. How many lives would have been saved, and how many attacks beaten back! It is always necessary in a fortress to prepare defensive positions in peace time, and this can be done conveniently as part of the training of the troops in garrison.

The fighting on Headquarter Hill cost us somewhat dearly. The Scout Detachments of the 5th Regiment lost more than half their strength—160 men and one officer (Second-Lieutenant Andreiev); the two naval companies suffered a loss of 30 men each; the remainder, represented by companies of the 13th Regiment and of the 4th Reserve Battalion, were reduced by quite 15 per cent. of their strength. The 11th and 12th Companies at Pan-lung Shan did not have many losses, but three officers were placed *hors de combat*—Major Katishev being wounded, and Second-Lieutenant Merkoulev and Ensign Moukin killed.

CHAPTER V

WE had to work absolutely under the enemy's very nose, mostly at night, although we took the opportunity of working in the day-time whenever the enemy's fire slackened a little.

It was a good thing that the 5th Regiment had learnt something about trench-making, so that the officers, and even the non-commissioned officers, knew exactly how to go to work without any instruction from sapper specialists, of whom we did not possess a single man.

General Kondratenko did not propose recapturing the advanced hills, as they were not exceptionally important positions, and it would have cost us dearly to hold on to them.

After August 15, things were fairly quiet on our side, but bullets, and even shell, rather frequently passed over the quarters of the regimental staff. We had, therefore, to move them farther back, to a small river running along the road from the town towards 203 Metre Hill, and as a large mess tent would have been visible from a great distance, we decided not to pitch one.

The Japanese had not got off lightly in their attacks on the advanced hills, and their losses must have been reckoned in thousands. They lost particularly heavily in storming Height 426, where they stumbled blindly upon the wire entanglements and made repeated attacks. There were piles of dead heaped up round these entanglements. The fact must be noted that we were driven out of these positions by gun fire, and not by the Japanese infantry.

Events here made it clear to every one what preponderance in artillery really means. The side that silences the enemy's guns can capture his positions without particularly hard fighting, for, having once got the enemy's fire under control, one can choose a point of attack, concentrate the whole of one's artillery on it, and then take it by storm with comparatively small numbers. For this, however, a numerous, well-trained, and efficient artillery is essential. To win a battle with badly trained or inefficient artillery is now a matter of extreme difficulty. I will not venture to lay down the exact proportion of guns necessary per 1,000 infantry, but there must be, at any rate, not less than 6 guns per 1,000 (*i.e.* one battery to each complete battalion).

What an error we committed in posting our artillery on the crests of the hills! The Japanese punished us very severely for the mistake, but it was too late then to change our dispositions.

The Japanese batteries were completely concealed, and fired on our skirmishers as deliberately as if they were at practice on their artillery ranges. They had a lot of work in front of them yet, of course,

8

as we could still hold on to those positions we had spent some time in fortifying, and the 5th Regiment had yet many trying moments to live through.

Much had to be done on 203 Metre Hill in order to enable our troops to hold out under a veritably hellish fire, with which our gunners were powerless to cope.

From the capture of the advanced hills until the morning of August 19 we worked on our positions almost without molestation, the enemy devoting all his attention to 174 Metre Hill (See Map II.). Being convinced that the next serious attack would be made on that hill, we did all in our power to put it into a good state of defence.   The left flank was covered by a wire entanglement, the front was strengthened by a 3-foot revetment, and the right flank had a double line of trenches, the upper tier of which was blinded.

On the top of the hill solid shelters were built for the gunners and a round trench was made, with a considerable number of blinded traverses, which were not, however, very solidly constructed.

The summit of the hill on the left flank (which we called the Connecting Ridge) was lined with trenches. On the reverse slopes of the hill a magazine, very solidly made, was constructed for gun and rifle ammunition, and cover was also provided there, sufficient for a whole reserve company.   In rear of the hill (174 Metre Hill) there were four field mortars, and on the crest, for long-range firing, two long naval guns (I do not remember their exact calibre, but I think it was 150 mm.) with steel shields, in a well-constructed battery, and behind the crest four field quick-firers. On the saddle between 174 Metre Hill and Connecting Ridge were Lieutenant Tsvietkov's two quick-firers.

The garrison of 174 Metre Hill consisted of the 5th and 9th Companies of the 5th Regiment (about 300 men), while the 6th, 10th, 11th, and 12th Companies of the same, and one company of the 24th Regiment were on Connecting Ridge.

There were on Namako Yama at this time: on the left flank, the 1st Company of the 28th Regiment under Major Sakatski, the 11th Company of the 13th Regiment, the 5th and 6th Companies of the Kuang-tung Battalion, and the 12th Company of the 13th Regiment. It must be admitted that the trenches here were not sufficiently strong to afford much protection against the Japanese Shimose and shrapnel, and heavy losses were expected. But what could be done ? We had neither the time nor the tools necessary to deal with that rocky soil, and thus to improve matters.

A battery had been placed on the top of 174 Metre Hill, instead of an infantry redoubt. This battery was in position before the 5th Regiment occupied the hill. I wanted to convert it into a redoubt, but my senior officers refused to sanction the proposal, as, in General Bieli's * opinion, there was no other position for long-range guns. How much time and trouble we spent on completing this battery, while the real defenders had to crowd into the small unfinished trenches ! I may add that the guns posted in this battery had a large area of dead ground, and drew on themselves the fire of the Japanese heavy

* Commander of the Fortress Artillery.

artillery, which considerably interfered with our work. I was nearly killed by a shell bursting near me, and escaped by a miracle with no greater hurt than a blow in the side from a large clod of earth.

On the fall of the advanced positions the garrison of 174 Metre Hill had to live in the trenches, whereas before they had been encamped on the reverse slope of the hill. Field kitchens had been well built in a ravine, and others on the reverse slope.

The men lived in large field tents, and the officers in an improvised barrack, built of planks.

Strenuous efforts had been made to construct a road leading from the top of the hill, and an enormous amount of energy had likewise been expended in making roads to the principal hills—203 Metre, Namako Yama, and Akasaka Yama. To this end we had been working hard ever since the arrival of the 5th Regiment at 174 Metre Hill, at which time there existed only one small path over 203 Metre Hill.

By its fire, and by the posting of a detachment to prevent Height 426 from being outflanked from the left, 174 Metre Hill was a source of considerable annoyance to the Japanese, so, in attacking the advanced hills, they did not forget it.

On August 14,* at 4.15 a.m., the enemy opened a tremendous fire on 174 Metre Hill, and kept it up till 5 o'clock in the evening. On this day Captain

---

* Our Official History states that "mist and rain prevented an effectual bombardment on this day," and no real assault took place. The bombardment of 174 Metre Hill on the 15th was evidently only done to cover the attack on Height 426 (described in the last chapter), as no serious attack was made on 174 Metre Hill till the 19th.

CONSTRUCTING THE ROAD ON THE REVERSE SLOPE OF 203 METRE HILL.

Andreiev, commanding the artillery on the hill, was wounded by four splinters.

At 1.15 a.m. on August 15 the enemy advanced on 174 Metre Hill from the front and from the left flank. Firing continued till 3.15 a.m., when the Japanese retreated, but a heavy bombardment broke out again at 4.30 a.m. and continued till 9 o'clock.

This bombardment was renewed at 4 p.m., continuing till 7 p.m. As a result some of our splinter-proofs were destroyed and also part of our trenches.

On August 16 the Japanese did not fire at all, possibly through want of ammunition, we ourselves taking advantage of the occasion to rebuild our trenches. About 9 p.m. desultory rifle fire broke out under the hill, and the enemy's skirmishing line appeared about 1,200 paces away, while behind, in complete silence, marched the storming columns. The defenders of the hills threw down their digging tools, stood to their posts, and opened fire in volleys.

The storming columns moved away, now to the right, now to the left, and finally took cover in the defile on the left. This was at about 11 p.m., and our men sat in the trenches all night expecting another attack. We expended 12,000 rounds of ammunition.

On August 17 and 18 our men rebuilt the trenches under heavy rifle fire.

On the 17th the trenches were completed to the required profile, but a heavy bombardment was then opened on the hill. Our guns tried to answer the fire from the hills, but could not locate the batteries that were destroying them, and the Japanese soldiers only showed themselves when out of range. Our field guns were therefore put under cover, and I still regret that it was impossible to put those 150-mm. guns under cover as well.

On August 18 the firing upon the hill increased considerably in volume, and our trenches and splinter-proofs began to suffer severely. Lieutenant-Colonel Leesaevski, who was commandant of the hill, reported that he expected an attack, so I moved our reserves to 203 Metre Hill.

At night fierce hand-to-hand fighting took place round the base of the hill between the Japanese and our patrols who were forming the outpost line—a sure sign of a coming attack.

On the night of August 18–19 the Japanese moved in great strength up to 174 Metre Hill and lay down behind the crests of the nearest hillocks. Lieutenant-Colonel Leesaevski had the whole garrison on the alert, and opened fire as soon as the columns showed themselves over the crests beyond. The enemy made several attempts to come to close quarters, but without avail. On the alarm sounding, star-rockets were fired from 203 Metre and Division Hills, and our search-lights came into play for the first time. The scene was a terrible, but, at the same time, an exhilarating one. Discovered by the beams of light, the Japanese hastily retired over the crest, leaving a great number of dead in front of 174 Metre Hill. After several attempts they ceased their attacks, and the rest of the night passed in petty encounters and outpost skirmishes.

Early on the morning of August 19, just as day was breaking, I was awakened by a fearful cannonade. Running out of my room, I saw a pall of smoke from bursting shrapnel hanging over 174 Metre Hill. In order to find out what was happening, I galloped over to Akasaka Yama. However, when I got there, I was no better off than before, so I went to the left flank of Namako Yama. A dense skirmishing line was advancing on the right of 174 Metre Hill, and lines of skirmishers and columns of troops were moving towards the centre, occasionally taking cover in the valleys and then again appearing on the ridges. The rattle of rifle fire from our companies on Connecting Ridge could be heard on the left flank. The main attack was delivered against the left of 174 Metre Hill, but it was not within my field of view. The lines advanced so skilfully that our guns were unable to range on them, though they suffered heavily from rifle fire. Orderlies with reports were galloping away from 174 Metre Hill.

In order to meet them, I again returned to Akasaka Yama, where Colonel Irman joined me.

Wishing to be at the centre of the hills attacked, and within easy reach of orderlies, we changed our position to a hillock situated between Namako Yama and Connecting Ridge. We also thought that this would be a favourable point for making observations, but, as a matter of fact, it was rather the reverse, because all shell falling "over" landed in this very locality. We posted the reserve (the 7th Company of the 28th Regiment) behind the left flank of Namako Yama.

From 203 Metre Hill we sent a telephone message to the officer commanding the artillery, directing him to concentrate every available gun on the slopes in front of 174 Metre Hill.

In a quarter of an hour our guns boomed forth, and shells of every size began to fall on the ground indicated by us. The Japanese gun fire smothered 174 Metre Hill, and a continuous stream of wounded flowed back towards 203 Metre Hill, where the chief dressing station was situated. This fierce bombardment continued until about four o'clock. We had lost heavily. The whole of the rear of the hill attacked was literally strewn with shell. I was rather badly hit in the left side by a stone thrown up by a bursting shell.

Seeing that the right flank of Connecting Ridge was the most probable point of attack (there was a good deal of dead ground from our guns in front of it), and that a very heavy artillery fire was now being directed there, I sent the 7th Company of the 28th Regiment, under Major Frantz, to stand in reserve behind it.

About four o'clock the firing reached its zenith. The Japanese advanced to the attack, not in columns but in large groups, but they failed to get up to the trenches. Hundreds of them were mown down, and it seemed to me that the attack had failed everywhere. What was our surprise, when we received a report from Major Astafiev, commanding the 10th Company, * that his half-company had been wiped out, save ten men, and that the Japanese had occupied his empty trenches during the attack. The remaining ten men, however, had not retreated (they were separated from the captured trench by a cliff), but had stuck to their trench. I then and there

* This company was on Connecting Ridge and had been sent to reinforce the 5th and 9th Companies on 174 Metre Hill.

made a mental vow that the deeds of these heroes should eventually be put on record in letters of gold as a perpetual memorial to the 10th Company, and I now redeem my pledge.

The trench occupied by the Japanese was under the cliff, and it was a very difficult matter to climb down into it. As we had no further reserves available, I sent to 203 Metre Hill for two half-companies (2nd and 4th of our regiment), hoping to drive the Japanese out of the trench with these men. I also sent to General Kondratenko for reinforcements.

Lieutenant-Colonel Leesaevski reported from 174 Metre Hill that the Japanese had run up one by one, had established themselves within a few paces of the trenches, and were throwing stones at our riflemen, who returned the missiles.

At about six o'clock we collected two companies of the 13th Regiment, and made an attack on about 100 Japanese then in the trenches of the 10th Company. The companies quickly reached the top of the cliff, but got no farther, as it was a big drop down below. The Japanese artillery, noticing them, at once opened a heavy fire, and as it thus became impossible to remain there in the open the companies retreated again into the valley.

At about seven o'clock General Kondratenko joined us, and four companies of the 13th Regiment arrived, the 2nd, 6th, 7th, and 9th, under the command of the battalion commanders Majors Goosakovski and Gavreelov.

We decided that the Japanese must be driven out of the 10th Company's trenches, and, with that object in view, I reinforced these men, who had already resisted several attacks, with one more company. The attack was repeated, but with the same result (it was a big jump down, right on to the bayonets of the Japanese, who were invisible from the top, while the guns from the heights beyond mowed down the attackers). This time half of the men lodged themselves behind stones on the top, and I now felt sure that the Japanese would not take the hill, as it would be very difficult for them to climb up the cliff. In order to minimize our losses from gun fire, I decided on a night attack, and sent one company, under Major Goosakovski, to carry it out.

I ordered back half a company of the 5th Regiment to its original position.

It transpired that the 7th Company of the 28th Regiment was not in its correct place, having for some reason retired behind 174 Metre Hill. I did not see when Major Frantz carried out this movement.

All this time the firing and bombardment on 174 Metre Hill continued, and our forces dwindled away rapidly.

Reinforcements being demanded, a Scout Detachment under Captain Osmanov, which had only just come up, was sent there. This detachment, with its commander at its head, steadily and quietly ascended the hill, five men excepted, who tailed off at the foot of the hill, evidently afraid to go on. I did not order them to ascend the hill, knowing from experience that the presence of a few cowards may unsettle the very bravest company.

The stream of wounded from the hill increased, and many of these poor sufferers expired while being carried across the shell-strewn ground. We saw

one wounded man, who was being carried by two of
our clerks, killed by a shell falling right on top of him.
One of his bearers was killed too, but the other escaped as by a miracle. A large group of wounded
now went past me, and behind them an officer on a
stretcher. He was a very young gunner, and he
kept waving his sword in a frenzy and muttering
something. I do not remember what he said, as
my attention was attracted by another stretcher,
on which was an officer whom I thought I knew.

When the stretcher came close, I recognized in
the wounded man Lieutenant-Colonel Leesaevski,
who had been commandant of the hill. He was
covered with blood and dust. A bullet had shattered
his lower jaw and tongue, and another had struck
his hand. He could not speak from loss of blood.

In his absence things might go badly on the hill.

This seasoned warrior had always shown extraordinary energy combined with method. He was nick-
named " General Fock " in the regiment, which for
some reason displeased the real general, so, instead
of commanding a regiment, Lieutenant-Colonel Leesaevski was given the command of the 2nd Battalion
of the 5th Regiment. General Fock never recognized
the great spirit animating this man, which showed
up so prominently in the defence of 174 Metre Hill.
The old Colonel was indeed a far finer soldier than
many of the younger ones.

He fearlessly walked about the hill, encouraging
the men and directing their fire, closely following
the movements of the enemy, and then, bringing up
his small reserve just at the right moment, he scattered
the thick columns of attackers like chaff before the

wind by a few well-directed volleys. When the men wanted to take him to the dressing station, he said : " Leave me alone, my lads ; I want to die with you." With a heavy heart I accompanied the stretcher, fearing that a stray bullet or shell might end the career of this magnificent old soldier. But, thank God ! he got safely across the pass to 203 Metre Hill, which meant that he was out of harm's way. In his place I appointed Captain Bielozerov, commanding the 9th Company of the 5th Regiment, one of the bravest of our officers.

Towards evening more reinforcements were called for from 174 Metre Hill. The defenders were so worn out that they could not repair the damage done, which was considerable. The upper battery was destroyed, all the field guns were dismounted, and the gun-pits reduced to ruins. Nearly all the splinter-proofs in the trenches were destroyed, as well as half of the parapet. The whole of the overhead-cover against shrapnel was also wrecked by shell fire.

It is difficult to defend such places without casemated works. On a hill commanded from all sides what can riflemen do against heavy artillery, and the high-explosive shell of field guns ? During this day the 5th and 9th Companies of the 5th Regiment lost half their strength.

Gun fire slackened. The stream of wounded also ceased, and we breathed more freely. Our party on the central hillock was joined by some reserve officers, and eventually we even had something to eat.

Meat, bread, and hot tea were supplied to the men in the lines, and the field kitchen on the other side of 174 Metre Hill, which had escaped untouched, got to work.

General Kondratenko brought up two more companies to the reserve and sent two companies of the 13th Regiment to the hill to work at the trenches.

We laughed at the Japanese who had taken the 10th Company's trench, and must by now be feeling like rats in a trap. The half of the 1st Company of the 13th Regiment who had been left there, and the ten men of the 10th Company, prevented them from spreading along the trench, while in front their road was barred by those standing on the hill, so that it appeared inevitable that they must all be killed that night.

Meanwhile night had already fallen. The usual night firing had started between the outposts at the foot of the hills, and the resulting noise would cover the advance of our attacking companies. I sent to ask why the attack had not commenced, and was kept waiting for an answer for a very long time. The night was very dark. Everything was quiet, till now and again the enemy's bullets, like birds of the night, hummed high overhead, or our star-rockets, strange hissing monsters, like fiery snakes shot up into the sky and burst into a thousand dazzling stars, brilliantly illuminating the dark hills and valleys.

" The spirit is willing, but the flesh is weak." This proverb was exemplified in us and in our men. How many times have we not been witnesses of the truth of it! how many times have not the Japanese taken advantage of the utter exhaustion of our troops, fallen upon them when they lay asleep, and captured important points in our position (as at Ta-ku Shan, Miortvaia Sopka, * and other places) !

We realize now what it means to defend a fortress lacking a main line of defence and having an insufficient number of permanently fortified positions. Now I can clearly see that open field works, even though prepared for some time in advance, and with trenches strengthened with glacis parapets (as Glinka-Yarnchevski proposed at one time), will not give the defenders facilities for sufficient rest; and rest is a very important factor.

We were so tired that day—a fact not to be wondered at—that we lay down where we were and went to sleep. Heavy rifle firing brought us to our feet again. Star-rockets shot into the air and lit up the place, and caused the firing to die down once more. We received word from those on the hill that they had been firing on the Japanese, who had destroyed some of the wire entanglements. There were not many of them, but they had nevertheless caused a good deal of damage, and then had crouched down near the line of wires. It was unfortunate that they had succeeded to such an extent. I sent orders for the damage to be repaired as far as possible, but I knew our men on the hill were handicapped owing to lack of barbed wire.

This barbed wire was literally worth its weight in gold, and I was always delighted when we succeeded in getting some for the defence of this or that point, but there was great need of it everywhere.

* Meaning "Extinct Volcano"; situated about midway between 174 Metre and Division Hills.

There were several of these alarms during the night, but all this time Major Goosakovski's attack on the Japanese failed to come off.

However, I received a note at last, saying that he had decided to attack at daybreak.

Having quietly thought the matter out, I came to the conclusion that the Japanese might be left in the trench. These 100 men could not climb up and take the hill, which was defended by a whole company, neither could they be reinforced, as any reinforcements would be annihilated before they reached them. I told Colonel Irman, who was sitting near me, what I thought, and as he quite agreed with me, I sent an order cancelling the attack, and withdrew the companies, except the one behind the rocks, to a more sheltered spot between 174 Metre Hill and Connecting Ridge. One of these companies I placed in reserve behind 174 Metre Hill, so that there were now three companies in the reserve, *i.e.* at the immediate disposal of the officer in command on the hill. The two companies which had arrived in the evening I assigned to the general reserve. There were a few hours left till dawn, of which we took advantage to get some sleep, repairing to Namako Yama, so as not to be disturbed by the groans of the badly wounded men as they were being carried along the road.

Our bearers (bandsmen, regimental clerks, and volunteers from the town) sought them out during the night in the ravines, trenches, and ruined blindages, * and carried them to 203 Metre Hill.

* A blindage is a covered trench with a roofing at least sufficiently strong to afford protection against rifle and shrapnel bullets.

Before the sun had risen, the enemy's guns began their work of destruction, the worst of it being that they did it without receiving any punishment in return.

Little by little, rifle firing broke out. When it was quite light, the companies on Connecting Ridge noticed a Japanese battery coming into action at very close range. They opened fire in volleys, and the battery retired with heavy loss. Second-Lieutenant Bitzouk, who was for the second time wounded in the leg, was chiefly responsible for the destruction of this battery.

After this battery had retired, the infantry commenced their attack, and towards seven o'clock there was very heavy rifle firing.

All the company commanders on Connecting Ridge were placed *hors de combat,* and the three companies were commanded by Acting Ensign Agapov. I called for volunteers from the staff for the command of these companies, and in response to my call Lieutenant Vaseeliev and Second-Lieutenant Galileiev at once stepped forward.

At 8 a.m. General Kondratenko arrived, and found that everything was satisfactory. But the firing and bombardment had not slackened.

About 11 a.m. it was reported from the hill that the enemy was attacking from the left flank, and that Acting Ensign Shishkin had been killed.

I immediately telephoned to the officer commanding the artillery to again concentrate his fire on the valley in front of 174 Metre Hill, and soon our shells were streaming in the required direction. But still the Japanese guns vomited death.

A report now came in from the troops on the hill that their trenches were absolutely destroyed. They asked for not less than one company to reinforce them, as there were very few of the original defenders left. I myself saw that their last reserves had been used, and a long line of wounded streamed down from the hill, amongst whom was the new commandant, Captain Bielozerov. When brought to my vicinity, he was in a fearful condition ; a bullet had struck him on the right side of the chest and, passed right through, his shirt being soaked with blood. He passed quite close to me and whispered to me : " Send up a company at once. Put Second-Lieutenant Ivanov in command."

Second-Lieutenant Ivanov was one of my bravest officers. When volunteers were called for to collect the wounded on Height 426, he said he would go with twenty-five men who had also volunteered under Lieutenant Alalikin of the battleship *Poltava*. When they reached the Japanese outpost line, they saw that it was impossible for the whole detachment to get through, whereupon Second-Lieutenant Ivanov crawled through the enemy's lines alone and found a wounded artillery non-commissioned officer, whom he hoisted upon his shoulder and brought back. On his way back he met Serpukov, a lance-corporal of the 9th Company, who had got through safely, and between them they carried the wounded man to their detachment, and thence to 174 Metre Hill.

I immediately sent an order to Second-Lieutenant Ivanov to consider himself in command on the hill.

The loss of Lieutenant-Colonel Leesaevski and Captain Bielozerov was irreparable. The latter was

9

a real hero. On August 20 there was a moment on
174 Metre Hill when the sections of the 28th and
13th Regiments * on the left flank wavered and turned
their backs. Captain Bielozerov rushed in amongst
the fugitives, and with a few impassioned words,
pointing out to them the shame they would bring
on their regiments, made them return to their posts.
Captain Bielozerov was wounded when he sprang
out of the trench to see where the enemy was and
what he was doing.

It was only possible to hold the hill at the price
of heavy losses, but we decided that it was worth it.
Hence I resolved to go myself to the hill, and to send
up our last reserves.

At this moment E. P. Balashov, the medical officer
in charge of the hospital, rode up with his assistant,
M. Tordan, a French subject, and accompanied by
General Fock. These unexpected arrivals put new
spirit into us.

We were all struck with the bravery and coolness
of E. P. Balashov, who was a great favourite in the
regiment. Bullets were whistling by in sufficient
numbers to try the nerves of any man who had not
previously been under fire, in spite of which our
civilian general † and his companion did not appear
to experience the slightest sensation of fear.

General Fock did not fail to give us his opinion on
the position of affairs, and he declared that the hill
must be held anyhow till nightfall. This was already

---

* Sent up from Namako Yama to reinforce 174 Metre Hill.

† Officials in Government employ in Russia have civil " rank " just
as officers in the army have military rank. Hence the term " general "
here.

quite obvious to all of us. It is a very nasty thing to retreat by day under the fire of an enemy who is only a few paces off. But General Kondratenko expressed the wish to hold the hill for an indefinite length of time, notwithstanding the fact that it would be more than difficult to remain there under a hail of large and small shells without any cover from their murderous effect.

About twelve o'clock a rifleman ran down from the hill with a note from Second-Lieutenant Ivanov. He demanded immediate reinforcements, and as many as possible, saying that both officers and men were beginning to waver; hence it was obviously necessary to send up help at once.

I knew that Second-Lieutenant Ivanov would not ask for reinforcements without good reason. I reported this to General Kondratenko (we had one company left in the reserve), and it was decided to send the required reinforcements. But General Fock heard the order given, and fired up at our " inexperience."

" What does this mean ? " said he. " You want to hold on until nightfall, and yet you send up your last reserve ? "

" It is absolutely necessary," I answered.

" It is not at all necessary," declared General Fock.

" All right, Nicholai Alexandrovitch," said General Kondratenko, turning to me ; " we will wait a little longer."

I saw that General Fock's assurance had overruled General Kondratenko's judgment, and I had not the moral courage myself to contradict him and insist on the despatch of the last company, the more so, as

Colonel Irman, my immediate superior, did not give
me any support.

About half an hour passed since the reinforcements
had been asked for.   Balashov and M. Tordan
departed saying that they had had quite enough of
it, and General Fock also rode off.   Meanwhile the
struggle grew fiercer and fiercer, and now the first
signs of wavering became evident.

I noticed three riflemen running away from the
hill, and three men without rifles behind them.   I
drew General Kondratenko's attention to them, and
he evidently realized his mistake, for he said to me:
" Ah ! now it is too late ! "   Then behind the second
group of three men there quickly followed about
twenty others, and soon an entire company poured
down the hill after them.

On the hill itself men were running in all directions,
like ants whose hill has been disturbed, but a group
of about fifty men rushed into the upper battery,
stood upon the breastwork, and fired straight down
on the enemy below.   In front of this group,
holding his naked sword in his hand, I saw our Acting
Ensign Shchenakin, and my heart swelled with pride
for the 5th Regiment.   All these men belonged to
the 5th Regiment, and they had not lost hope of
holding the hill, although every one else had fled.

At this moment the enemy opened a hellish fire
on this group of heroes, wreathing the hill in clouds
of smoke ; the Japanese, by the way, never thought
twice about firing over the heads of their own men.
I did not see what was the end, for we all—General
Kondratenko, Colonel Irman, and myself—galloped
off to stop the retreat, and, though the task was not

an easy one, we nevertheless succeeded. I placed the reserve near our central hill, and the troops who had retreated occupied a position in touch with this reserve, from Namako Yama to Connecting Ridge. A telephone message was sent off at once, ordering the artillery to direct as many guns as possible on 174 Metre Hill.

The yellow-caps had already shown themselves on the crest and opened a fairly heavy, though not very accurate, fire on us.

At this moment the crest of the hill was swept by such a terrific storm of our shells, that everything living was destroyed in a few seconds, and the Japanese did not dare to show themselves even after the firing had ceased.

It is a very difficult matter to hold ordinary field trenches against siege artillery placed at short range.

With the fall of 174 Metre Hill we saw that it was impossible to hold on to Connecting Ridge, which had, therefore, to be evacuated. General Kondratenko gave the order to do so, and then went home, as he was utterly worn out and could hardly stand, Colonel Irman going away with him.

Taking advantage of the fact that the Japanese did not dare to show themselves on 174 Metre Hill, I quietly withdrew the companies from Connecting Ridge, and posted them for the time being behind Namako Yama and Division Hill.

On August 19 and 20 the 5th Company lost 62 killed and wounded, about half its then strength. The 9th lost 120 men, and had only 48 left in the ranks. Our companies were the last to retreat.

Our losses during the defence of 174 Metre Hill

amounted to 1,000 men, of whom about one-third were killed.

Considering that this loss was incurred chiefly on 174 Metre Hill and Connecting Ridge, where only four companies (800 men at the most) could act at a time, the loss of 1,000 men at one point will give some idea of the volume of fire developed at this spot by the Japanese.

If we had decided to retake the hill, it would not have been a difficult matter, but it would have cost us more than 500 men a day to hold it, as we should not have been able to reconstruct the trenches to keep pace with the amount of damage done day after day ; my regiment would only have sufficed for four days, since, including the details from the 28th Regiment, our strength was no more than 1,800 men.

As is evident from the foregoing narrative, when necessity arose, units from other regiments were sent to me, but they were often required for other positions of the defensive line.

Besides 1,000 casualties, we lost 2 long 150-mm. guns, 4 field guns, 2 machine guns, and 4 field mortars. However, two of these were recaptured by us during the final attacks at the foot of 174 Metre Hill.

With the fall of 174 Metre Hill it became immediately necessary to strengthen the trenches on Division Hill, Namako Yama, Akasaka Yama, and 203 Metre Hill.

These trenches were far from complete, except those on 203 Metre Hill, where they were made with splinter-proofs and light cover from shrapnel shell, and were furnished with wire entanglements.

But our experience on 174 Metre Hill had taught

us how weak our earth-works were in comparison with the destructive power of the enemy's shells, and so it was evidently necessary to strengthen considerably all the fortifications on 203 Metre Hill.

All this should have been done earlier, but want of tools and men had prevented us during the defence from working at any but the advanced positions. 203 Metre Hill was an exception, as, being one of the most important points if not *the* most important, on the defensive line, it had received my special attention.

We had to set to work again night and day. This is what I proposed to do : to throw the four trenches on Namako Yama into one long trench the whole length of the hill; to make several communication trenches back to the rear of the hill, where splinter-proofs were to be built and tents erected for those defending the hill; to build kitchens and establish a dressing station at the foot of the hill close to the battery of long 6-inch guns; to construct a magazine for small-arm ammunition, shell, and cartridges, and also make a dug-out for the commandant. I furthermore proposed to convert the trench on the top of Akasaka Yama into a redoubt, and to make several trenches in front of it along the hill; to strengthen all the splinter-proofs on 203 Metre Hill; and to place solid timber baulks to hold up the head-cover, so that the splinter-proofs would remain standing, even though the parapet was blown away.

We set to work on our task the first night after the capture of 174 Metre Hill.

The troops on the positions occupied by us were ⌐isposed as follows : On Division Hill, the 5th, 7th, and 11th Companies of the 5th Regiment, with the 2nd and 3rd Scout Detachments of the 5th Regiment and the 9th Company of the 27th Regiment, under Major Beedenko. On Namako Yama, two companies of Marines, under our own officers, Afanaisev and Siedelnitski, both companies under the command of Lieutenant Shcherbachev ; the 7th Company of the 28th Regiment and the 2nd Scout Detachment of the same regiment, under Major Sokkatski; also one company of the 13th Regiment and the 9th Company of the 5th Regiment.*   A section of Marines defended Extinct Volcano. On 203 Metre Hill, as before, there were the 2nd and 4th Companies of the 5th Regiment, and I had three companies of the 4th Reserve Battalion in reserve. All worked at night, and slept during the day.

We were very much stronger now that our defensive line was so much smaller, and I no longer feared sudden attacks. But the following regrettable incident again disturbed my peace of mind.

Early on the morning of August 23, I was awakened to hear a report that the Japanese had taken Extinct Volcano in the night.

I would not at first believe it, as the firing must have been heard, and the night had passed absolutely quietly.

When I said so to the orderly, he told me that there had been no firing, as the Marines had been caught asleep.

It turned out afterwards that they were not asleep, but were working, and had been taken by surprise because they had failed to put out outposts.   Extinct

* Consisting of 101 men.

Volcano had two trenches on it—one near the foot, for a half-company, and the other on the crest, for a section. Three days before, I had sent half a company of Marines to this hill for work and defence.

Owing to their ignorance of outpost work, they had put out no standing sentries by night, but were content with a few sentries on the trenches themselves.

Noticing their negligence, a small body of Japanese had crept up to the drowsy sentries, surprised them, and sprung into the trench.

Our Marines only grasped the situation when the majority of them had already been killed. The remainder fled to the upper trench, where there was one sub-division of riflemen (I do not now remember to whom they belonged—possibly the 7th Company of the 28th Regiment, as they occupied the right flank of Namako Yama). The Japanese ran up behind them and burst into the trench at their very heels, thus taking Extinct Volcano without noise or firing.

Major Zimmermann—a hero in the true sense of the word—in command on Namako Yama, hearing what had happened, immediately organized a counter-attack, and when the men had somewhat recovered themselves, set them an example by rushing forward with drawn sword. The soldiers followed him to a man, and Extinct Volcano was retaken. Unfortunately, Major Zimmermann was wounded in the arm and breast, and had to relinquish his command.

Ten minutes after the recapture of the hill, the enemy's artillery opened a terrific fire on it.

By this time I had reached the scene of action,

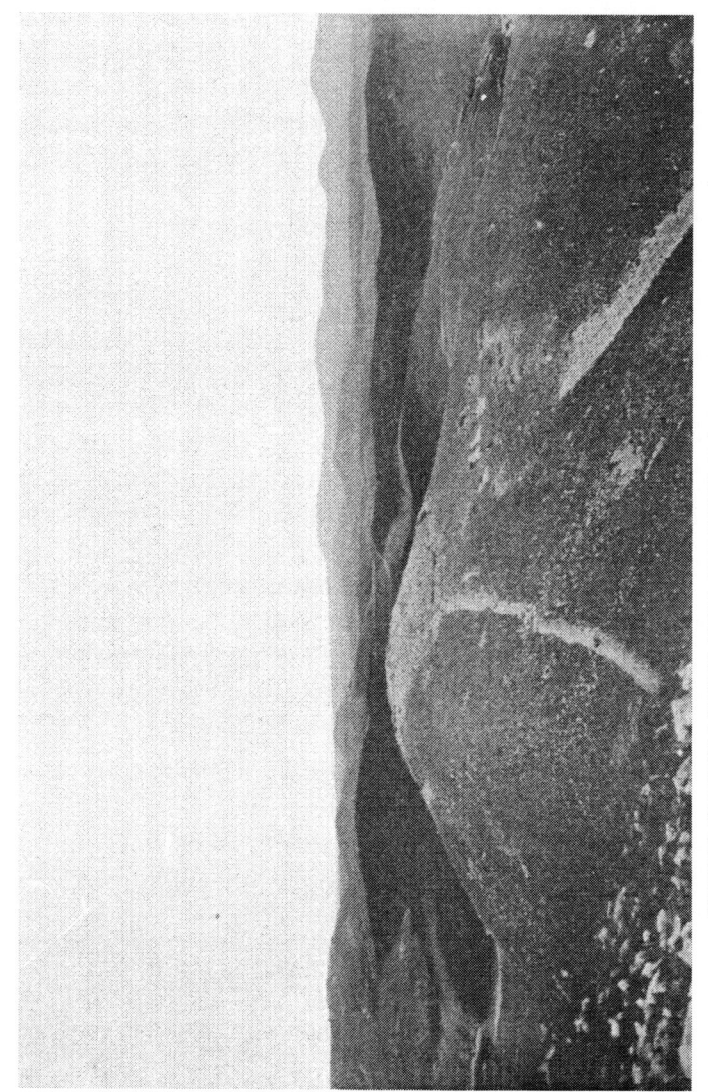

EXTINCT VOLCANO: TAKEN FROM THE RIGHT FLANK OF NAMAKO YAMA.

having with me one of the reserve companies, which I ordered to remain on the site of the former bivouacs of the regimental staff, near the graves of Colonel Petrov and Major Schiller.

Reaching the top of Namako Yama, the nearest point to Extinct Volcano, I saw that the yellow-peaked caps were on its summit. This meant that the enemy's fire had driven us off the hill, which proved, indeed, to be the case.

I sent a report to that effect.

At this moment Colonel Irman arrived with his adjutant, and told me that he had sent for three companies from the general reserve.

But at least an hour would pass before they could arrive, and in that time the enemy would be able to dig himself in, and it would be very difficult to drive him out again.

We therefore decided to attack the hill without delay, and with this object I ordered the 1st Scout Detachment to come to me immediately (it was stationed near Fort Yi-tzu Shan). Everything was quiet there, and I felt I could withdraw troops from that position without the fear of any hostile attacks.

Colonel Irman telephoned to the officer commanding the fortress artillery to open fire on the top of Extinct Volcano with as many guns as he could get to bear.

Our guns thundered out, and a hail of shell swept the top of the hill. In a moment the hill was wreathed in smoke, and the yellow-peaks disappeared.

In order to see what was happening on the reverse side of the hill, I went into a ravine in front of the left flank of Division Hill. Our cannonade continued.

Just as I reached my new point of observation, I had a very alarming experience. I heard the shriek of a heavy shell over my head, and a moment later it fell about 10 paces from me ; the earth shook from the deafening reverberation of the explosion, and I was thrown heavily to the ground, covered with sand and lumps of clay. It was some time before I recovered from the shock and could continue my way.

This was due to one of our own 11-inch guns on the coast forts. It was laid on the hill occupied by the enemy, but the shell dropped near me—by no means the first instance of our coast-defence guns giving us an unpleasant surprise. An 11-inch shell once landed in the 6th Company's trench on Division Hill. Luckily, there were no serious consequences from these mishaps.*

On reaching the left flank of Division Hill, I found that the valley was not visible to me. I shouted up to Division Hill, telling those there to inform me if there was anything to be seen behind Extinct Volcano, and soon received the answer that there were no hostile troops in the valley.

The Japanese, however, caught sight of me from their trenches and lost no time in firing at me, which was pleasant indeed. They even started shelling me with their field guns ; they had, seemingly, an enormous supply of rifle and gun ammunition, and certainly used it freely.

* These shells must have come either from Golden Hill Battery or No. 7 Battery on the Tiger Peninsula, each of which had 11-inch *howitzers*. (See Map III.)

When I returned to Colonel Irman, our scouts had already arrived, and we decided to attack without delay. The scouts, with one company from the reserve (the 5th of the 27th Regiment), were to advance directly on the hill, while one company from the garrison of Namako Yama moved from the flank. It was a hard climb up the high steep hill, and continued for some time without the enemy firing a shot, our guns meanwhile sweeping the summit. When, however, the scouts got close up, and likewise the company from Namako Yama, our guns ceased firing, upon which the yellow-peaks immediately again crowned the hill.

The companies rushed forward. They reached the parapet under a very heavy fire, but went no farther, and lay down near it among the hollows in the ground.

The opposing forces were so close to each other, that they could easily throw stones across. The yellow-peaks took cover behind the parapet, and our men began to throw stones, as there was no possibility of reaching them with bullets. The Japanese replied in like fashion, and this continued for some time.

We were quite accustomed to rifle and gun fire, and it did not have much effect on us now, but this stone-throwing produced a most childish impression; it was annoying to think that there was not one man sufficiently brave to show his comrades an example by mounting the parapet, and the whole procedure appeared futile to one anxiously awaiting an assault.

Eventually our men stopped throwing stones, and were evidently preparing for a bayonet charge.

Several men dashed forward—an officer and some non-commissioned officers.

"Now, God with you!" said I to myself. "At last they have pulled themselves together and are swarming over the parapet."

The yellow-peaks showed for a moment over the crest of the parapet, then they were hidden by our fellows, and with a wild "Hurrah" our companies poured into the trench. Then all was silent.

"They've got it," said Colonel Irman.

"Yes, we had it once before," I answered, "but nothing came of it, as their artillery drove us off again. I reported Major Zimmermann's success that time; but now we will wait and see." I had scarcely finished speaking, when the Japanese began to sweep the top of the hill with fire from their heavy artillery.

We felt that nothing could be achieved until these cursed guns were destroyed. But, forced to husband their ammunition, our artillery hardly put up any fight against the hostile batteries.

Shells of every calibre literally covered the top of the hill, but our men did not come out of the trench. It seemed strange indeed, as there were no splinter-proofs in the small trench, and such a fire must destroy all the defenders.

Ten minutes passed and there was no sign of movement. Another ten minutes and no retreat.

At last the enemy's artillery ceased fire.

"Now," I thought to myself, "the hill is ours." But a Japanese soldier with a flag suddenly appeared on the parapet.

"What's the meaning of that? Surely our men

are not all killed ? " But it was practically so. The few that were left broke their way through to Namako Yama. And the Japanese stood on the parapet and waved his flag.

Just then reinforcements came in sight—a scout detachment of some regiment. At their head was Lieutenant Evstratov, a strongly built, tall, fair fellow with a reddish beard. The men marched quickly and joyously ; but there were not more than eighty of them.

" How is it you are so few—they promised me three companies ? "

" Here are the three companies, Colonel," said the Lieutenant.

" Where ? " I asked.

" Here," and he pointed to his men. " These are worth more than three companies ! "

We decided to add another small detachment that came up behind the scouts, and attack as before, sending yet another company from Namako Yama on the flank. We accordingly sent an orderly to Namako Yama with the necessary instructions. The men who had just arrived did not know the ground, so I took them on to the hill myself, and went with them until they could all see how and where they were to attack.

Our artillery again opened fire on Extinct Volcano, and we saw the man with the flag jump down from the parapet, while the summit of the volcano was wreathed in smoke from our bursting shells. We were evidently getting our revenge. After this I returned to Colonel Irman.

There were very few attackers, and we impatiently

awaited reinforcements, but none arrived, and already the scouts had nearly reached the top, and firing had commenced. The officer leapt on the parapet and fired at some one with his revolver. All his men followed him, and lay down on the glacis without jumping down into the trench. Obviously the Japanese were there.

No reinforcements had yet reached us. I could not stand it, and ran to a hill lying behind us to see if the companies were coming up, or if they had halted anywhere.

To reach this hill I had to run across a fairly broad ravine. As I went down into it, I heard the Japanese firing on the hill, and as I reached my point of observation I saw the reinforcing companies hurrying towards us.

I returned to Colonel Irman with the good news, but he soon put a damper on my spirits. " It's no good now, our men are all killed by shell fire." Looking towards the hill, I saw nothing but the dead bodies of our gallant comrades.

The reserve companies reached us completely tired out. Colonel Irman and I could not help acknowledging that it was now impossible to retake the hill.

Having come to this conclusion, Colonel Irman sent a report to that effect to General Kondratenko.

I heard afterwards that that splendid officer, Lieutenant Evstratov, was wounded by a fragment of shell and died in hospital.

Extinct Volcano remained in the hands of the Japanese, and the piles of bodies, both Russian and Japanese, served for the rest of the siege as a reproach to our gunners, who were not strong enough to prevent the enemy from coming into action at decisive ranges.

The defence of this hill was shorter than that of 174 Metre Hill; of course, there were reasons for this. In the first place, the top of the hill was ten times smaller than that of 174 Metre Hill, the trenches only accommodating one section; and, secondly, there was not a single splinter-proof on it, and the line of trenches was beyond our general line of defence, and had a certain amount of dead ground in front.

Our riflemen had no cover from artillery fire, and if they did not retreat, were destroyed to a man. But if we gave up this hill to the Japanese, we hoped that they would not occupy it, because our artillery could sweep them off, as theirs did our troops when we were in possession. However, it did not turn out so.

When we told our gunners to drive the Japanese from this hill, they answered that they had very few shell and must keep them for more important targets.

So the Japanese held our trenches unpunished, and repaired them, making communication trenches and cover from our bullets.

Colonel Irman gave me the companies that had come up at the finish for strengthening the defences on Namako Yama, and they were badly needed by me.

What an enormous influence one man, whether officer or private, can have on the issue of a battle!

In many battles I have noticed and studied the psychological effect produced on an ordinary man who is brought face to face with death.

The desire to escape from the danger threatening

him is so great, that he is scarcely able to exhibit the strength of will of even the average individual.

Overcome by this feeling, a man loses his power of weighing circumstances, and he either acts from force of habit, or else follows the example of his commander or his neighbour. (This is a well-known phenomenon, but it is brought home only to the man who has been among soldiers during a fight.) Now, supposing this neighbour loses his head and runs, there are very few who will not follow his example; the average man will take to his heels too, his neighbour follows him, and so on, until the whole detachment is retreating in disorder.

A disorderly retreat is always started by one man, and in most cases this man is physically weak and sometimes, though rarely, an obvious funk. Therefore it is essential to recruit soldiers from men who are physically strong, for almost every weak man will be a cause of retreat and, consequently, of defeat. A hundred picked men are preferable to two or three hundred weak ones, even though the latter are equally well trained.

I would add that men must learn how to husband their strength. On a long march fatigued soldiers are worse than useless. So I say that we must discard most of what our soldiers now carry in their knapsacks, and retain only the following articles: 1 shirt, 1 pair of trousers, 1 pair of putties, 1 pair of socks, a ball of lint, a butter-tin, some needles and thread, and sugar for two days. All the other things are absolutely superfluous. Have your supply columns perfect; but the soldier must go as light as possible, and must, moreover, look smart, so that an enemy

10

will not dare to call him a " ragged beggar." * Make
a soldier so smart that even a sloven will become
a rather fine-looking fellow. A smart outward appearance raises the spirits of the troops.

It is also indispensable to teach the infantry
soldier field fortification thoroughly, so that he be-
comes the equal of a sapper and needs no supervision
in war time. In the 5th Regiment, not only the
non-commissioned officers, but the men also, could
point out where trenches should be constructed,
and of what depth and length they should be.

Our men blamed the sappers for making trenches
with elbow rests, as they knew by experience what
the loss of that width of earth meant along the firing
line. They said that the sappers did it because they
had not themselves been under shrapnel fire, and
did not know how to take aim from behind cover.

* The average Russian soldier of the infantry of the line, with his
loose jacket, loose breeches, battered peaked cap, and invariable
slouch, does not look what we call smart, and this is what General
Tretyakov is probably referring to.

RED HILL ON THE RIGHT, WITH THE TOWN AND BAY IN THE VALLEY. IN THE FOREGROUND ARE SEEN THE HEADQUARTERS OF THE 5TH REGIMENT.

p. 146]

CHAPTER VI

Continuing the work of fortifying the various hills—End of the first
general assault, August 22 and 23—Attacks on Namako Yama
from August 24 to September 19.

As soon as Extinct Volcano had been surrendered to
the Japanese, I determined to strengthen our present
defences by means of trenches and wire entanglements,
and had the trenches on Namako Yama and Division
Hill extended and deepened accordingly.

I placed the 10th Company in the valley between
Extinct Volcano and Division Hill, hoping thereby
to fill up the gap between the hills occupied by us.

This done, we had next to set to work to fortify
Akasaka Yama, taking the task in hand without a
moment's delay.

I had already commenced a redoubt capable of
accommodating one company on the top of Akasaka
Yama, which now required finishing, and, in addition,
it was necessary to build trenches round the hill for
five companies.

Keeping in view the possibility of the enemy
breaking through across Extinct Volcano, I fortified
the ground between Fort Yi-tzu Shan and Riji Hill *

* Meaning Red Hill; situated right in the rear of 203 Metre
Hill.

147

and made Division Hill and Namako Yama into two independent commands. We also had to safeguard our communications with Division Hill and Namako Yama which might be exposed to attack. For all this work we wanted tools, material, and men, and we were again short of all three. Luckily, at this difficult time Major Gemmelmann of the Engineers, as well as several non-commissioned officers, was attached to me, so I was able to get some sleep at night. I collected a large store of *matériel* near the regimental headquarter camp.

After many urgent messages the authorities concerned began to send us wire, bags (for sand), all sorts of iron and steel, and a few tools, and, as before, we procured whatever else was wanted from the stores in the town and from the railway people.

Our regimental horses became quite worn out from hauling heavy materials, such as beams, planks, rails, etc. We had very few carts and wagons for carrying these things, as our baggage wagons were mainly required for bringing up regimental necessaries and stores needed to meet our daily wants.

It is an extraordinary thing how an important fortress like Port Arthur could have been left almost without any vehicles for general service, a want which must be seen and felt to enable one to understand rightly what sufficient transport means in a fortress, and how indispensable it is.

Towards the end of the siege a light railway was laid as far up as my headquarters, but was never worked, probably owing to the want of trucks. I saw the rails, but trucks were conspicuous by their absence. A fortress, like an army, must have its own transport and the horses necessary for it, or, preferably, be provided with good powerful motor vehicles.

I wanted to construct a splinter-proof observation post for myself and Colonel Irman on one of our hills, but again for want of transport we had to remain throughout the siege at an observation station exposed to the enemy's fire. We always spent the night at the regimental headquarters, where Colonel Irman's staff (he was in command of the whole of the western front) also stayed. Our quarters were buildings belonging to the Artillery Headquarters Offices on Red Hill, and a large marquee pitched there served as a mess-room, in which quite a number of us sat down to dinner.

We seldom received any official visits from the town, as we were not out of range of the enemy's bullets and shell. Two bandsmen were killed near the building, and two wounded, as was also my orderly, Private Ravinski.

However, General Nikizhin rode out fairly frequently to sup with us, and we always looked forward with pleasure to his visits. At all times in the best of spirits, he was a clever and entertaining conversationalist, and invariably brought us some piece of interesting news, so that while he was with us we forgot the monotony of our existence. From him we learned how things were going on in the other sections of the fortress, what attacks had been beaten back, and the latest news of Kuropatkin's Army.

We used to get through an extraordinary amount of tea, of which the officers, both regimental and staff, had a plentiful supply, thank God! Our

dinners were, however, becoming somewhat meagre
—rice soup and roast horse-flesh, with rice garnished
with rancid butter or tallow. Supper was of much
the same type. Occasionally when the men brought
us up a canteen full of "goltsies" (small, dark
fish), which they had caught in the horse-ponds, we
had a regular banquet.

When I went up to take observations from Red
Hill I often shot small birds sitting in the bushes
on the slopes of the hill, which we ate with
great relish. I think night-hawks, particularly,
are most delicious, and I do not know why we do
not eat more of them in the ordinary way of
living.

There was a small fir-wood behind Red Hill, towards
its northern side, which became my favourite place
for resting, and was a splendid observation point.
One could walk through this wood and breathe the
air, heavy with the odour of firs, and at the same
time see all the positions. On a bright sunny day
every man on the hills round could be seen, and the
occupations of the various units defending the positions could be clearly observed. There, on Division
Hill, they would be preparing dinner in the kitchens
of the 7th Company ; a little to the left, the dinners
of the 6th Company had already been served out;
and along the communication trench a whole company was moving in relief of our scout detachments on
the left flank of Division Hill, who were in constant
touch with the Japanese.

Under Red Hill was a row of small ponds, used
as watering places for the artillery horses. They
were a source of real pleasure to our men, who

frequently bathed in them and fished, in spite of bullets and shells constantly splashing into them.

Everything was quiet on 203 Metre Hill, and I was thankful that the Japanese were giving us time to fortify it.

There was a harmless bombardment of Forts Yi-tzu Shan and Ta-an-tzu Shan, all the shells falling short of the former and passing over the latter.

With what terrific force they burst! The gases are not very noticeable, nor do they collect in one large puff, but are whirled away in little streaks scarcely visible to the eye, and then above a cloud of black smoke is seen.

It was a remarkable thing that where the first shell fell " short," the others all fell short likewise ; if " over," then the remainder fell over.

There was a road between Forts Chi-kuan and Ehr-lung. Standing on this road, one could watch the practice of a certain Japanese gun. The shells, coming across the road from behind the hill, always struck in exactly the same place, which was fought shy of by every one, and this continued throughout the siege, from the beginning to the end. The soldiers used to joke about it, and say that it was some gunner calibrating his gun.

Very few shells burst near my walk through the wood. They all fell on the battery on Red Hill, where Lieutenant Kornilovitch, a most gallant officer, who came from Kiev to Colonel Petrov's battery, was killed.

I spent much time in the wood on Red Hill, living

again through all that had passed, and trying not to think of either the present or the future. I always used to say to the men : " Never think about what is *going* to happen to you, but only about what *has* passed."

I was frequently accompanied in my walks by our doctor, Theodore Troitski. He was ever in good spirits and full of jokes, could always find something interesting to talk about, and so was much sought after. In my spare time, when everything was quiet, I often used to go to the dressing station and drink a bottle of stout with Troitski, which he had managed to get by secret means from some treasured spot. Though many envied him his privileged position, no one could ever find out whence he got his stout.

In order to strengthen the positions, we had to construct, in addition to the trenches, various kinds of obstacles at the most important points.

The favourite device, and the most effective one, was the wire entanglement, but there was very little barbed wire in the fortress.

Certainly, an enormous quantity of barbed wire had necessarily been used for strengthening the main inner defensive line, but when it came to blocking the intervals between the forts (before our arrival in Port Arthur) no one seemed to have thought of fortifying 174 Metre Hill. I do not say this in any spirit of criticism of those who fortified Port Arthur. Naturally they had to strengthen the main line of defence first, and they had not sufficient material for 174 Metre Hill as well.

THEODORE SEMENOVITCH TROITSKI, REGIMENTAL DOCTOR,
5TH REGIMENT.

p. 152]

The following were covered by wire entanglements : 203 Metre Hill, the left flank of Akasaka Yama (a very short piece), the left flank of Division Hill, and the right flank of Namako Yama. (The space between Extinct Volcano and Namako Yama was strengthened by planks with spikes in them.*) To prevent the enemy breaking through between Falshivy Hill † and 203 Metre Hill, fougasses were laid, as also between Akasaka Yama and Namako Yama, and on the left flank of Division Hill. These fougasses were much dreaded by the Japanese, and for that reason, perhaps, they did not once attempt to force any of the valleys, but always elected to climb up the most impossible cliffs.

We had suffered many defeats from August 14, and continued to do so until September, the Japanese, thanks to their superiority in artillery, taking hill after hill from us.

Nevertheless, I did not despair, and often consoled General Kondratenko, pointing out to him that the nearer we drew towards our main defensive line, the more effective would become our defence, by reason of the greater facility of communication between the defenders of the various positions.

Anyway, in the centre,‡ where the main Japanese attacks were directed, we successfully defended

* Compare with Official History, Part III., p. 31.

† Meaning False Hill (south-east of and closely adjoining 203 Metre Hill).

‡ This refers to the north-eastern section of the defence. The Japanese captured the East and West Pan-lung Redoubts, but obtained no other advantage for a total loss of 15,000 men. Hence the " successfully defended." (See Map III.)

ourselves, and our successes there raised our spirits considerably.

There were no sheep left. We had eaten them all. We had lamb occasionally for dinner, cut up into very small portions and served as tit-bits, but we lived mainly on rice soup.

It was always very hard to get hay for the horses, and very soon it would become impossible to buy any, and we should have to indent for it. The Government forage stores had not yet been touched.

We sent Lieutenant Bogdanovitch to Pigeon Bay to get us some fish. He brought back a good many, but all were rockfish, which none of us would have looked at a few months before.

As I have already said, on the capture of 174 Metre Hill, we evacuated Connecting Ridge, which the Japanese immediately occupied and began to fortify. They also constructed a strong line of trenches designed to sweep the rear of Namako Yama.

On August 15, I was placed in command of the forts and batteries in the defensive line from Fort Yi-tzu Shan to Fort Ta-yang-kou North.

I had constantly been on all these positions and forts. Fort Ta-an-tzu Shan was the only one completed, while Fort Yi-tzu Shan was finished in the interior, but there were no traverses, and the garrison had to construct some with the help of sand-bags. There were also no caponiers in the ditches, and one could come out on to the gorge * from the ditch on the left flank and climb up on to the parapet.

* Rear part of work.

Therefore the men composing the garrison themselves made an open caponier at the front corner (chief salient), blocking the approach to it by iron gratings.

Fort Ta-yang-kou North was worked by the garrison throughout the siege. All that the enemy could see was a gigantic pile of hewn stone, in front of which was a ditch about 4 sagenes * deep, with vertical escarp and counterscarp cut out of the rock. A bare slope ran down into this ditch from the entrance of the fort. It was intended to have made a gate, but, as there was not time to cut it out, any one was free to come up out of the deep ditch on to this slope, and so, from both sides of the ditch, straight up through the entrance of the fort. Casemates or splinter-proofs were entirely wanting. There was also no defence on the right flank, so that the interior of the fort was plainly visible from the enemy's artillery positions. The front face and entrance were splendidly flanked, but the left flank was taken completely in reverse by very many Japanese batteries.

With the assistance of some workmen sent up by us the garrison strengthened the right flank with blindages. In the centre of, and behind, the entrance a strong bomb-proof was built, sufficiently large to accommodate the entire garrison. The roof of this bomb-proof was specially made to withstand shells of large calibre (I myself saw the damage caused by an 11-inch shell on the right front of a corner of it, but the bomb-proof itself was not touched). Splinter-proofs for officers and gun detachments were

* A sagene is about 7 feet.

built under the ramparts, and near the right flank a large search-light, with a big steam engine, was placed without any cover whatever.

The space between Forts Yi-tzu Shan and Ta-yang-kou North was covered by an unbroken line of wire entanglements, supplemented by a large number of fougasses, and above them again a line of trenches, which were, however, very shallow and had very thin parapets. We were only able to complete them after our retreat from 174 Metre Hill to our main positions.

Threatened from the side of Extinct Volcano, and enfiladed from Connecting Ridge, Namako Yama was in a dangerous position, the more so, as the trenches on it were absolutely devoid of overhead cover from shrapnel fire. It was a good thing that after the capture of 174 Metre Hill we had constructed long traverses the whole breadth of the hill, so that the enfilade fire from Connecting Ridge had little effect. When the rear of Namako Yama began to suffer from the firing from Connecting Ridge, I posted two quick-firing guns near the road leading up the hill. They demolished the trenches on Connecting Ridge and caused the Japanese to stop their annoying and dangerous fusillade. In order to ensure Namako Yama against night attacks, I blocked the road running along its rear with a row of fougasses, wire entanglements, and *chevaux de frise* made out of planks (an excellent obstacle when there is no artillery to demolish it). To prevent a turning movement on the right flank, I laid fougasses there, and extended the trenches on the right flank of Akasaka Yama, where I posted two companies in well-constructed trenches.

In spite of all these measures Namako Yama was very weak, as the trenches were very shallow and unprotected by head cover from shrapnel. Besides that drawback the near slopes of the hill could not everywhere be swept by the fire of the defenders, a serious failing when one had to deal with an enemy such as the Japanese. All this showed me that Namako Yama was in a very precarious state, although defended by six companies.

Taking everything into account, I set to work to strengthen the defences on Akasaka Yama, but want of tools and men delayed the work, more especially so as we had at the same time to strengthen the left flank of Division Hill, which was sadly in need of it. It was possible to see, not only the heads, but even the heels of the riflemen defending the trenches from the direction of Extinct Volcano. It was also impossible for us to reach the hill, so we had to dig at least two long communication trenches. All this required an enormous number of tools and men, and the difficulty of making fortifications was increased by the scarcity of everything needed.

It was fortunate that we had an abundance of rain, yielding streams full of clean, cold, fresh water, and providing bathing and washing places for nearly every company on the position.

203 Metre Hill and Namako Yama were worse off in this respect. The men had to go from there to the artillery horse-ponds near the headquarters of the staff, not accessible without some danger. Second-Lieutenant Ivanov was wounded in the leg there by a stray bullet. There was, however, no other less exposed place available.

On August 22 and 23 the Japanese main assault *
on the centre of our defensive line was beaten back,
the enemy losing very heavily. We were told that
all the slopes of the hills attacked were piled up with
Japanese bodies, and that the stench was becoming
unbearable, from which cause we also suffered, owing
to the number of dead on Extinct Volcano.

When Major Zimmermann was wounded on August 22, I appointed Major Moskvin, who had been
in charge of administration, to command on Namako
Yama. I had great faith in this gallant, energetic
officer, and felt assured that the defence of Namako
Yama would be safer in his hands than in those of
any other man, all our own officers being utterly worn
out and requiring immediate rest. Apart from that
consideration, they were nearly all wounded.

About this time the following occurrence took place.
Lieutenant Frost, our paymaster, Captain Felitzin,
and Father Vasili Slounin were put up in my former
quarters near the bazaar in the New Town. In
the morning (I do not remember at what time)
they had only just got up and were drinking tea,
when a shell burst in the room in which they
were sitting. Captain Felitzin was wounded in the
head, as was also Father Slounin (he had some of his
hair singed off), and Lieutenant Frost was severely
wounded in the head, besides receiving several other
minor wounds in the face. Thank God! none of
them were killed, and all were soon quite well again.

Very many of our horses were killed in our two-
wheeled carts and company wagons while taking

* Chiefly directed against the East and West Pan-lung Redoubts.
(See Map III.)

FATHER VASILI SLOUNIN, CHAPLAIN OF THE 5TH REGIMENT.

p. 158]

supplies up to the positions. The horses killed were eaten, thus helping to keep up the physical strength of the rank and file. Many of them did not fancy horseflesh, but, following the example of others, they ate it, and felt all the better for it. The following incident will serve to prove that horseflesh was eventually much sought after. I do not remember exactly when it was, but a horse was killed on one occasion near our staff headquarters. That day, for want of men, we did not remove the carcass, and in the morning the horse had gone, a few bloodstains only showing where it had lain. We learnt afterwards that the men on Red Hill had come over, cut it up into chunks, and divided it amongst themselves.

I got up very early on August 24, drank a cup of tea, and, seeing that all was quiet, went to take my constitutional in the wood on Red Hill. It was a glorious morning, and I could plainly see the men on the positions going down to wash.

The smoke of the field kitchens rose up into the clear air ; it promised to be a magnificent day.

I cannot remember how long I sat there amongst the fragrant green trees, but I should have stayed some considerable time if I had not been hailed from below. Some one called to me to go with Colonel Irman to Fort Ta-yang-kou North, upon which I quickly descended the hill, found my horse already saddled, and in a few minutes we had reached the fort mentioned by the town road. It would not have been safe to have gone straight across.

About half-way we passed a battery of 42-mm. guns (No. 4 Redoubt).

I pointed out to the commander of this battery the end of a Japanese trench, where our scouts said there were some Japanese machine guns which interfered with our sorties. The embrasures for these guns were plainly visible through glasses.

Our guns were quickly laid on the target, and after a few ranging shots the shells began to fall with extraordinary accuracy.

The dangerous end of the trench was destroyed, but I think the guns remained untouched, perhaps because the Japanese, anticipating the impending bombardment, had removed them to another spot. It would, however, give them a whole night's work to put them into position again. The 42-mm. gun is a very accurate weapon, and it is a pity that the effect of its high-explosive shell is so slight as to render it good only for dismounting the enemy's pieces. The gun is sufficiently mobile to be capable of quick and sudden concentration on any fully exposed hostile battery, a contingency which would, however, rarely occur, as nowadays all batteries are carefully hidden from the enemy's view. Pieces, however, of this type are incapable of coping with heavy guns, and one would not advocate having many of them in a fortress. Their real place is in reserve, and not in batteries on the main fighting positions.

The enemy did not fire a single shot in reply to the 42-mm. guns and we quietly rode on to Fort Ta-yang-kou North, which we reached a few minutes later.

Everything was quiet at the fort. The men worked steadily and without hindrance, but there was an enormous amount to be done, the task undertaken by the garrison being to construct a covered trench as well as some splinter-proofs. Splinter-proofs for the gun detachments and officers had already been constructed, so the fort became more or less self-contained and able to put up a good defence.

Our riflemen had originally been posted outside the fort, but, with the completion of a large bomb-proof and covered way with traverses inside, it was possible for them to occupy the real defensive line and live in the fort. As always, the officers received us gladly, gave us tea, and then took us on a tour of inspection. Every one was at his post. The work was going on apace, and Captain Versi, of the Naval Construction Department, who was superintending the work on the fort, displayed great energy and resource. The exits from the ditch were covered, and the flank ditches well enfiladed from both sides.

A large bomb-proof, impervious alike to rifle and shell fire, was being constructed for the reserve, but the ground was solid rock, and so the work was slow. We had finished our inspection and were talking to the commandant in a splinter-proof, when we heard a loud crash, caused by the bursting of a large Japanese shell somewhere near.

We all followed Colonel Irman out of the shelter. The gun detachments were working at their guns, laying them on some far-distant point from which the enemy's shell had come. It was dangerous to stand in the open, so with Colonel Irman I ran to the nearest gun, where the signaller could always give warning of the coming of a shell. Ere the guns had been correctly laid, the signaller shouted : " Look

11

out ! " I ran quickly down into a traverse with some
sailors.   The enemy's shell screamed over our heads,
and burst with a tremendous report on the traverse
of No. 2 gun.   In the twinkling of an eye, the sailors
were at their places and the two 6-inch Canet guns *
roared forth.   I jumped up to see where our shells
fell, and clearly saw two puffs of smoke on a very
far-distant hill, right behind the Japanese positions.
" Do you mean to say there is anything there ? " I
said to the gun captain of No. 1 gun.   " Yes, sir, it is
there all right, we noticed it a long time ago."   Again
the signaller shouted : " Look out! " and we again
rushed under cover while the shell shrieked over us,
but this time it went a long way over and burst somewhere behind the fort.   Almost before it had struck,
the sailors were at their guns and two more
shells were sent towards the same spot, and then
other forts joined in adding to the death and
destruction.

This artillery duel continued for a long time.   We
alternately came out to observe and ran back under
cover.   Colonel Irman was much more indifferent to
danger than I was.   It seemed to me that my position
behind the traverse was not a particularly safe one,
and I decided to change it for a bomb-proof.   At
the next shout of " Look out ! " I put my idea into
execution, but with unfortunate results.   A number
of men rushed with me towards the point of safety,
we tumbled one on top of the other, and I found
myself among those who had not time to get into the
bomb-proof before the enemy's shell fell behind us,

* These guns were taken from the ships of the fleet, and were manned
by naval gunners.

burst with a deafening report, and buried us in smoke, stones, and dust.

Luckily, none of us were badly hurt, but I had a large bruise on my back to carry away with me as a memento of the occasion.

We had paid no attention to the other hills during this bombardment, but now we saw that the Japanese were evidently preparing for something very important.

When peace reigned again on Fort Ta-yang-kou North, we noticed that 203 Metre Hill was wreathed in smoke from bursting shell. Apparently, instead of the usual daily allowance of two or three dozen shell, the Japanese had already expended more than a hundred rounds on it. This caused us much anxiety, and we galloped off as hard as we could go to the position of the staff. When we arrived, we received a message from 203 Metre Hill from Major Stempnevski to the effect that the enemy was sweeping the hill with artillery, and that the left flank of our trenches had suffered severely from shell fire.

Namako Yama was also being heavily bombarded, and it was evident that an assault was imminent. It would be difficult to hold this hill, as it was swept from front to rear and from flank to flank. We could hear very heavy firing from the north-eastern section too, where the situation was evidently even more serious than with us. Namako Yama was fairly strongly held by six companies.* On the right flank were two 6-inch guns and one quick-firing gun, with Lieutenant Kolmakov in command. On 203 Metre Hill there were only two companies, the 2nd

* See p. 136.

and 4th of the 5th Regiment, and two quick-firing guns (I do not count the two short 6-inch guns, as they had been silenced long before). Fearing for the safety of 203 Metre Hill, I sent another company there from the reserve.

Compared with other points, the position of the defenders there was serious. Food could only be taken up to them at night, and there being no water at all on the hill, that had to be carried up at night also. It was impossible for any one to show himself on the sky-line. As the enemy was within a stone's-throw of the defenders, eight patrols of six men each had to be furnished at night. There were no junior officers in the companies, and gun ammunition was very scarce.

Foreseeing the capture of 174 Metre Hill, we had actually begun to fortify Namako Yama on August 11. The work itself was very heavy, besides which the rocky nature of the soil and the want of tools hampered us greatly. A battery for two long 6-inch guns had been previously constructed on the hill and a road made leading up to it. The men only worked at night, as it would have been madness to do so in the daytime in face of the enemy's heavy fire. It was even dangerous to move about, and every day we had several men killed there. The total number of defenders amounted to about 500 men. By day one section out of each company was in the trenches and furnished sentries for observation purposes, while three sections slept behind the slope of the road, which ran the whole length of the hill, where small splinter-proofs had been made out of planks. After dinner at night the garrison of the post started work, covering itself with a line of outposts.

On the night of August 25–26 I was awakened by heavy rifle firing in the direction of Division Hill. Soon an orderly galloped up with the report that the Japanese were climbing up Namako Yama. I threw on my clothes and galloped off towards Namako Yama, ordering two reserve companies, posted near the regimental staff quarters, to proceed there immediately.

Having reached a spur of Akasaka Yama, I began to watch the battle. The weather was as bad as it could be, a strong wind was blowing, and it was raining as well. I felt quite confident, knowing that if the enemy had not succeeded in coming up unobserved and taking our men by surprise, he would certainly be beaten back.

At this time our batteries opened fire, at Colonel Irman's orders, on the valley in front of Namako Yama, and the whole foreground was lit up by our star-rockets. In another half-hour our reserve companies came up, and Colonel Irman also arrived.

Several wounded men who were being carried back from the hill told us that the Japanese had not climbed up any farther, but were firing from below, which meant they had been driven off.

In half an hour the firing ceased, and Major Moskvin reported that the assault had been beaten back with heavy losses to the enemy, who tried to take us by surprise, but was discovered in good time by the standing sentries, whose warnings had given our men time to get to their posts.

We had 4 men killed and 16 wounded.

After this attack we made a communication trench from the road above along the hill to the advanced trenches, because all our casualties had occurred as our men were running to occupy their trenches.

On the night of September 1–2 the Japanese again tried to take Namako Yama by surprise, but were driven off by rifle fire and retreated behind 174 Metre Hill after suffering heavily. We had Lieutenant Afanaisev and 6 sailors wounded.

For the repulse of these two night attacks, Major Moskvin received the thanks of the General Officer Commanding, in General Orders, and he and a number of other officers were recommended for rewards, but they never got them, owing to the list of rewards recommended being lost.

After these attacks Colonel Irman and I proceeded to Namako Yama on a visit of inspection, as the Japanese had evidently chosen it as their point of attack.

This inspection left me with a very bad impression. The trenches were still very shallow, of overhead cover there was practically none, and the enemy had posted some batteries behind 174 Metre Hill and on the slopes of the hills in front of it at a very short range from us; but our men were in splendid spirits, in spite of the constant heavy fire.

On September 8 the company of Marines on the right flank was relieved by No. 7 Company of the 28th Regiment. This company had not shown up very well during the fighting on 174 Metre Hill, but I had no other unit to send up, and I thought that it would be anxious to redeem its reputation.

From September 8 to 17, things were fairly quiet

on Namako Yama, but at the dinner hour, about twelve o'clock, on the 17th, the Japanese (about one company) made a rush from Extinct Volcano against the right flank of Namako Yama, and captured the trench occupied by the 7th Company of the 28th Regiment without firing a shot. The men of the company were having their dinners at the moment, and had not time to seize their arms before the Japanese were in the trench. Hearing of this by telephone from Division Hill, I immediately telephoned an order that the Japanese were to be driven out of the trench, and received an answer to the effect that Major Moskvin had ordered the 7th Company to re-occupy their trench without delay. This company, however, proved unequal to the task.

An attack by the 1st Company of Marines was also not wholly successful, as, though a part of the right flank of the trench was retaken, the Japanese held the other end, and blocked it with rocks and sand-bags.

Alarmed at such a state of affairs, I went with Colonel Irman to the hill. I personally inspected the place where the Japanese were lodged. They did not show themselves at all, and there was not a sign of life anywhere. They had built up a strong barricade, so high that a man could not climb up it without the help of another.

We could easily have dislodged them with hand grenades, but we had none. It was absolutely essential that we should drive them out, and as it seemed to me that it could best be done at night, I gave orders to that effect accordingly. For some reason, however, the attack did not come off, the commandant contenting himself with fortifying a small knoll on the right flank of the Japanese.

On the morning of September 18 the enemy opened such a terrific fire on the hill with rifles and five guns that came into action at a very short range, that all our trenches were knocked to pieces, and we suffered heavy losses.

On this day that splendid officer, Captain Saltovski, commanding the 9th Company, was killed, and the company itself lost 26 killed and 49 wounded.

The enemy attacked the hill during the day and captured the advanced trenches of our 9th Company, but the gallant fellows, quite unaided, reassembled on the crest-line, charged with the bayonet, and recaptured their ruined trenches. The hill was in a hopeless plight. Surrounded on all sides, it was an impossible position.

Colonel Irman and I sent a report to this effect to General Kondratenko, and then rode off to Akasaka Yama to observe and discuss the chances of holding the hill if it continued to be deluged with such a fearful fire from all sides.

Apparently there were sufficient men to defend the hill. To send up reinforcements only meant subjecting them to the enemy's deadly fire, as all cover had been demolished, and, moreover, the commandant did not ask for help, although expecting an attack every moment.

The Japanese concentrated under the hill in considerable numbers, concealing themselves very cleverly in the folds of the ground. However, we moved the reserve nearer the hill, but kept the 10th Company, which was placed on the right flank of Akasaka

Yama, in its former position. Thus the whole day passed. Our 9th Company fought minus officers. The *moral* of the troops under this deadly fire was extraordinary. Towards evening the firing died down, dinners were sent up to the men, and one company (the 12th of the 13th Regiment, I think) was sent as a reinforcement to help to hold the place during the night.

Early on the morning of September 19 Colonel Irman and I proceeded to our observation station. Firing had already commenced, especially against 203 Metre Hill and Namako Yama. We received a report that the Japanese were moving in force against these hills, so we expected an attack on both of them simultaneously. I therefore moved my reserves to the hollow behind Akasako Yama, so that they should be under my hand and easily despatched to either 203 Metre Hill or Namako Yama. The situation was unchanged, but our men were suffering severely from the artillery fire. Hence we came to the conclusion that the Japanese intended to leave things as they were, and compel us to evacuate the hill without making an attack.

Towards evening Colonel Irman and I became convinced that the Japanese did not intend to attack, as I had received no reports to the contrary from the hills. The only report sent in by Major Moskvin was to the effect that he was organizing an attack on the trenches occupied by the Japanese, and that, by enfilade fire from the left of the hill, he had annihilated 1,000 Japanese who had been lying down under 203 Metre Hill.

I was delighted at this success. About 6 p.m.

Captain Sirotko, of the Frontier Guard, who was attached to my regiment, joined me on Akasaka Yama. I immediately sent him to command our 9th Company on Namako Yama. In the evening the firing again slackened, dinners were sent up, and a reinforcement of one company of the Reserve Battalion detailed for assisting in the night's work. That night I inspected the works on 203 Metre Hill and Namako Yama. Those on the former were practically undamaged, but on the latter all were destroyed. I spent the night with my orderlies in a ravine behind the 10th Company, in the dug-out of the officer commanding the 10th Company, and slept for three hours.

CHAPTER VII

Continuation of the struggle for Namako Yama, and abandonment of the hill, September 20—The first attacks on 203 Metre Hill, September 19–22.

ON the morning of September 20 the cannonade commenced very early, reaching its zenith at about midday. Our men kept low in their trenches during this veritable hell of fire, which continued for about two hours. "Will they hold on, or not?" I thought to myself, looking towards the right flank of Namako Yama, which was being subjected to the full fury of the bombardment. Our gunners failed to locate the enemy's batteries, and thus remained impotent witnesses of the slaughter of our companies.

Just then I saw the top of the right flank of Namako Yama covered with grey smoke and the men there rushing headlong down the hill. The Japanese were using hand grenades charged with pyroxylin and Melinite, this being the first instance of their use. I immediately sent a report of what was happening. After the men on the right flank (they were the 7th Company of the 28th Regiment) had run, the others from the battery and the enemy appeared simultaneously on the crest. A few minutes later, from the left of the battery behind the crest of the hill, appeared a group of our men, who opened fire on the Japanese and drove them off the top.

Unfortunately, our men did not remain where they were, but also ran back down the hill. Colonel Irman came up just in time to witness the complete evacuation of the position. It all happened in a very few minutes. We immediately sent all the officers and orderlies near us with orders to the retreating companies to stop on Akasaka Yama and occupy the trenches there, and I also moved the whole of my reserve there.

Our artillery was evidently watching the course of the fight on Namako Yama, for, as soon as we had evacuated it, our shells feel like hail on the summit, and the Japanese disappeared like smoke before the wind. This enabled us to occupy Akasaka Yama at our ease, and in the night we fortified ourselves strongly.

I think it would be interesting to describe the action of our 9th Company during the last minutes of the defence of Namako Yama.

When Captain Sirotko arrived, he found the company in a critical position. Acting Ensign Anikin of the 27th Regiment was in command. The trenches were in ruins and enfiladed from two sides by rifle fire, and from 174 Metre Hill by gun fire as well. Piles of dead bodies were heaped up all round, blocking the trenches at various points.

The right flank of the company's trench was connected with that of the 7th Company of the 28th Regiment, of which the enemy now held possession,* and from which was enfiladed the trench

* Namako Yama was defended by two tiers of trenches, an upper and a lower, and this was part of the lower line that had been captured (see p. 174, where the upper tier is mentioned).

of the 9th Company. Lower down, behind the rocks in front of the trench, was another small party of Japanese.

Wishing to find out in what strength the enemy held the 7th Company's trench, Captain Sirotko called for volunteers to attack them. Twelve men came forward and made a rush, but they were met by a volley from about 100 Japanese, losing five men, whereupon they retired. Having reported this to Major Moskvin, Captain Sirotko received an order that the 7th Company of the 28th Regiment and one company of Marines were to attack and drive the enemy out of the trench.

About 8 a.m. three Japanese batteries of heavy guns, posted in a valley behind 174 Metre Hill, four quick-firing guns from 174 Metre Hill itself, and five or seven heavy guns that came into action on Connecting Ridge, near the Chinese temple, all of them concealed from our batteries, opened fire with high-explosive shell and shrapnel.

By about 2 p.m. only 48 men were left out of the original 155 in the 9th Company; many of them were wounded, and nearly all more or less injured by stones and clods of earth. The trench was quite full of the bodies of the fallen.

Captain Sirotko asked that an emplacement to his left might be occupied, so Major Moskvin sent 50 men of the Reserve Battalion for that purpose. These, however, occupied a communication trench near that of the 9th Company instead of the position assigned to them, and subsequently ran off precipitately the moment a few shells fell near them. Just then the gun fire slackened, but firing continued on the right flank, and strong columns were seen advancing from Extinct Volcano, one of which began to turn No. 9 Company's right flank.

Captain Sirotko could not see a single man in the upper tier of trenches above him—they had all retreated. Then he ordered the remnants of the company, and also Melinkov with his 30 Marines, to abandon the trenches. At this time there was not a single non-commissioned officer on Namako Yama, except those left in the splinter-proofs. In the trenches of the 12th Company of the 13th Regiment there remained only a sentry and one non-commissioned officer, who had been forgotten by their company and did not know that their comrades had retreated. Akasaka Yama was alive with retreating men. Captain Sirotko, with the remainder of his company, opened fire on the Japanese who showed on the crest of the hill, compelling them to take cover, and thus giving all those left alive time to retreat quietly on to Akasaka Yama.

The First Attack on 203 Metre Hill

The Japanese commenced their bombardment of 203 Metre Hill and Namako Yama simultaneously. I thought that they were going to attack Namako Yama first, but was mistaken. I must mention in this connection that the fortifications on 203 Metre Hill were now so strong as to be practically impervious to 6-inch shells, and a heavy bombardment with projectiles of that type would make but slow progress. From this it was inferred that an assault on 203 Metre Hill would have to be somewhat later than the one on Namako Yama, which was defended

PLATE I

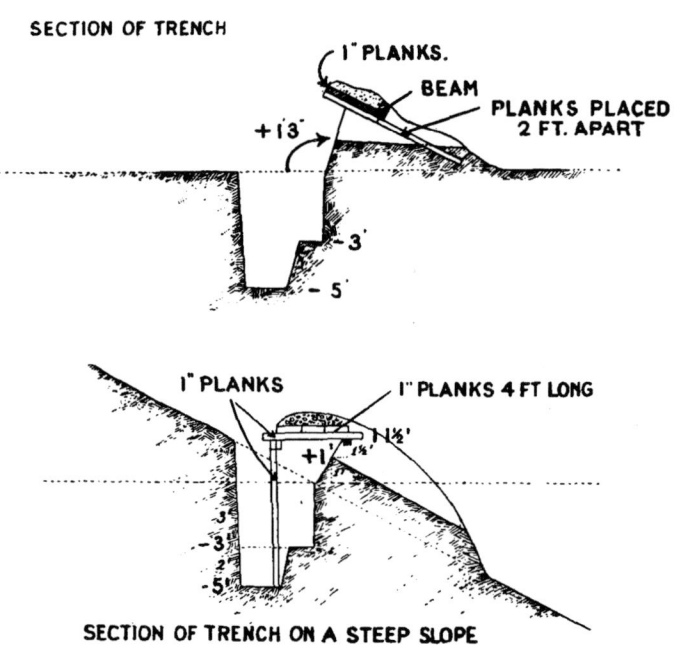

SECTION OF TRENCH

1" PLANKS.

BEAM

PLANKS PLACED
2 FT. APART

+13"

3'

- 5'

1" PLANKS

1" PLANKS 4 FT LONG

1½'

+1'   1½'

3'

- 3'

2'

- 5'

SECTION OF TRENCH ON A STEEP SLOPE

[p. 175

by but weak entrenchments.   It would not be worth while, we thought, for the enemy to indulge merely in "sweeping" fire.*

About 3 p.m. on September 5 a Japanese battery had opened fire on 203 Metre Hill, and on the 6th it was observed that the enemy had during the preceding night placed two guns in a covered position behind 174 Metre Hill, with which he began to sweep the rifle pits on 203 Metre Hill (see Plate I.). From the 7th onwards it was noticed that the enemy was massing troops behind Siedlovy (Saddle) † and 174 Metre Hills, until he had there, by September 14, about one brigade of infantry, with a squadron of cavalry; and from this date the enemy began to fortify himself strongly on Connecting Ridge and its offshoots.

At daybreak on September 19 two companies attacked ‡ our outposts on the spurs of 203 Metre Hill, captured their positions, and began to dig themselves in.   Our artillery and rifle fire several times put a stop to their work, compelling them to take cover, but they nevertheless finally made good their hold on the trenches and began to pour in a hot rifle and gun fire on 203 Metre Hill.

From all this it could reasonably be concluded

* Probably the author means that to effect anything an assault would be necessary, as the defenders, safely ensconced in their now well-constructed trenches, had nothing to fear from a mere bombardment.

† In future references the term "Saddle Hill" will be used.   This position is the saddle joining the southern extremity of 203 Metre Hill to Connecting Ridge.

‡ No mention of any *attack* is made on this date (19th) in our Official History; this was probably a preliminary movement to the main assault fixed for the next day.

that they had decided to make an attack. When, therefore, Major Stempnevski (sen.), the commandant of the hill, asked for reinforcements, I sent him the 1st Company of the 28th Regiment, under Second-Lieutenant Protasevitch, who reached the hill at 6 p.m., the 11th Company of the 27th Regiment, under Captain Churbanov, and the 7th Company of the 27th Regiment, under Major Jeltkevitch, both of whom arrived at 8 p.m. Altogether there were on the hill on September 19, 480 bayonets, 50 gunners, 2 miners, 6 telephonists, and 6 Marines.*

Of guns, there were the following: two 6-inch, two heavy battery, and two quick-firing guns on the col between 203 Metre Hill and Akasaka Yama, also two 37-mm. guns, four machine guns, and one mortar for throwing pyroxylin bombs.

About 5 p.m. on the 19th the mortar was dismounted by a shell, and one 6-inch, one heavy, and two machine guns were disabled.

On the arrival of the companies the commandant disposed them as follows: the 1st Company of the 28th Regiment, and half the 11th Company of the 27th Regiment in the trenches on the right flank, the remainder in the reserve.

At 8.30 p.m., as the enemy was seen advancing on the left flank, the commandant sent half the 11th Company, 27th Regiment to occupy the stone-hewn

---

* The numbers here given again differ widely from those given in our Official History. Here 500 is about the total, and the Official History gives 1,500 (Official History, Part III., p. 61)—a considerable difference. Note the numbers on p. 181. Assuming that companies were at this time about 140 strong only, the total of these five comes to 714 (700 + 2 + 6 + 6), which, with gunners, gives a total of 764.

trenches on the very top of the hill, so that it could pick off the Japanese as they climbed up on to the roofs of the bomb-proofs along the main trenches.

At that time there were no redoubts on the top of 203 Metre Hill.

The 7th Company, 27th Regiment was placed in reserve behind the 11th half-company.

The enemy did not for a second cease his rifle and machine-gun fire from Saddle Hill. He commenced his attacks at 10 p.m., advancing always in dense columns. Though our riflemen and gunners from the neighbouring batteries and trenches caused fearful havoc among the attackers, the Japanese nevertheless reached the wire entanglement and cut it in two places ; however, they could not get any farther, as our volleys swept them away by the hundred. Our 8th Company, which was occupying False Hill, and was thus acting on the enemy's flank, rendered great service in destroying the enemy. A few Japanese, however, succeeded in reaching our trenches, but, when there, were killed by hand grenades. Throughout the night the enemy's infantry continued their attack, supported by fire from every kind of gun, but at about 9 a.m. they retired into the ravines and valleys behind Connecting Ridge. In these attacks the Japanese lost more than 1,500 men in killed alone.

At 7 a.m. on the 20th the enemy's artillery swept the hill with fire, but about 10 a.m. changed its objective to Namako Yama, which was finally captured at 2 p.m., as already described. At 4 p.m. fire was again directed on 203 Metre

12

Hill, and the enemy's infantry began to concentrate behind Connecting Ridge.

The troops in question were collected in order to relieve those that had attacked the hill on the 7th. That night they made several attacks, one after the other, but each time were beaten back with heavy losses. We were greatly indebted to our star-rockets for the repulse of all these night attacks. However, a section of Japanese fought its way into our trenches, and occupied one large bomb-proof and one small one where we had a Maxim.*

The news of this reached me at daybreak on the 21st, on Akasaka Yama, where work was proceeding on the trenches, and whence I watched the fighting † on 203 Metre Hill. This intelligence was so alarming that I returned to the staff headquarters, where I found Colonel Irman, who, at Major Stempnevski's request, sent up one company from the reserve (our 6th Company).

Reinforced by this company, the garrison of the hill made a counter-attack and retook a large portion of the half-ruined trench previously seized by the Japanese. A small body of the latter, however, still held the two bomb-proofs, and could not be turned out, and thus the part of the trench between these two bomb-proofs also remained in their hands. Unfortunately, this was the identical piece of trench in front of which was " dead ground " to all our batteries. The enemy could consequently pass

---

* All this preliminary fighting is not described in our Official History, but the lodgment effected by the Japanese on the 20th in the Russian bomb-proof is mentioned.

† See p. 180.

freely and in safety to and from their comrades lodged in our trench. This was no novel experience for us, but I well knew the danger of it.

In order to prevent the Japanese from spreading along the trench, our 6th Company was ordered to occupy both ends of it. Our assailants tried several times to climb right up to the top of the hill, but were driven back on each occasion. Finally, the commandant sent a portion of the 6th Company there, and the gallant fellows, standing out in the open all day under shrapnel fire, prevented the enemy from reaching the summit of the hill. All this was plainly visible to the staff, who were tremendously impressed by our men's splendid behaviour.

That evening, at my orders, the top of the hill was surrounded with a ring of small trenches, and during the night these trenches were connected up with the batteries on the right flank of the hill, which measure rendered our position fairly safe.

Several desperate attacks were successfully repulsed, in spite of the fact that the first of them was made before the completion of the trenches, when our men had to stand up in them without any cover under a perfect storm of shells. They *had* to stand up, as they could not fire down the steep slope of the hill in a sitting position. The situation was critical. We were losing men so fast under the terrific fire that the companies were literally melting away minute by minute. An endless stream of wounded continued to be carried away from the hill all through the night. In view of this, Colonel Irman sent for reinforcements from the general reserve, all our local reserves having been used up.

Danger threatened 203 Metre Hill's other neighbours, especially the left flank of Akasaka Yama, where there was some dead ground right up under the trenches.

My own personal observations from early morning on September 20, from Akasaka Yama, were as follows : everything was quiet on the rear side of 203 Metre Hill, in spite of the shells bursting over it, as if the garrison were in no danger whatever. The companies were standing quietly in the trenches, visible to us. The trenches themselves were, apparently, very little damaged. Thank God ! only a few shells had pierced the roofs of the bomb-proofs. Only one bomb-proof on the right flank of the hill, facing 174 Metre Hill, was seriously damaged. There was not a single Japanese to be seen anywhere. They are indeed a wonderful people ! But the rattle of musketry did not cease for a second. The enemy was firing from the trenches surrounding the hill, chiefly from Saddle Hill. The dull reports of bursting shell did little more than deafen the men in the bombproofs. A veritable blizzard of lead swept the rear of the hill and the road leading along the top, and huddled up beneath the steep embankment of the latter sat some of the reserves.

Judging by present appearances, it seemed as though we were not in such a very bad way, though the part of our trenches occupied by the Japanese was a thorn in my side. I knew from experience that this foreboded the final capture of the hill, and incidentally the destruction of our fleet. Colonel Irman, I believe, watched 203 Metre Hill from the side of False Hill. No living man was visible

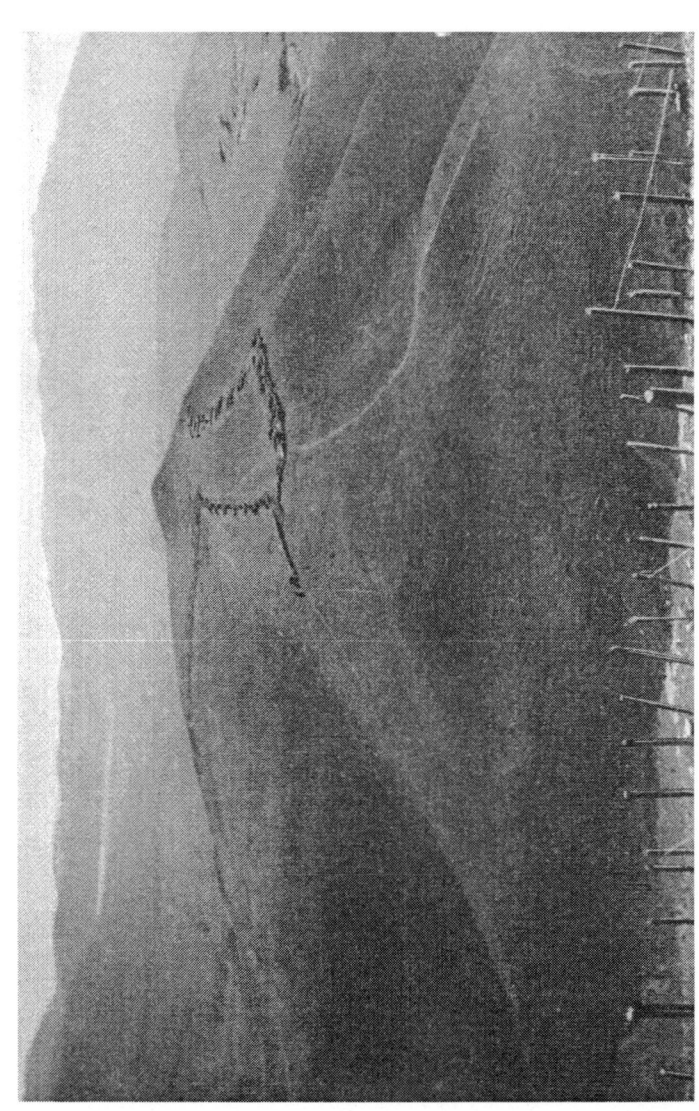

VIEW TAKEN FROM 203 METRE HILL, SHOWING WIRE ENTANGLEMENTS AT THE FOOT THEREOF, IN THE
FOREGROUND FALSE HILL WITH THE TRENCHES ON ITS RIGHT FLANK.

p. 180]

from that side, but from both Akasaka Yama and False Hill the Japanese dead were to be seen in piles. In the ravine at the foot of 203 Metre Hill there were hundreds, if not thousands, of them.

After half an hour's observation I returned to the staff. Everything was as quiet there as if the fortress was not threatened with any danger. But dark clouds were gathering.

A report came in from Division Hill that large bodies of Japanese infantry were moving towards 174 Metre Hill.

It became imperative to drive the enemy out of our trench on 203 Metre Hill. An idea occurred to me to roll a large naval mine down on the occupants, as some of the other forts had done. General Kondratenko and Colonel Irman approving of my scheme, I at once sent for Lieutenant Podgourski, who was a specialist in these matters. This was late in the evening, so he promised to come in the morning with some mines. Having little hope of success with the large mines, I asked him to bring, in addition, small ones (from 6 to 10-lb. bombs), and we decided to attack the Japanese in the bomb-proofs with these missiles.

Our losses during these two days (*i.e.* September 19 and 20) were as follows : In the 2nd Company, out of 141 men there were left, including slightly wounded, 83 ; in the 4th Company, 48 out of 167 ; in the 11th Company of the 27th Regiment, 96 out of 140 ; and of No. 7 Company of the 27th Regiment, and No. 1 Company of the 28th Regiment half their strength was *hors de combat*. During this time also the following officers were killed : Major Jeltkevitch, commanding the 7th Company of the 27th Regiment, and Ensign Diantrougov, the junior officer of the 1st Company, 28th Regiment.

It was an unfortunate idea of Father Slounin to bury the dead near the road leading from 203 Metre Hill to the staff headquarters. The sight of our dead heroes, lying in long rows along that road, was bound to leave a bad impression on those who passed by.

As evening drew to a close, taking advantage of a temporary lull, I sent another company from the reserve with tools and sand-bags to work on 203 Metre Hill; it was absolutely imperative to strengthen our trenches on the top of the hill by means of sand-bags. This company, being our last reserve, was to return in the morning. As far as I remember, it was on this night that two companies of the 27th Regiment arrived which we had asked of General Kondratenko for strengthening the works on Akasaka Yama. They were sent there forthwith, and remained until the end of the siege.

I was deadbeat that day, and when I got the chance, I threw myself down and snatched a few minutes' sleep. In consequence of the wide extent of ground covered by our command, both Colonel Irman and myself were utterly worn out.

On the morning of September 21 the enemy's fire against 203 Metre Hill increased in volume. We had a splendid view of the hill from the trenches near the quarters of the staff. As I was watching, I plainly saw a Japanese flag waving over the bomb-proof on the left. I ran to the telephone and asked what was the meaning of it, to which the commandant answered that he knew nothing about the flag, and that everything was all right on the hill. The Japanese were sitting quietly in their trenches. I gave orders for the flag to be taken down, and was glad to see that it had disappeared a few minutes afterwards. Some Japanese soldier had crawled up during the night and stuck it into the roof; but how he did it, no one knew. That morning 203 Metre Hill and the part of Akasaka Yama lying nearest to it were subjected to a tremendous fire from the Japanese heavy artillery, and we expected an assault every moment; the more so, as we noticed that the enemy had concentrated a very large force right under 203 Metre Hill. We also received a telephone message from Lao-tieh Shan telling us that a body of Japanese was in position in a large flat-bottomed ravine at the foot of 203 Metre Hill.

We were unable to see them from any point, but it was obvious that they had been moved there for the decisive attack on the hill in question. In response to a call for immediate reinforcements we received two companies, which I sent closer to the hill, so as to be within easy call. The roar of the cannonade round the hill increased meanwhile.

Podgourski now arrived with his mines, which were sent to the hill. The Japanese evidently intended to destroy, if they could, every living thing on the hill and then to occupy it. Anyhow, they delayed their attack, which we expected every moment.

Just then I received bad news. While attempting to take the trench occupied by the Japanese, Second-Lieutenant Pogdanovitch was killed instantaneously, and the attack failed; the 1st Company of the 28th

Regiment lost heavily, but fought magnificently.
The death of this gallant young officer was a
heavy blow to me. There were not many like him
left.

" Well, if Podgourski's mines are a failure, I don't
know what will be our next step. God grant that
we can hold on to our positions, and then it will be
time to decide that difficult question," I thought to
myself. Firing ceased; which meant the attack
was imminent. I ordered the reserve companies
to move right up to the foot of 203 Metre Hill; and
Colonel Irman reported this fact to General Kondratenko, and asked for two more companies to
reinforce him.

Colonel Irman and I rode to Akasaka Yama,
where one had a better view of the positions and of
203 Metre Hill, but though the attack was at its
height, we did not see a single Japanese. Apparently
they were attacking along the narrow strip of cliff
on 203 Metre Hill which was hidden from view from
all our positions. We concluded that the assault
was being driven home in small detached parties.

The rifle fire directed on 203 Metre Hill from all
the neighbouring hills occupied by the Japanese
was simply terrific. Bullets were flying in all directions; it was dangerous to stand out in the open,
even far away to the rear, and one of my horses,
which was in a place apparently quite safe, was
hit in the foreleg. Now one of the reserve companies had climbed up to the hill; in another hour
the second was almost there. It became necessary to think about further reinforcements. In
an unbroken line the wounded were being brought

back from the hill. At this moment I heard heavy rifle firing from Division Hill, but I had not a single man to send there. If the enemy were now about to attack there also, we should indeed be in a very bad plight.

It was now that Midshipman Doudkin opened fire with his small guns. Our telephones were silent. The strain was awful. If the Japanese took Division Hill, communication between 203 Metre Hill, Akasaka Yama, and False Hill would become extremely difficult. I reassured myself with the thought that Fort Yi-tzu Shan would prevent the Japanese from advancing too far. Meanwhile I sent an orderly to Division Hill to find out what was happening there. We had a splendid view of the rear of 203 Metre Hill, and could clearly see what every man was doing. We saw how the companies, on reaching the hill, wriggled along like snakes to the different parts of the trenches, and then disappeared into them, how every now and then a man would make a dash for the commandant's bomb-proof, and then pick his way back again to the top of the hill, how they carried the wounded back to the dressing station— in a word, every movement of the defenders was plainly visible from our point of observation. For a long time we received no reports, but at last one came in from 203 Metre Hill. Three attacks had been beaten back, with enormous losses to the enemy ; but the commandant felt sure that the attacks would be renewed, and therefore considerable reinforcements were indispensable. He also reported that they had found it impossible to roll the mines down upon the Japanese, and that things in general were in a very bad way. There were very few men left, and practically no officers.

Soon after Lieutenant Podgourski * came back from the hill with his sailors (we had by then returned to the staff headquarters) and promised to bring smaller bombs, from 6 to 10 pounds in weight, on the morrow.

Podgourski informed us that unless we sent up one company to 203 Metre Hill, it would be taken, as the men were physically and morally worn out. Fortunately, a reserve company arrived, and I immediately sent it to the hill, and Colonel Irman sent a despairing message for at least two more companies to reinforce us. We heard afterwards that the sight of the company coming to their help had had a most reassuring effect on the commandant, officers, and men.

The situation seemed to be so hopeless that one of the artillery officers suggested that the hill should be abandoned, since there was no hope of holding it. But Major Stempnevski was the first to say that, even though every one else left the hill, he would remain with his one company. Captain Alander supported him, declaring that if the 2nd Company remained, the 4th would stand by it. Just at this moment the reinforcing company was seen coming up. A ringing cheer went up, and the heroic defence continued. It was reported from Division Hill that the enemy had occupied a position in front of the hill and opened a very heavy rifle fire ; to which we replied that the enemy had apparently no reserves there, and that this was probably only a demonstration, as it eventually turned out to be.

* He had apparently failed to keep his previous promise (see par. 2, p. 181).

STAFF HEADQUARTERS OF THE 5TH REGIMENT. IN THE DISTANCE IN THE CENTRE IS 203 METRE HILL.

p. 187]

The Japanese attacking 203 Metre Hill did not merely restrict themselves to ground unswept by fire from any point, but would have crept up the northern side of the hill, had they not been driven back by the fire from Akasaka Yama and those trenches on 203 Metre Hill which were more or less undamaged. As a result they showed themselves there no more.

In the evening (September 21) two companies of the 14th Regiment arrived. Captain Yarsevitch, commanding one of them, was well known to all for his courage and enterprise. I gave him the necessary orders, and expressed the hope that his company would drive the Japanese out of the trench captured by them, and that the hill would be ours. Reinforced by these companies the commandant was to make a counter-attack, and I felt sure that they would clear the hill of the Japanese during the night. The companies of the 14th Regiment marched off. Having asked for permission to have a rest (he was utterly worn out), Major Stempnevski (sen.) came to the staff headquarters that evening. With him were relieved the 2nd and 4th Companies of the 5th Regiment, and the 1st Company of the 28th Regiment. The men of the last mentioned had lost heart somewhat, and were in a state of exhaustion after the three days' ceaseless fighting.

Colonel Irman and I met the gallant companies and showered on them thanks and praise. The men were in good spirits, but one could not see their faces for the thick coating of dust on them.

In place of the companies I had withdrawn, I sent the 2nd Company of the 13th Regiment and the

4th Company of the 28th, and appointed Captain Sichev commandant of the hill in place of Major Stempnevski (sen.).

Night fell. Everything was apparently quiet. At times the enemy fired a few heavy shell at 203 Metre Hill, at other times rifle firing broke out and then again ceased, while occasionally the star-rockets, fired from the hill, brilliantly lit up the enemy's positions, and the heavy guns on our hills fired a few rounds, the riflemen meanwhile opening fire on any Japanese caught out in the open.

Colonel Irman, Captain Baum,* Lieutenant Kostoushko,† and I sat in the staff headquarters, deliberating as to what was to be done with the Japanese who had got into our trench on 203 Metre Hill. It seemed to us that without very careful organization a counter-attack would not stand much chance of success by day. On the other hand, it was impossible to make this attack in the night, as the enemy could concentrate large reserves against us, follow us up the hill, and, completely outnumbering us, creep close up behind as we withdrew, and finally drive us entirely off the hill.

In view of the paramount necessity for decisive action on 203 Metre Hill, I had already sent Major Stempnevski (who had had a certain amount of rest) back with 20 men who had volunteered from the 2nd and 4th Companies of my regiment. As he knew every inch of 203 Metre Hill, Major Stempnevski was ordered to assist the new commandant

* Staff Officer to Colonel Irman.
† Orderly Officer to Colonel Tretyakov.

in organizing an attack on the Japanese then in occupation of our bomb-proofs.

Considering the importance of the intended attack, I wished to go myself to the hill. I sent to General Kondratenko for two more companies, but he refused to let me have them, proposing to undertake some movement himself. Thus it but remained for me to see in the morning from what part I could best withdraw two companies.

At this moment an officer was brought in on a stretcher, and I was horrified to see that it was our gallant Captain Yarsevitch, wounded in the chest. I ran to him and asked him if he was badly hurt, whereupon he pointed to his right breast, saying in a very feeble voice : " It's nothing—I shall get over it. It's all right on the hill . . . they can fight a bit longer . . . successfully . . . but they must be relieved . . . they have had no sleep and are deadbeat. Let them take me to the hospital." Having assured him that his wound was not dangerous, we turned away determined that we would get men, cost what it might, to relieve the garrison of the hill, knowing, however, that it was almost an impossibility, as *we* had no men, and in the centre,* where there were some reserves, they might be more needed than with us, seeing that there also the fighting had been very fierce. Not without cause had General Kondratenko left us to our own devices.

Captain Yarsevitch was wounded as he rushed at the head of his company on the trench occupied by the Japanese. Met by a hot fire, and seeing the

* This refers to the Japanese attacks and capture of the Water-works and Temple Redoubts. (See Map III.)

fall of their commander, the men picked him up and ran back. How important it is that a company should respect and love its commanding officer! The men did everything for him that could possibly be done.

Early on the morning of the 22nd the cannonade, with its resulting stream of wounded from 203 Metre Hill, recommenced. The reserves had not arrived, but we received information that the enemy was collecting in large force under 203 Metre Hill. One might almost say that we were helpless, as we had not a single man in reserve.

Then an order came from General Smirnov directing us "To send immediately two quick-firing guns to the rear against the Japanese collecting under 203 Metre Hill." Colonel Irman, Colonel Romanovski, Major Gobiato, and other gunner officers had a long discussion as to which guns were to be withdrawn. At last they decided to telephone to Lieutenant Yasinski to move from the Lao-tieh Shan positions through the *kao-liang* towards Pigeon Bay, to the rear of the Japanese. The message was sent, and Colonel Irman himself rode off in that direction, leaving me at the telephone. Scarcely two hours had passed before some one caught sight of him galloping towards our headquarters as hard as he could ride. We ran out to meet him. "Victory! Victory!" shouted our Colonel, riding up to the door. We deluged him with questions.

"The Japanese are in full retreat from under 203 Metre Hill and the trenches near it," he shouted as he dismounted. Lieutenant Yasinski had ranged on the very centre of them, in one minute had destroyed half of them, and in another most of the survivors. Completely demoralized, off they went helter-skelter, like partridges, and even evacuated their trenches on Saddle Hill.

We were like mad people ; I do not think I had ever experienced such a feeling of joy.

A little later Lieutenant Podgourski arrived with his small 6–10 lb. bombs. But as we had no reserves we could not withdraw a single man, the enemy being in force before all the hills.

Podgourski proceeded to 203 Metre Hill. Everything was quiet there now ; even the rifle fire had ceased. I still awaited the advent of the two companies which I intended to send up to drive off the Japanese, because I put such little faith in the efficiency of the bombs. It seemed to me that those who had to throw them would not be able to get near enough to the Japanese trenches.

Hardly an hour had passed since Podgourski's departure, when several terrific explosions were heard from 203 Metre Hill, followed by some dozen minor ones and then an outburst of rifle fire. We heard a " Hurrah ! " shouted through the telephone. The Japanese were decimated by the bombs, and the remainder shot as they ran down the hill. Our spirits rose, and a gasp of relief was heard on the receipt of this message. I immediately sent a report of the result to General Kondratenko.

This is what had taken place. On the arrival of Lieutenant Podgourski, Captain Sichev, Major

Stempnevski and Captain Kramorenko (to whose initiative the attack was mainly due) formed the following plan : to call for volunteers among the officers and men to attack the Japanese with the bombs, to divide them into two parties, and, on a rocket being fired, one party to act from one flank of the trench and the other from the other flank. Lieutenant Podgourski was to take charge of one party. As arranged, the two parties started off in absolute silence towards their objectives. Then Lieutenant Podgourski with three volunteers, Riflemen Trufanov and Butorin of the 4th Company of the 5th Regiment, and Fomeenitch, a sailor, wriggled up on their stomachs to the trench, and there set the fuses of their bombs. The distance was yet rather far for throwing, but as it seemed impossible to crawl any nearer without being observed, they decided to have a try. Fomeenitch was the first to throw his bomb, but it fell short. The enemy did not pay the slightest attention. As the signal had not yet been given, it was decided not to throw any more bombs for the present. Then, seeing that they were not in a good position for throwing, Lieutenant Podgourski and Fomeenitch crawled along to the other flank and joined Captain Kramorenko's detachment. They then succeeded in getting quite close to the bomb-proofs, and Lieutenant Podgourski threw his bomb, which, however, also fell short.

" Let me have another try, sir," said Fomeenitch to Lieutenant Podgourski, and the 10-lb. missile, hurled with a strong arm and true aim, fell right into the entrance to the bomb-proof. There was a

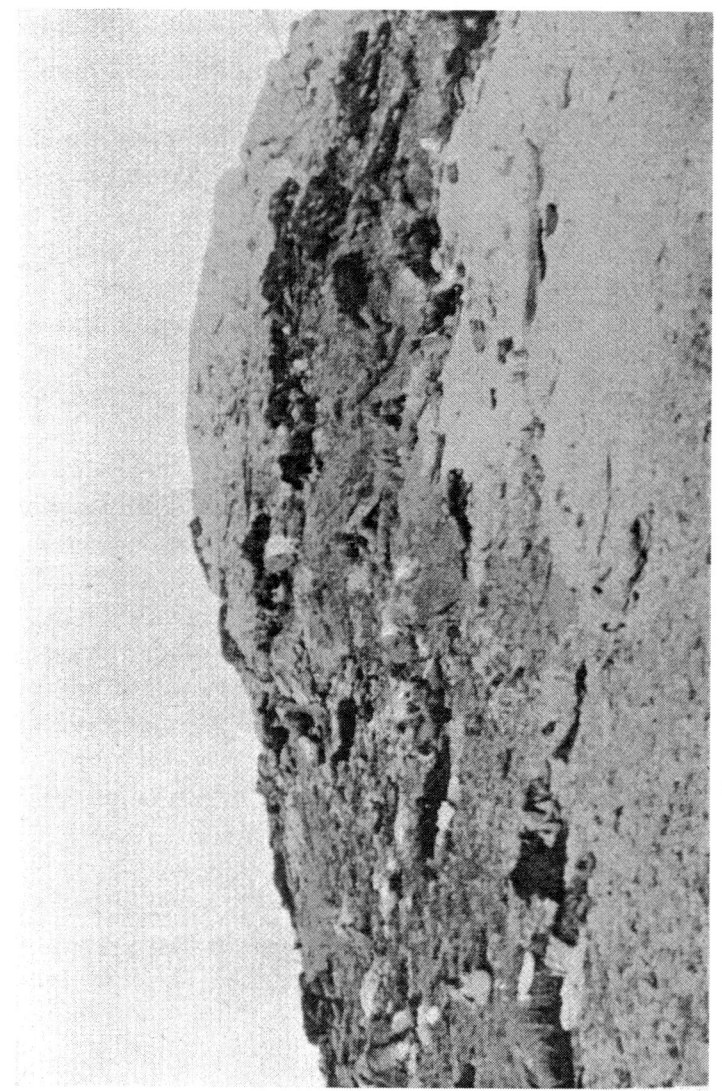

JAPANESE BODIES ON THE TOP OF 203 METRE HILL.

deafening roar, and a great column of smoke, combined with fragments of planks, beams, iron girders, and shattered limbs, shot high into the air. All the other men then ran out into the open and threw their bombs. With a terrific roar the bomb-proofs were blown to pieces. Clods of earth, pieces of planks and beams, and fragments of human bodies fell all round our brave fellows. Those of the Japanese who were left alive fled down the hill, but were all shot down by Captain Kramorenko's men. All was over in two minutes.*

Praise and all honour to Podgourski and Kramorenko! Our joy knew no bounds, whereas the Japanese were literally dumbfounded.

Their futile, but desperate, attacks had cost them some thousands of men,† whose bodies were strewn over all the slopes of 203 Metre Hill and choked the ravines at the foot of it.

On the following day (September 23) we collected a number of rifles and digging tools. We walked freely about 203 Metre Hill and its environs, and did not hear a single shot from the Japanese. The enemy's artillery also was silent, and if we had only had one more division, we could have retaken all our old positions, the Japanese having apparently abandoned them.

Parties of Chinese were sent out to collect the bodies on 203 Metre Hill, and they dug pits on the spot and buried the dead in them. Our men were laid to rest near the headquarters of the staff. Many

---

* Official History affirms that this was done with 15-lb. charges, but according to our narrative the heavier charges failed.

† The Japanese casualties amounted to about 2,500.

13

of the dead had lain for a long time in the trenches on 203 Metre Hill among its living defenders.

Rest ye in peace, brave men ! Your heroic deeds will bear such fruit on Russian soil that thousands like unto you will arise hereafter.

CHAPTER VIII

Making good damages, and strengthening and supplementing the works on the various hills.

THE following morning (September 24) the damage done to our trenches and batteries was thoroughly surveyed, and we at once eagerly set to work to renew those that had been ruined, and to complete those left untouched.

Several bomb-proofs had been shattered by heavy shell, while some had collapsed owing to the shells striking the parapet on which the baulks supporting the roofs rested.

The trenches themselves were so very shallow that one could not stand upright in the blindages. General Fock, who also came to the hill to inspect the works, was very much dissatisfied. He gave orders that the trenches should be deepened to 7 feet (the ground was solid rock), and the overhead cover of the blindages strengthened by a thickness of stone sufficient to render them proof against heavy shells ($3\frac{1}{2}$ feet stone and 14 inches earth); that the 6- and 8-inch beams holding the roofs should be supported on 8-inch uprights; that a bomb-proof should be made for the commandant and officers, and for the sergeant-major and the non-commissioned officers; that the battery on the right flank should be made into a redoubt ; that a redoubt should be hewn out of the rock on the left flank and supplied with an inner ditch, 3 feet deep, with vertical sides ; and that an abattis of wire entanglements should be constructed in front of it, and bomb-proofs with iron roofs inside it.

Throughout this day wagons containing every kind of material made their way to 203 Metre Hill. Workmen swarmed on the hill like bees, but the enemy did not disturb us by a single shot.

I was glad to find that two sapper officers were placed under my orders—Major Gemmelmann, and Ensign Yermakov, a capable and practical man. I detailed the latter to supervise the work in progress on the top of 203 Metre Hill.

His idea was to resort to blasting, and I was in complete accord, as our digging tools were almost worthless in the hard rocky soil.

I had already drawn the trace of a redoubt for one company on Akasaka Yama, the soil of which was similar, and had put Major Mousious there with his company to make it.

I gave orders for the existing trenches on False Hill to be bent back so that the slopes of 203 Metre Hill could be swept by fire from the south-west. Everywhere work was being pushed forward at top speed.

Paralysed by their defeats, the Japanese showed no signs of life for three days. During these three days the hundred or so of Chinamen whom we employed were unable to collect all the bodies, and it was hardly possible to breathe on 203 Metre Hill from the overpowering stench. The bodies of the

Japanese remained in the ravines near the hill until the very end of the siege.

I had succeeded in obtaining some hundreds of poods of barbed wire, and with this I hoped to be able to render 203 Metre Hill impregnable against all ordinary attacks. The work became interesting to the whole garrison, and especially so to the 5th Regiment, whose honour was bound up in the fate of that bloodstained height.

After the September attacks had failed, we had a fairly quiet time in my section of the defence, and my first thought was to give the companies occupying 203 Metre Hill every opportunity of resting.

We replaced them with others, and the defenders were quartered near the headquarters of the staff. O God ! I shall never forget the sight they presented as they descended the hill. Emaciated, ragged, and so caked with dirt that it was impossible to see the colour of their faces, but in splendid spirits nevertheless. All the companies had lost at least two-thirds of their strength in killed and wounded. Colonel Irman and I took it in turns to compliment and praise them. There were only 70 of my men left. On my recommending some of them for St. George's Crosses, I received the ironical reply from General Fock that " out of 70 men I had recommended half for rewards." General Fock forgot, of course, that these 70 represented one-third of the original strength, and that there had been more than 200 of them originally * on 203 Metre Hill.

Seeing that the Japanese had become quite list-

* The author is referring to men of his own regiment, two companies of which comprised part of the garrison of 203 Metre Hill.

less, we began to work openly by day. This made things much easier for us everywhere, and especially on Akasaka Yama and the left flank of Division Hill.

Almost the whole of the 27th Regiment was placed under my orders for the manning of our defensive positions and fighting line, which were, on the whole, very weak. As they did not come all together, but arrived by companies, they were posted on different hills, as were also companies of other regiments which were sent up at various times.

By General Kondratenko's orders the 5th Regiment was distributed over all the hills, in order to render the defence more stubborn.

Leaving us in comparative peace, the Japanese began to bombard the town on September 24, and it became dangerous to walk about in it.

Our central forts also had begun to suffer from the enemy's gun fire. We constantly saw big shells bursting near Forts Yi-tzu Shan and Ta-an-tzu Shan.

From the beginning of September it began to get cold at night, and we had to think of making winter arrangements for the troops. Again we had to collect material and carry it on to the position, but how could our horses do this work without fodder? It was not good for the men either to be without meat. We had had no beef from September 10, and were eating nothing but horse-flesh.

In the summer the men could be quartered in the actual fighting line; officers and men slept in the open air in their trenches, or in tents pitched in safe positions behind the trenches. But this was impossible in the winter. So, by my orders, warm

PLATE II

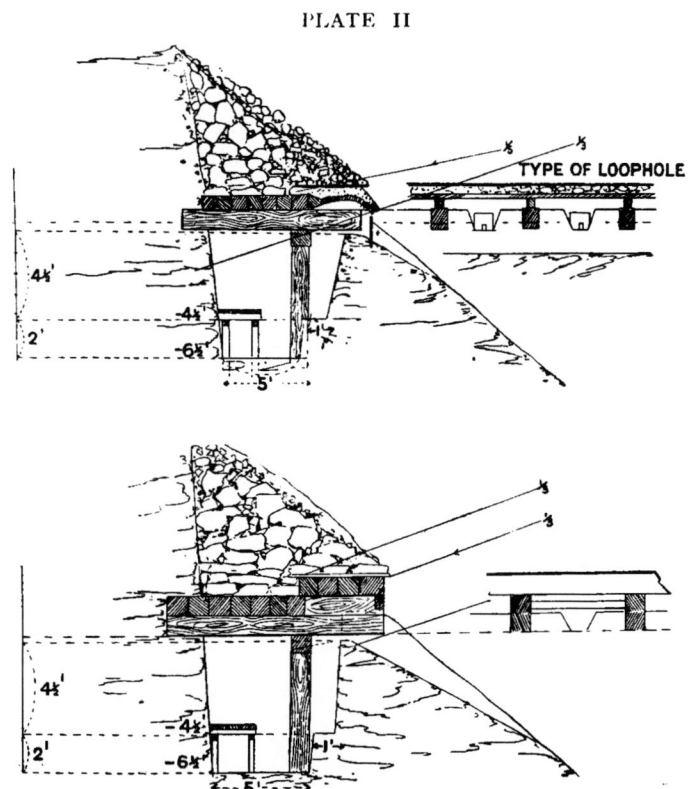

TYPE OF LOOPHOLE

TYPES OF TRENCHES WITH OVERHEAD COVER ON A VERY STEEP SLOPE IN ROCKY SOIL

bomb-proofs (of the type shown in Plate No. II.), designed by the company commanders themselves, were constructed in the trenches. We had also to make closed-in places for the company kitchens, and, lastly, we had to have baths, as the men were beginning to suffer greatly from vermin.

We wanted an enormous number of sand-bags for completing the trenches, and barbed wire for making entanglements. Our regimental supplies of material and tools had, therefore, to be augmented, and we had also to hunt about for carpenters.

The gunners were appealed to for help to bring up everything needed on to the positions, and in response they gave us several dozen four-horsed wagons.

Thanks to the short rest and peace that reigned in our section, both officers and men somewhat recovered their spirits. On various pretexts officers began to collect at the staff headquarters and in the quarters of the officer commanding the western front.

Various rumours, exaggerated of course, were recounted, the probable intentions of the Japanese were discussed, and interesting anecdotes related; in a word, we were all in the best of spirits in spite of the meagreness of our table, which boasted little more than horse-flesh and horse-radish.

With what zest did we not devour that bitter root! There was plenty of vodka and wine to be had, but I hardly ever saw any one drunk.

The enemy now turned all his attention to our centre,* and the roar of gun and rifle fire rolled down

---

* The north-eastern section. This refers to the preliminary movements of the Japanese against Forts Erh-lung and Sung-shu. (See Map III.)

to us continuously from that quarter. I often, during my tour of inspection round the positions, saw curling puffs of smoke from bursting shrapnel over the forts in the centre.

It was not by any means pleasant in the town. Shells fell not only on the houses, but on the hospitals. A shell bursting in the town wounded our Paymaster, Lieutenant Frost, in the face and head, Second-Lieutenant Bobirev in the head, Father Vasili slightly in the head, and Captain Felitzin also. I therefore ordered the horses to be picketed on the left flank, near the staff of the 28th Regiment, as it was unsafe to leave them in their old places on Red Hill. The advantage of the strong bomb-proofs which I had made for the reserves behind Red Hill, and on the right flank in front of the naval barracks, in the very heart of the town, was now apparent.

On October 1 we learnt that the enemy had brought up 11-inch howitzers. This was serious news for us. One could feel that 203 Metre Hill was practically safe against 6-inch projectiles, but 11-inch were a very different matter. I had thought that the enemy would never be able to take 203 Metre Hill and Akasaka Yama. What was to be done now?

Colonel Irman and I thought long and earnestly over this difficult question, but we could see only one solution—to delve deeper into the rock. We decided to do so, hoping that the accuracy of the 11-inch howitzers would not be very great, though I must acknowledge that I did not put much faith in this supposition. Report said that the 11-inch shells were coming from behind Feng-huang Shan, which was only 5 versts from our positions, and I knew what our long 10-inch guns could do at 10 versts.

That evening a large number of officers gathered in the staff headquarters, officers of all arms being present, among whom there was much discussion and talk about the 11-inch howitzers. Finally they comforted themselves with somebody's remark that Port Arthur would not be taken by one 11-inch gun.

Thereupon some began to protest against such an argument. "Why do you think," they said, "that the Japanese have only one 11-inch gun, and not a dozen?" "Because it would be a very difficult and long business to bring them up and put them in position; and besides, where would they get them from?" "Then where have they got the 700,000 men from, instead of the 350,000 we gave them credit for?" This question was unanswerable.

The Japanese had made no move for some time, but now they again began to show signs of activity. It was October 3; on 203 Metre Hill our men were sitting round the samovars,* which they had placed on the road, and were cleaning their clothes and mending their boots, which had suffered sadly on that stony ground. I went to the upper redoubt, where I found that good progress had been made, thanks to the successful blasting. Only a short time ago we had made the trace † of the redoubt, and now it was fully capable of defence. The drainage and water-supply systems on the top of the hill were nearing completion. Colonel Doubeedi, of the

* Tea-urns.

† The "trace" or "outline" of a work is its general shape in plan.

Naval Construction Department, who had at my request been detailed to supervise the construction of the fortifications in my section, procured for us many tools and much material. He had obtained a steam-engine and pipes for pumping up water, and promised that in a week there would be a tank on the hill with as much water as was needed ; and, judging by the present rate of progress, this seemed very probable.

That night our sentries reported that great numbers of the enemy were working between Saddle Hill and Namako Yama, and when I came to look next morning I saw an unbroken line of trenches, revetted with sand-bags, stretching from Saddle Hill to Namako Yama. On a not far-distant hillock, lying to the west, I noticed a short length of trench, also revetted, and the enemy was apparently working at it from both sides. It was a sap !

From three points of the trench between Akasaka Yama and Saddle Hill the Japanese had begun to make passages for sapping operations. Hurrah ! the enemy had had enough of direct attacks and was going to undertake regular siege works against our trenches.

I went from 203 Metre Hill to Akasaka Yama. Good progress had been made there, and now it was possible to live in the trenches, and a stubborn defence might be reckoned on. From Akasaka Yama I had to cross over to Division Hill. This had to be done as quickly as possible, as the Japanese always fired on men crossing in the open, and the need of a communication trench between those points was becoming very pressing. I was very tired after my tramp through the trenches, and by the time I reached the 7th Company on Division Hill I was panting for breath. All the enemy's works against my section were to be clearly seen from here. Every hill and mound that were so familiar to me were crowned with Japanese trenches. They had closed in towards us considerably, and the approaches between the front and rear lines of trenches were plainly visible. Behind Extinct Volcano I saw a typical sap with traverses, leading straight up towards the left flank of Division Hill. Through my glasses I could actually see the men at work.

I explained the significance of these works to officers and men on all the hills, and ordered the former to call for volunteers and make sorties, to destroy the sap-heads and the men working in them ; in this way I gave full scope to Russian enterprise, which I always encouraged in every way I could think of.

The capture of Namako Yama made intercommunication along the rear of our positions extremely difficult. Now we had to construct a regular network of communication trenches, entailing very heavy work. I was fortunate in having Major Gemmelmann, Ensign Yermakov, and Lieutenant Fetter with me to assist me with my field fortifications.

It was not necessary for me now to point out the position of each trench, for our officers fully understood the end and object of sappers' work, and were themselves competent to undertake it.

The fearful effect of small hand grenades demon-

strated to us the necessity of having a store or magazine of them, so Colonel Irman applied to General
Kondratenko, who lost no time in giving the necessary
orders.

Lieutenant Melik-Porsadanov was ordered to construct a melinite factory, and was given the necessary
men for working it. In a few days we were able
to test the efficiency of this factory. Before, however, we utilized its products, our gunners proposed
that they should fire some of these small shell at
the enemy from their mountain guns, using time
fuzes. Some hundreds were immediately supplied to
them, with instructions in their use. They were
distributed among the gunners in the advanced
positions.

From this time, in the evenings, we set to work to
devise a means of replacing the slow-match in the
grenades by some kind of firing mechanism. Our
miners showed the highest inventive powers and
thought out and tried several excellent designs. It
is a pity that they took such a long time to make,
as Bickford's slow-match remained to the end of the
siege practically the only method of ignition. The
soldiers, as was natural, were all for having grenades
that would burst on impact.

A grenade with a slow-match is a very imperfect
weapon. One has only to put oneself in the place
of a rifleman, almost face to face with the enemy,
lighting the slow-match of the grenade in a wind.
The match is blown out—he lights another ; but the
enemy is all the time climbing up closer and closer.
At last the slow-match catches, the grenade is thrown
amongst the enemy, in a second there is a fearful

explosion, and the foe has disappeared. There is nothing left but a pall of black smoke, and over it, high into the air, fly scraps of clothing and portions of human bodies—arms, legs, and heads. That is roughly the effect of a 5-lb. pyroxylin bomb. Our men give a shout of "Hurrah!" and the survivors of the stupefied enemy fly headlong down the hill and hide in their trenches. But it sometimes happens that the slow-match goes out, or the bomb bursts after the enemy has passed it. For the future, before the outbreak of war, some kind of practical mechanism must be fitted to pyroxylin and melinite grenades.

On October 19 our gallant Colonel Irman rode into the staff quarters wounded in the thigh. I had told him times out of number not to expose himself in the trenches.

Whilst going from one trench to another on False Hill he had had a good lesson for the future! Thank God! the bullet did not touch the bone. He was a very brave man, our Colonel, but somewhat foolhardy, and as the officer commanding the whole of the western front of the defensive line he should have been more careful.

I was nearly always with him, and formerly it was most exceptional for me to be on one of the positions without him. But as time passed, it became evident that one of us must always be near the telephone at our headquarters, so that orders could be passed along without a moment's delay.

The first section of the western front was mine, but as other sections under Colonel Irman's command were as yet out of reach of the enemy's fire he made his headquarters within the circle of my section, and when the enemy compelled me to move my headquarters to a less dangerous spot, I had them placed in line with the headquarters of the officer commanding the western front, which was altogether a better arrangement.

After the 27th Regiment had occupied Akasaka Yama and the companies of the 4th Reserve Battalion were distributed over various parts of the defensive line, they began to send sailors into the reserve. They were very fine men, these sailors, but where patience, forbearance, and knowledge of infantry tactics are essential, they should never be sent, as they are then worse than useless.

For instance, the left redoubt on 203 Metre Hill was occupied by some sailors. Tea-time came, and the sailors, under the very eyes of the enemy, left the redoubt one by one and descended the hill without even posting sentries. I do not remember what I wanted, but I had sent an orderly to the redoubt. A minute later he came hurrying back, fully understanding the danger of the situation, and reported : " There is no one at all in the redoubt, sir ! " Of course I sent some men of the reserve there at once, and sent all the naval officers—who refused to believe that their men could have been capable of such folly—after the sailors.

I had a lot of trouble with the sailors. Sometimes they had no kettles, sometimes they had no warm clothing and had to be supplied from the regiment, at other times they were tired and wanted rest, and so on, and so on ; but they were splendid fighters, especially if they were led by good officers.

However, now we had to consider what was to be done about the Japanese saps, gradually lengthening in our direction. After careful inspection we found that they had made the following: against 203 Metre Hill, parallels from the west and north; a long approach from beyond Namako Yama, right across the valley; against Division Hill at some distance from it, several separate parallels.

About two days after the construction of the parallels under 203 Metre Hill we noticed several sap-heads, the parapets of which were made entirely of sand-bags; apparently the rocky nature of the soil made it impossible to dig down deeply.

About two days later the approaches under 203 Metre Hill were plainly visible. There were five of them—two from the west and three from the north.

From the rear of Extinct Volcano one approach had been made towards the left flank of Division Hill. Thanks to the use of sand-bags made of straw the enemy got on fairly quickly. Sometimes more than a sagene (7 feet) was made in a night.* We carefully watched their progress.

Sorties on a small scale, organized by the commandants of the hills, were made to try to hinder

---

* The usual rate of advance of a sap is from 2 to 4 feet per hour, depending on the nature of the soil and the amount of excavation necessary. The latter must, of course, depend on due cover for the party being provided. The Official History states that breastworks, or, more correctly speaking, "parapets" had to be built up, 5 feet high and 4 feet thick, with sand-bags, as ordinary digging was impossible in the rocky formation of 203 Metre Hill. This accounts for the slow rate of progress. Though it is not clear from the narrative, the type of sap was probably that known as "double."

the work.   We also decided to ask General Kondratenko from time to time to order all the howitzers
in the fortress to concentrate their fire on those
points where the enemy was making headway with
his sapping operations.   This would have been
excellent if the fire of the howitzers had been more
accurate, but we ourselves sometimes suffered from
their bad shooting.   We were particularly afraid of
the large naval guns, whose shells frequently fell
inconveniently near us.   However, they caused the
enemy, too, a good deal of annoyance.   It was
unfortunate that, owing to the scarcity of ammunition, they were not able to keep up a continuous fire.
If work on the saps was noticed by day, we kept up
a heavy rifle fire on the sap-heads.   The bullets
evidently penetrated the sand-bags, as the enemy
stopped putting them up, and only began work
again, with much caution, when firing ceased.   In
order to prevent them from working at night, I
ordered supports to be made for the rifles, which
were laid with the greatest care on the sap-heads,
and all night firing was kept up from these rifles.
On General Fock's advice we clamped the rifles
down with sods and earth so that they could not
move out of position.*

As we could use our field guns with effect against
the sap-heads on the left flank of Division Hill,
I obtained one gun and placed it on the top of
Division Hill, absolutely screened from the enemy's
view, and opened fire on the head of the sap.   The
third shot struck it fairly, and, scattering the sand-bags,

* It will be remembered that regular rifle clamps were used
during the South African War for firing at night.

opened up the trench inside. In about three days the excellent practice made by this gun compelled the enemy to stop working that sap altogether, and I felt in consequence considerably easier in my mind about Division Hill. But the sapping proceeded surely and steadily round 203 Metre Hill. Our sorties were the only effective means of checking the work.

I forgot to mention our successful sorties against the saps on the left flank of Division Hill. We had there our 1st Scout Detachment and the 3rd, 7th, and 12th Companies of the 5th Regiment. Our Scouts under Acting Ensign Elechevski, a fine officer of our regiment, made two very successful sorties, besides several rather fruitless ones. On each occasion the Japanese were annihilated by grenades and bayonet charges, and their earth-works demolished. After these sorties, and the excellent firing of my field gun, no further progress was made with that sap; but the firing from Extinct Volcano and Namako Yama gave us no rest. In order to secure the left flank of Division Hill, and to afford means of communication therewith, we had to dig trenches in rear and communication passages at least 2 versts in length. The work was carried out under Lieutenant Kostoushko (who was my orderly officer towards the latter end of the siege) with only a limited number of men. It was very heavy work. Owing to the carelessness and indifference to danger of our men never a day passed without some casualties.

During the first weeks of October the Japanese made themselves very strong opposite our centre

14

(Fort Erh-lung, and West Pan-lung Redoubt, and the valley of the Lun-ho), and, as with us on 203 Metre Hill and Akasaka Yama, rifle firing there did not cease day or night, and Japanese shell from every kind of gun fell constantly round the positions.

When making my inspections, I often watched the enemy's movements against our central positions from Division Hill. I had an excellent view of the ground in front of Forts Erh-lung and Sung-shu. On one occasion I observed something very interesting and instructive, which I will now describe.

While selecting a position for a field howitzer and one quick-firing gun on Division Hill, I went over to the extreme right flank and saw in front of me the following picture. Forts Erh-lung and Sung-shu were literally swept by a storm of shell, and from the ravines below great masses of Japanese infantry were climbing up towards the forts in question, and we could clearly see their lines of skirmishers on the open ground. This movement was apparently unnoticed from Forts Erh-lung and Sung-shu, but from Fort Yi-tzu Shan everything must have been visible quite plainly.

" Why," I thought to myself, " does not Fort Yi-tzu Shan fire ? " I asked the question by telephone, and was informed in reply that ammunition was scarce in the fort and had to be reserved exclusively for beating off assaults. I immediately gave orders for fire to be opened on the enemy advancing on Fort Erh-lung.

Fire was opened, and I had the pleasure of seeing that our shells compelled the Japanese skirmishers to take cover in the folds of the ground. After this

WATCHING A BOMBARDMENT OF FORT ERH-LUNG. COLONEL IRMAN IS SHOWN ON THE RIGHT IN A FUR CAP, AND GENERAL TRETYAKOV ON HIS RIGHT.

our firing ceased and the lines again came out and began climbing up towards the fort and the battery.

I gave orders for the firing to be renewed, but received the answer that all ammunition had been expended and more would not arrive before nightfall, even if sent for immediately; and this when the Japanese had already got almost up to the glacis and had begun digging themselves in right under the eyes of all our artillery.

Surely, under such circumstances, this was absolutely irrational. If they had only had some ammunition at Fort Yi-tzu Shan, the Japanese would have been swept away from the ground in front of Fort Erh-lung like dust before a broom, as there they were within short range of our guns. In reality, however, they were in an untenable position, facing as they were the heavy long-range guns in Fort Erh-lung, and being enfiladed from Fort Yi-tzu Shan, which was also well armed. In consequence of a similar economy in gun ammunition they had also been left in undisputed possession of Namako Yama and Extinct Volcano.

Report has it that great numbers of shell were taken after the surrender of the fortress, so why was the enemy allowed to remain, unmolested by artillery, in positions close up to our lines?

It is true that the heavy guns on Fort Ta-yang-ku North did on several occasions damage the Japanese trenches on Extinct Volcano, but a continuous fire should have been directed at this hill, so as to prevent the enemy from attacking the left flank of Division Hill and firing at our men in the communication trenches in rear.

CHAPTER IX

Fortifying 203 Metre Hill—Situation at the beginning of November
—Mining operations.

ON my inspections now I had to run and jump like a goat from traverse to traverse, and even crawl on all-fours. I had indeed good reason for complaining more often perhaps than any one else of the inaction of our artillery.

Not long before this the Japanese smashed up our water-cart as it was wending its way to Division Hill. Well, we ate the horses, but the cart itself was shattered to pieces, and all because our guns allowed the enemy to get too close up to our positions.

Thank God! the Japanese could not see our staff headquarters, or otherwise the structure would have been razed to the ground. Stray shells alone caused a certain amount of damage to it, so one can imagine what would have happened if the opposing artillery had actually ranged on it.

A short time ago, when the Japanese sent up a balloon, I climbed on to the roof of one of the buildings to see if we were visible to the men in its car.

I could see the balloon distinctly through my telescope, but it seemed very doubtful if the Japanese could see the chimneys of our houses, so we no longer worried about their safety.

I have already said that the Japanese sapping operations near 203 Metre Hill were progressing apace, and consequently we were now racking our brains to devise means of impeding their work. I proposed making a sortie on a large scale. In order to ensure its success, I took a photograph from 203 Metre Hill of our own and the Japanese works, and told Major Fofanov, the officer commanding our 5th Company, whom I had selected to lead the sortie, to make a careful study of the ground himself, but in the end our senior officers refused to give us permission to make any sortie on a large scale. We had, consequently, to be content with a series of small ones. Numbers of men always volunteered for these sorties, of whom Acting Ensign Makurin and Rifleman Stoliarov of the 1st Scout Detachment especially distinguished themselves.

One of their sorties was brilliantly successful. The Japanese in the saps and trenches were bayoneted, the trenches were wrecked, and a quantity of digging tools was captured, while our own losses were insignificant. One sortie, however, made by Makurin on the night of October 20–21, was a failure, probably for the reason that the Japanese had anticipated it, and our men were thus met by rifle fire and hand grenades. Our losses were heavy, Makurin himself being severely wounded in the arm.

These sorties were our only means of combating the Japanese sap work, until at last we discovered a new method—one that had been tried by Midshipman Vlassev in the centre of our positions. A description of the procedure was given us when we were all drinking tea (of which we always had a plentiful supply) in the staff headquarters, and we promptly decided to try the experiment ourselves.

The following day we dragged a 42-linia * gun to 203 Metre Hill, mounted it in a trench and, with General Kondratenko's permission, asked Midshipman Vlassev to come over. Under his direction a stick about 4 feet long was fixed into the base of a cylindro-conical shell of calibre 41·5 linia. This wooden tail was pushed down the bore of the gun, which was previously charged with a small quantity of powder. On firing, the shell with its tail flew towards the enemy's sap, where the 20-lb. charge of pyroxylin exploded, and destroyed all the enemy's works as well as the men engaged in constructing them. Midshipman Vlassev and Major Gobiato (a gunner) undertook to try this method of firing. Though the first few shots were not successful, the wooden tail being either burnt up or broken, and the shell failing to drop where it was intended, they nevertheless struck fear into the hearts of the Japanese! Afterwards firing became more accurate, and the shells frequently fell right into the trenches.

For future fortress warfare some practical means must be devised for throwing 20-lb. charges a short distance with precision, and then close approach will be rendered so difficult as to be almost an impossibility.

Having noted the position of this dangerous gun, the enemy directed a tremendous fire upon it, but it took him a month to dismount it, and then only because it was impossible for us to protect it in the trenches from the constant fall of heavy shell.

* The linia is a Russian unit of measurement, and equals $\frac{1}{10}$ inch; hence the calibre of the gun was 4·2 inches.

BLINDAGE ON THE LEFT FLANK OF 203 METRE HILL. THE MEN ARE RIFLEMEN OF THE 2ND COMPANY, 5TH REGIMENT.

p. 215]

The discharge of these great tailed shell was watched with the greatest interest by our riflemen. But the enemy, not to be outdone, also began to discharge large mines at us, the effect of the explosion of which was considerably greater than that of his 11-inch shell, but their striking effect was weak and limited to a terrific roar and an indescribable volume of smoke.

During the last month the work of fortifying 203 Metre Hill had made rapid progress. One could walk freely about the trenches now, without the risk of knocking one's head against the cross-beams in the blindages. Dug-outs had been made in the rear face of the trenches, so that a third of the defenders could turn in at night and obtain proper rest. The blindages in the most exposed places had been strengthened with rails and $\frac{1}{2}$-inch iron plates, with earth and stone piled up on them to a height of about 6 feet, and the loop-holes were furnished with $\frac{1}{2}$-inch iron shields, with a cross-shaped aperture in the middle for the rifle, so that the men felt themselves fairly safe when exchanging fire with the Japanese.

Unfortunately, however, the enemy began noticeably to increase his fire on the hill from 11-inch howitzers. One shell hit a traverse 9 feet thick, blew it to pieces, in spite of the fact that it was nearly all solid rock, and wrecked all the passages round it. I went to see what damage had been done, and saw that it would need a great deal of work to repair it. The passage round the traverse had been blown out to a depth of 7 feet. Three riflemen, who were standing alongside the traverse near an embrasure, were killed.

I asked the men : "Well, how do you like this kind of visitor ? Do you find it trying ? " " Not a bit, sir. They seldom do much damage, beyond singeing us a bit—look there ! " and a soldier pointed to one of the hills near the Shipinsin Pass where a puff of smoke was hanging. In another second a huge 11-inch shell screamed over the hill, and, striking somewhere behind, burst with a tremendous roar. Thousands of splinters flew in all directions. " M-iles over," drawled one of the men unconcernedly.

" That is why they have put you here," I continued. " Every one knows what splendid men you are—that you will not surrender ; you must be proud that you are so honoured by the whole garrison. Men of the 5th Regiment are posted in all the most dangerous positions."

" We *are* proud, sir," answered a chorus of voices.

That is how things were when no attack was proceeding. But the end was bound to come. The enemy's saps had come half-way up the hill, and we continued to strengthen our positions.

203 Metre Hill had by now a complete belt of wire entanglements round it. To further strengthen this obstacle, I gave orders for abattis to be constructed in it. Trees were cut down near the staff headquarters and dragged up to the hill. In this way an open attack was rendered an absolute impossibility. The redoubts and trenches on Akasaka Yama were also completed. Acting Ensign Yermakov and Major Mousious surpassed themselves. General Fock came to Akasaka Yama and was very satisfied

with the work done there, which I believe he has mentioned in his "Notes." *

I had many companies of other regiments on the positions in my section. As I have already said, these companies were sent up as they were needed, and so they became rather intermixed. This was in every respect most undesirable, as, whenever anything went wrong, it was impossible to determine who was really to blame.

It became very evident to me that it is not by any means the same thing whether four companies of different units hold a position, or whether it is defended by one battalion, under its own commander.

In view of this, the whole of the 27th Regiment, with the exception of the 1st Company, was ordered to concentrate on Akasaka Yama and the 5th on Division Hill, 203 Metre Hill being defended as before by the 2nd, 4th, and 6th Companies of the 5th Regiment, with four machine guns, the 1st Company of the 27th Regiment, and the 7th Company of the 14th Regiment under Lieutenant Vanikovski. These men were all familiar with their various positions, and had become indifferent to constant danger and quite accustomed to looking down from the top on the enemy digging below without any particular feelings of alarm.

---

* General Fock wrote a number of "Notes" during the siege, which were published from time to time and distributed throughout the garrison. As many of them contained severe criticisms of commanders of regiments (which were read by junior officers), General Fock was charged at the court-martial, held in St. Petersburg, in 1908, with conduct to the prejudice of military discipline, and General Stessel was also blamed for allowing them to be published. Compare Official History, Part III., p. 144 (3).

I must acknowledge that in view of past experience I did not like changing my tried companies for new ones. I therefore organized them in reliefs —two days' rest near the staff headquarters to one on the position.

Interval Hill was occupied by one company of the 25th Regiment under Major Veselovski. In the reserve I had the companies of the 4th Reserve Battalion.

Towards the end of November the fortifications on all the hills were complete. On 203 Metre Hill was a huge redoubt, with two keeps, completely surrounded by wire entanglements.* The interval between 203 Metre Hill and False Hill was covered by several rows of fougasses. Akasaka Yama was encircled with a well-built line of trenches, and had a strong redoubt on the top, with two weaker ones on the right flank. On Division Hill there was a large redoubt with two retrenchments, the fire of which was directed towards Extinct Volcano, as an attack, we thought, was certain to come from that direction.

The communication trenches to Akasaka Yama and Division Hill were well screened from view and impervious to rifle fire. False Hill was also surrounded by well-constructed trenches, with covered communication passages leading to them.

The space between False Hill and Fort Ta-yang-kou North was the only piece in the section resembling a fortified position in the ordinary sense of the word, and it was held by only two companies,

* See Map V.

and four guns of small calibre. All the hills were self-contained and capable of making a separate resistance, and in case of need I could reinforce any one of them by two or three companies from the general reserve.

The men on the positions lived now in much greater comfort than before, particularly since there was room for all in suitable covered dug-outs at night.

They all had good kitchens, and on Akasaka Yama even baths had been made. In the matter of food there was, however, little variety, neither butter nor beef being available. Where had the artillery horses been taken? We saw none of them. We often ate mules and horses that had been killed on the positions, but some regiments were unable even to get them. The garrison was, in consequence, beginning to suffer from scurvy, and eventually this cursed disease stealthily found its way in among us also, and laid low many of our best men.

While we were, so to speak, having an easy time of it, important events were taking place in the centre.* Time after time we received reports from there of the defeat of the enemy's attacks and his heavy losses. But we also knew that the enemy's approaches were within striking distance of the forts, and that it would not be long before mining operations would commence.

On the evening of November 8, I received a note from General Kondratenko, inviting me to come and

* This refers to the repulse of the Japanese second general assault (October 26–31).

examine the mining work at Fort Chi-kuan, *
where they could already hear the enemy's miners
working. The main object of this examination was
to ascertain how far off their work was going on.

That evening I rode into Port Arthur and met
Colonel Grigorenko.† Having had tea with him and
a fairly large gathering of officers, who made one
feel quite at home, we all set out in carriages for
Fort Chi-kuan, where we arrived without any
mishap.

In company with General Nikizhin, Colonel Reiss,
and several staff officers we passed through the north
gate of the town, where the sentry was inclined to
stop us, because, as he said, he had received no order
to let us through.

The road passed through some dark ravines, and
by a way which was quite unknown to me. In half
an hour's time we reached General Nadyein's headquarters, which consisted of two barrack rooms, surrounded on all sides and roofed over with several
rows of sand-bags.

General Nadyein had taken some time in building
this splinter-proof, and had used thousands of sand-
bags over its construction. Inside it was comfortable
and light. It stood close under a steep cliff. On
the way to it we had heard a good many bullets
whistling around, but the staff quarters themselves
were in an absolutely safe place.

Telephone wires on service poles radiated in all
directions from the headquarters office.

---

* The last direct attack on this fort had been repulsed on October 31,
since when mining operations had continued.

† Commanding the Engineers.

General Kondratenko and Colonel Irman joined us here and accompanied us to the position, to the advanced lines of which we proceeded on foot.

There was a continuous rattle of rifle fire from all sides, and it was already quite dark. We proceeded along the narrow communication passages, sometimes coming out into a deep ravine, and thence into the fighting trenches, where our riflemen were standing in silence with their overcoats half thrown open (a coat turned inside-out looks like a rock from a distance, and the men in my section always wore their coats like that). Occasionally some of them would take aim and fire into the darkness.

Just as I was going past one of the men, he literally deafened me for the moment with the report of his rifle. "What are you firing at?" I asked. "Into the trench there, sir." "What are you firing into the trench for?" "I saw something moving there," he said. I looked over the parapet. The enemy's trench was indeed very close, * but I doubt if it were possible to see anything moving in it.

In this way we went on for a long time, now crawling along on the ground, now standing up to our full height, Colonel Reiss suffering most inconvenience of all. He had to bend the whole time, as he was so tall that otherwise his head would have been quite a foot over the top of the parapets of the trenches.

At last we stopped. "What's the matter?" we asked of those in front. "We have to run one by one across this piece of open ground." I took my turn

* Only 40 yards now separated the assailants (see Official History, chap. xix., p. 81).

to run across. There was a good deal of firing going on here, I suppose in order to let the Japanese know that we were on the alert. The rifle firing, however, was accompanied by fairly frequent discharges of what appeared to be heavy guns.

Having made one more turn, we saw before us a magnificent spectacle, which at once explained the firing we had heard. It was not gun firing, but the bursting of the Japanese hand grenades hurled at Fort Chi-kuan. I thought how pleasant it would be to be hit on the head by such a projectile.

But it was indeed a wonderful sight. From behind the breastwork of Chi-kuan (we were near the gorge) hissing streams of fire, either singly or in " bouquets," shot high into the air and, falling into the fort, burst with a report like that of a heavy gun.

For about five minutes we watched this wonderful firework display. An officer who had been farther to the front explained that the missiles were pyroxylin or melinite cartridges, to which was attached some wadding saturated with kerosene. The wadding was lighted and the cartridge thrown into the fort by some mechanical means, and there it burst as soon as the " slow-match " had burnt down.

The Japanese hoped by this means to set fire to the sand-bags, planks and beams that were piled up in stacks at the entrance to the fort.

Not knowing how long this display would last, we went across the entrance of the fort into a bomb-proof on the other side without any one being injured. Thanks to the light of some small lanterns and the flames of the wadding which was blazing everywhere, I was able to see that the fort was almost completely wrecked; parapets and traverses presented an absolutely ruined appearance, everywhere pieces of planks and beams from blown-up bomb-proofs were heaped up, and there were numbers of deep, wide holes where 11-inch shell had burst.

I noticed several riflemen on the parapet lying behind sand-bags. They were sentries. I also noticed a well-built retrenchment in the principal salient of the fort.

As I followed the others as quickly as possible into the stone bomb-proof, I became conscious that a moment before I had been somewhat uneasy as to whether I should escape without having my face damaged (just before I had seen a soldier with his face and arms horribly burnt).

The large vaulted casemate we had entered was filled with soldiers, quietly seated all round it. We passed through it and turned to the left, and then proceeded farther through several doors until we suddenly found ourselves in the brightly lit casemate of the officer commanding the fort. We had a short rest there. Colonel Grigorenko explained the situation, making it clear to us that the enemy's mining parties, drilling their way through in two directions, had already got very close to the wall of the semi-caponiers which were placed in the chief salient of the fort, while we had counter-mined in two places.

It was now necessary to determine how near we were to the enemy's miners and to calculate the charge required. There were very few expert miners among officers or men. The sapper company had been but lately formed, and its commander was a pontoon expert, while all the other officers were young. Major Linder (commanding the company) had never had any experience of mining operations, and the only people who knew anything about them were Colonel Grigorenko and Lieutenant-Colonel Rashevski. The former had served with me in the 6th Battalion and knew that I had for some years practised offensive and defensive mining operations at the Engineer College at Kiev, and for that reason he had asked me to come and help him at this critical moment. According to the officer who was superintending the work in our mines, the enemy was extremely close, but just then they could only occasionally hear the sound of very cautious digging.

After hearing this report, we all went into the semi-caponier. We proceeded for a considerable distance through some dark casemates, and then came to the place where the mining was being done. We ordered every one out of the mine and climbed in to listen. Colonel Grigorenko and Lieutenant-Colonel Rashevski were with me. We began to listen, but our movements and breathing prevented our hearing well, so my two companions went out and I was left alone. Putting my ear close to the wall nearest the enemy, I held my breath and listened intently, but not a sound broke the dead silence.

I acknowledge that when my comrades climbed out of the mine, which dropped down steeply in the enemy's direction, I felt none too happy.

Supposing the enemy had laid his charge and was just about to explode it! There would not be much of me left!

In my imagination I conjured up some very disquieting pictures, and all the time not a sound from

the enemy. This rather confirmed me in the correct-
ness of my supposition.

Long and intently I listened, several times changing
my position, as my legs got stiff and cramped owing
to my not being able to stretch them out. I strained
my ears, . . . not a sound. Suddenly . . . a blow, a
very careful one, then . . . another and another; I
tried to guess the enemy's direction, and how far
off he was. Though the formation was somewhat of
the nature of sand-stone, still one ought to be able to
judge fairly accurately. The man was working very
cautiously with a pick, and I could hear it from
all sides of our mine. As if it were now (one does
not forget such moments!), I remember that the
blows sounded near the left side of the passage
and a little above it. The distance was less
than a sagene (7 feet), but more than an archine
(28 inches).

Though the worker was very careful in using his
pick, yet he scraped away the loose earth and stones
rather noisily.

This scraping sound was plainly audible through
the intervening rock, but it was thought very probably
that an enemy on the other side could not hear it.

When I had quite decided how attacker and
defender were situated with regard to each other, I
climbed out of the mine and reported the result
of my observations. Colonel Grigorenko and his
miners accepted my conclusions, and decided to
lay their charge. A report was made to the commandant of the hill, who had himself heard the
enemy at work, and he personally exploded our mine,
which completely destroyed that of the Japanese,

15

and, bursting along the gallery, hurled planks, tools, and men to destruction.

However, having once laid open part of the caponier, which was now quite unprotected by earth, the Japanese blew it up with dynamite and became masters of part of the interior, and from this time there was a continual struggle for the possession of this place, which lasted for a very long time. Some one who was actually there must, however, describe what happened. I only know about it from what I have heard, and cannot give any reliable information except as to what I personally saw on a visit to the fort after the Japanese had blown up the roof of the gallery.

I do not now remember why I went to the fort that day, but I think it was simply out of curiosity. The roof of a large bomb-proof inside had then been wrecked by an 11-inch shell, and I noticed the amount of damage done. I saw the wooden wall dividing the ruined part of the casemate from the unharmed and habitable portion, near which General Kondratenko and seven of General Gorbatovski's best officers were killed.

When I left the semi-caponier, it was thick with smoke from our rifles, though it was possible to breathe in it. Near the sand-bag wall dividing the portion occupied by the Japanese from ours stood two riflemen, who continued to fire through the embrasures at the enemy hidden in the dark on the other side. There was a huge heap of empty cartridge cases piled up round them, reaching almost as high as their waists.

The enemy in my section worked away at his

GROUP OF OFFICERS AT DINNER. AT THE END OF THE TABLE COLONEL SEMENOV, ON HIS RIGHT GENERAL KONDRATENKO, ON HIS LEFT GENERAL GORBATOVSKI (WITH CROSS), AND NEXT TO HIM COLONEL IRMAN.

p. 227]

saps, and we continued firing at the sap-heads, throwing grenades into them, and frequently making sorties, the majority of which were most successful. Many of the men who took part in these sorties were deserving of, and recommended for St. George's Crosses; but General Fock did not credit the 5th Regiment with any particular bravery, and kept back the reward lists (ordering them to be curtailed and combined on one general sheet), so that, when eventually the fortress fell, they were probably all lost, and many heroic deeds passed unrewarded.

Availing ourselves of this period of comparative quiet, we varied occasionally the every-day routine work by riding into the town, or visiting other portions of our line of defences. However, a drive into the town was no great treat, as it was continually swept by fire, and once my horses were nearly killed by a shell bursting just ahead of them.

I generally went to see Colonel Grigorenko, but I also visited, though rarely, the commandant (General Smirnov) and General Stessel. We could always have tea with them and hear the latest news about everything.

It was most interesting to go to Golden Hill, whence they were continually firing on the enemy's torpedo-boats, and where latterly an attack by fire-ships was expected. The search-lights were kept going all night, and if one of the Japanese ships happened to cross the illuminated area, she fared badly. All the shore batteries would open at once a terrific fire on the unfortunate vessel, and the sea round her would boil and spout columns of water thrown up by the falling shell. In the town the firing sounded like thunder, and as the bombardment nearly always continued at night, the flash of the guns produced the effect of lightning; indeed, when one heard the low, unceasing rumble and crash, and saw the frequent flashes, it seemed as if this were not the work of man's hand, but a grand natural phenomenon. But this display cost us hundreds of precious shells which we were unable to replace.

The Japanese kept a very keen look-out at sea, and even Chinese junks found great difficulty in slipping past them. Imagine our surprise and delight, when one night a *steamer* came into Pigeon Bay. The general conjecture was that it had brought machine-guns and shell.

We were told that the vessel had brought some supplies, and that my wife had sent me a large quantity of foodstuffs from Tientsin; but Major Dostovalov, the officer in charge of stores and transport, would not tell me what kind they were, or how much there was of them. Everything that had been brought was commandeered by the commissariat staff, and several days passed without a word being said about our presents.

So I went to Major Dostovalov and asked him to let me have what had been sent me.

"Yes, I have got something for you," he said, "but I have not been able to send it to you yet. If you like, I will give you five Westphalian hams and we will consider everything square, eh?"

I did not expect to get so much as that, I must

confess, and my mouth watered at the thought of the five hams.

"Rather," I said. "I shall be quite satisfied."

I received my five hams and returned home in triumph.

The officers were even more pleased than I was, and we demolished the hams with the greatest relish, feeling very well disposed towards Major Dostovalov, who had added as I went away : " I am sorry you have come a bit late, Colonel, as I would have let you have more, but I can't now, as all I have left is for the generals."

I heard afterwards that my wife had sent me twelve hams, some fruit, sausages, coffee, and so on— 300 roubles' * worth altogether. So after deducting the five hams I actually received, there was a good deal left, all of which was snapped up by the senior officers.

Though we were rather sore about it, and there was a good deal of grumbling, yet we blamed Major Dostovalov and our Chi-fu Consul (Tiddeman) even more for not sending us some newspapers.

* About £30.

CHAPTER X

By about November 23 the saps made by the Japanese against the left flank of 203 Metre Hill had reached nearly as far as the lower line of the wire entanglement, but those in front were still very far off. We thus concluded that there was no likelihood of an attack on the hill yet awhile ; and as to an attack on the centre of our positions, in General Gorbatovski's section, we certainly anticipated none, since it would be more advantageous for the Japanese, having such vast superiority in numbers, to attack the fortress along the whole of its front at the same moment.

However, notwithstanding our deductions, we noticed from our observation points that on November 23, 24, and 25 some unusual movement was being carried out on the enemy's side. Apparently new troops were arriving. The same was observed from our positions and batteries.

Troops were being sent across to 174 Metre Hill. "They are meant for *us*," we said to ourselves. The bombardment of all our positions by heavy guns became fiercer, and our left flank on 203 Metre Hill suffered severely. The enemy made a trench extending away to the right from his first sap, and as

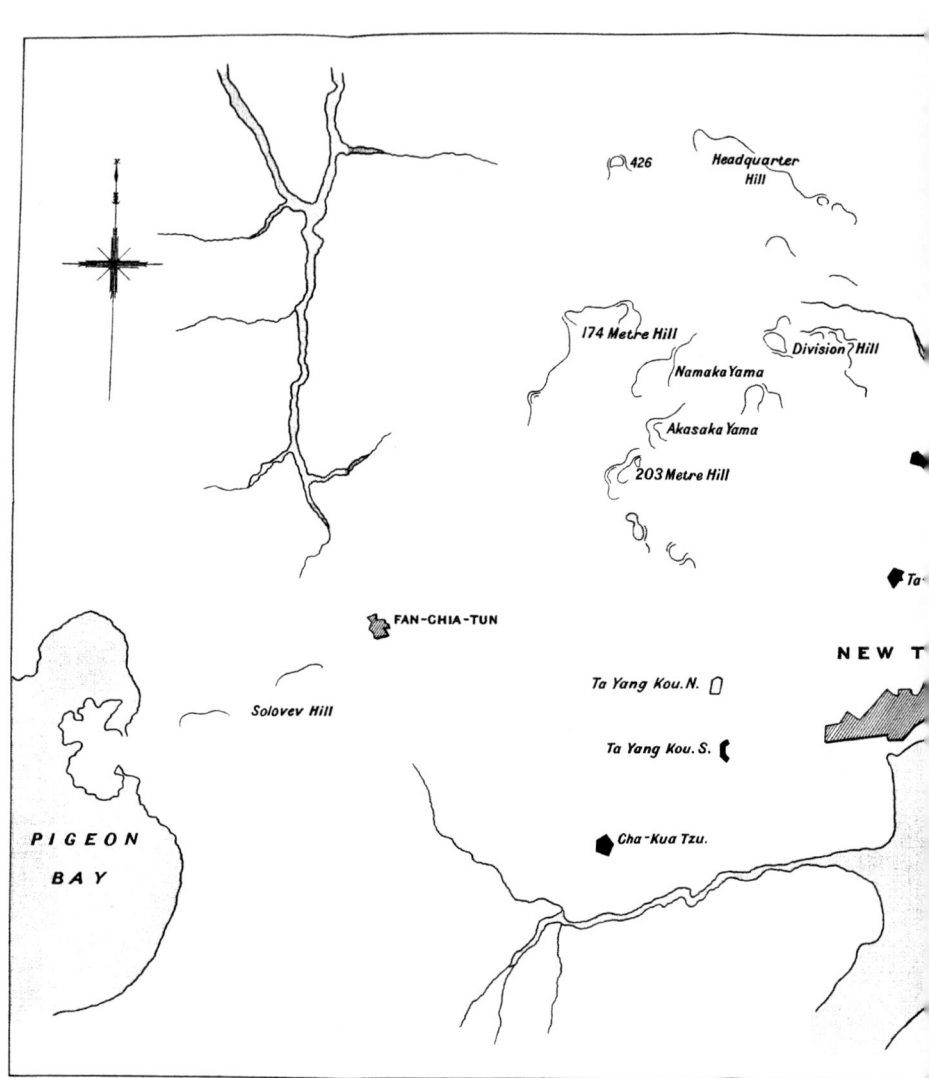

426   Headquarter
         Hill

174 Metre Hill   Division Hill

Namaka Yama

Akasaka Yama

203 Metre Hill

Ta

FAN-CHIA-TUN   NEW T

Ta Yang Kou.N.

Solovev Hill   Ta Yang Kou.S.

PIGEON   Cha-Kua Tzu.

BAY

London :

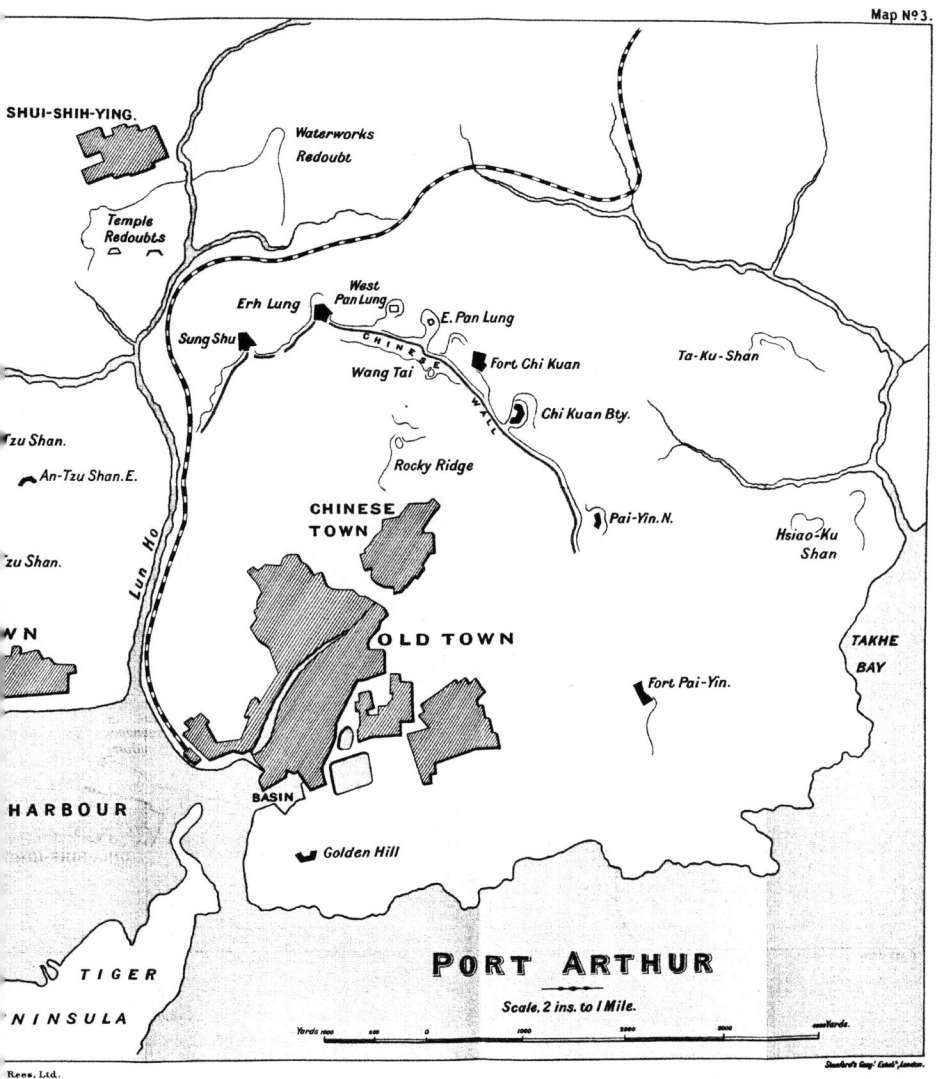

SHUI-SHIH-YING.

Waterworks
Redoubt

Temple
Redoubts

Erh Lung

West
Pan Lung

E. Pan Lung

Sung Shu

CHINESE

Fort Chi Kuan

WALL

Ta-Ku-Shan

Wang Tai

Chi Kuan Bty.

'zu Shan.

An-Tzu Shan. E.

Rocky Ridge

Pai-Yin. N.

Hsiao-Ku
Shan

'zu Shan.

CHINESE
TOWN

OLD TOWN

TAKHE

N

BAY

Fort Pai-Yin.

BASIN

HARBOUR

Golden Hill

TIGER

PORT ARTHUR

NINSULA

Scale, 2 ins. to 1 Mile.

Yards 1000   500   0   1000   2000   3000   4000 Yards.

from there he could very probably see into the harbour we decided to make a sortie to destroy it.

On the 26th the bombardment of 203 Metre Hill and of the central forts of our position became heavier still, so that it became clear that an attack was imminent, and we made preparations accordingly. From this moment we kept our stormers, *i.e.* the troops detailed to resist the assault, in the trenches. Those suffering from scurvy were detailed for this duty, and as it was very hard on men afflicted with this disease to have to remain in the trenches, we used to send them away to the rear, out of danger, where they could bask in the sun. As soon as an attack was anticipated, the order was sent down : " Stormers to their posts ! " upon which they had to leave their place of concealment and climb up the hill into the trenches.

A telephone message came through to the effect that our centre was being attacked.*

I went to Akasaka Yama, and found that the earth-works on its left flank had been badly damaged and the fortifications in front had been wrecked as well. I recognized at once that, in spite of the solidity of our works on 203 Metre Hill, they would not protect our men from the destructive force of the 11-inch shell.

On November 26 the enemy fired twenty-five 11-inch shells, eight 6-inch, 60 mines, † and 300 shells

---

* The third Japanese general assault, mainly directed against Chi-kuan, Ehr-lung, and Sung-shu forts. (See Map III.)

† This must refer to the missiles from the wooden mortars used by the Japanese. These Japanese wooden 5-inch and 7-inch mortars threw " mines " (really large hand grenades), weighing 4½ and 16¼ lb. respectively.

of small calibre. The redoubt on the left flank of 203 Metre Hill was much damaged.

From the right flank of 203 Metre Hill we watched a terrific bombardment directed against Forts Erhlung and Sung-shu. We heard the rattle of rifle fire from all sides, but I saw no signs of an assault. On returning to the staff headquarters, I heard the good news that all the attacks had been repulsed with enormous losses to the enemy. This news I immediately telephoned to all our hills, and ordered the garrisons to be prepared for attack. In order to further secure our line from being broken through, I called up the non-combatant companies * of the 5th, 13th, and 28th Regiments, and with them occupied a second line of defence.

The enemy literally swept 203 Metre and the other hills with fire. From various signs on November 26, we concluded that the Japanese were preparing to attack my front, so I moved up the reserve, and gave orders for all to be ready to meet the impending assault.

---

* There is in every regiment a certain number of men not armed with rifles—transport drivers, joiners, carpenters, clerks, harnessmakers, wheelers, and shoeing-smiths—and to these are added assistant-surgeons and hospital orderlies under battalion and regimental doctors. The company thus formed is commanded by the regimental Quarter-Master.

For inspection purposes these men are formed into one company, but on service the clerks and medical assistants form two separate companies and act independently, the former under the command of the Adjutant, and the latter under one who has passed the " Oko-lodok " (i.e. the lower standard in the Medical School of Instruction), so that the Quarter-Master has the transport drivers and joiners, etc., left in his charge.

All the men of the non-combatant companies are armed with revolvers, with the exception of the transport drivers, who are unarmed, but have to go through a course of rifle practice and instruction.

Early on the morning of the 27th,* 203 Metre Hill resembled a volcano in eruption. Apparently the enemy wished to sweep it off the face of the earth with his shells. Telephone messages were received from the commandant every minute, reporting the fearful damage done by the 11-inch projectiles.

Finally, by about 8 a.m., all the telephones were out of action, and at about 9 a.m. an orderly galloped up and reported that the hill was in the hands of the Japanese. This was apparently a mistake, as we could see no signs of our retirement from the hill, and everything there appeared to be as before. As a matter of fact, the works on the hill had been almost completely wrecked, but the losses had been small, as only sentries and small reliefs were in the trenches.

At 5 p.m. the Japanese attacked, but were repulsed. The commandant, however, sent for reinforcements and more officers, of whom very few were left. I sent up some reinforcements, and with them Naval Ensign Deitchman, already known to us as an exceedingly brave officer, whom, with the approval of Colonel Irman, I appointed orderly officer to the commandant.

It was already dark when Deitchman reached the hill, and on his arrival he found that all was not well. It transpired that the attack had not been entirely beaten back, and that a small body of Japanese was lodged in a blindage near the central battery, there awaiting reinforcements. The commandant

* The operations here described were evidently preliminary to the main assault, which, according to our Official History, opened at 8.30 a.m. on November 28.

immediately summoned a council of war, which at once decided to drive the Japanese out of this stronghold. Acting Ensign Yermakov, being thoroughly acquainted with the positions of all the fortifications, was detailed to organize the counter-attack. He formed three groups of volunteers with which to carry out his plans. The first, under Fleet Ensign Morosov, was to attack the Japanese from the right flank ; the second, under an officer whose name I have not learned, was to do the same from the left flank ; and the third, under Deitchman, was to rush the enemy from the front. On the signal being given, all the columns made a rush on the blindage, but Ensign Deitchman was shot in the head and killed on the spot. However, grenades were thrown into the blindage and annihilated the Japanese. Fleet Ensign Morosov was the first to rush in.

That day the enemy discharged thirty 11-inch, about three hundred 6-inch, and a great number of shell of smaller calibre at 203 Metre Hill.

At daybreak on November 28 the Japanese continued to bombard the hill, and destroyed everything that had been repaired during the night. From early morning the firing increased, and eventually the Japanese moved to the attack.

By midday they had completely wrecked the trenches on the hill with their shells, and as General Kondratenko had come to the staff headquarters, I prepared to go to 203 Metre Hill personally to direct affairs. During the day we repulsed two attacks and I sent up all my reserves in support— the 6th Company of sailors and the non-combatant companies of the 14th and 16th Regiments.

A number of officers of various corps had collected at headquarters, all eagerly watching the course of the fighting on 203 Metre Hill through their glasses.

At 4.30 p.m. on the 28th the Japanese again attacked the ill-fated hill. Our decimated remnant was cut to pieces, and the enemy captured both the upper breastworks.*

On Akasaka Yama also things were not going well, and at about 2 p.m. I sent up the 7th Company of the 27th Regiment, which had only just arrived.

At 5 p.m. I mounted my horse and rode to 203 Metre Hill. Father Vasili gave me a small silver crucifix as a charm, which I put on.

I reached the foot of the hill. In the ravine near the dressing station was a countless crowd of wounded and unwounded men. The rear slopes of the hill were covered with men lying in different postures, wounded men who had died on their way back. The reserve company was standing under arms, the men flattening themselves close up against the cliff, while shells were exploding all around. The top of the hill was wreathed in smoke from the bursting of every kind of projectile.

Having left my horse near the dressing station, and called up all the unwounded men who were taking shelter under the hill, I started to climb up, and reached the top of the road without a scratch.

Here a truly awful scene of ruin met my eyes.

* General Tretyakov speaks of "redoubts," but according to our Official History the works on 203 Metre Hill were really of the less formidable nature of "breastworks," which term is, therefore, substituted in this translation.

The light plank bomb-proofs, which were built out from the steep side of the cutting along which the road ran, were almost all destroyed and were choked with mangled bodies and torn fragments of human limbs. The whole road was simply blocked with broken beams and dead bodies.

Stepping over all this, and slipping about on the planks, which were saturated with blood, I reached the telephone bomb-proof, which had by some marvel been left untouched. Here I found the commandant and several officers, all apparently at a loss as to what action to take.

In a few words the commandant explained the situation to me. It was even worse than I had anticipated, and something had to be done instantly.

All the reserves had been used up, so we formed one out of the men I had brought with me. Although both breastworks were in the hands of the Japanese, our men were holding on like grim death to the ground in rear of them, the blindages, narrow passages, and communication trenches. The whole of the space between the two breastworks was still in our possession. The lower, circular trench was almost completely wrecked, but our men were still firmly lodged in the few untouched parts of it. It thus seemed to me that we must drive out the Japanese by one well-directed blow, and that, moreover, this would not be a difficult matter.

In order to put my plan into execution, I formed the men I had brought with me into one command, had hand grenades served out to each man, and, having given them a short harangue, sent them off, some against the left breastwork, and some against

BLINDAGES ON 203 METRE HILL, WRECKED BY SHELL FIRE.   THE MEN ARE SITTING AMONGST THE RUINS OF A
BLINDAGE COMPLETELY DESTROYED BY A 11-INCH SHELL.

the right. Seeing that all was not yet lost, and led by young officers, the gallant fellows rushed upon the works with a wild cheer. This was about 7 p.m.

The left one was taken in a single rush. The other did not fall at once, and the men came to a standstill before it, but again rushed forward on their own initiative and drove the enemy out, many officers, including Lieutenant Yermakov, witnessing their action. Hand grenades were freely used and once again proved themselves invaluable.

I immediately sent a report to General Stessel and General Kondratenko. The former had given orders to me personally to let him know by telephone all that happened on 203 Metre Hill, and I now received a message of congratulation from him. As soon as the Japanese had been driven out of the breast-works, the enemy's artillery fire became fiercer, and was directed mainly on the left flank of the circular trench and on the breastwork above it.

In order not to expose needlessly those of my men who were holding the now completely wrecked lower line of trenches, I ordered them to make their way round to the upper road at the rear, and form the reserve. We abandoned the ruined circular trench, with the exception of its left flank, but the enemy, unaware of this, continued to complete its destruction, expending thousands of shell.

I sent for sand-bags and reinforcements to make good at once the damage done to the trenches and breastworks on the top of the hill. A few hours later two companies of sailors and a two-wheeled

cart with hand grenades arrived. I placed the
sailors in the reserve dug-outs (deep ditches—one
above and one below the lower road), which were
practically immune from fire.

Lieutenant Fenster, a sapper, arrived on the hill,
and proposed to repair the trenches and the breastworks during the night. The north face of the left
breastwork, and the bomb-proof in it, were so ruined,
that I could not climb across them to its western
face, and the left end of the trench connecting the
breastwork was levelled to the ground, but the rear
face of the work remained intact.

It was imperative that all this damage should be
at once repaired with sand-bags, provided there
was no attack meanwhile.

All the enemy's trenches round the hill were full
of Japanese.

Night was falling on November 28, when hand
grenades began to burst in the left breastwork,
and a soldier ran up with the report that the Japanese
were attacking. We rushed out on to the road where
the reserves were. The communication passages
from all the fortifications on the hill met there, and
there was also a hollow in the ground, used as a
dressing station. But the explosions of hand grenades
suddenly ceased and all grew quiet, save for the roar
of the cannon ; our hand grenades seem to have driven
the Japanese back into their trenches. But how
would it be at dead of night when it was impossible
to see how far off the enemy was ? I was afraid
there would be a panic. In repulsing the enemy's
attack so easily, we had had great assistance from the
detachments led by Lieutenants Siromiatnikov and

Nejentsev which had taken the enemy in rear from the direction of Major Soloveiev's position.

That night (November 28) was a dark one, and everything was apparently quiet since the last attack, only the occasional roar of an exploding hand grenade breaking the stillness. I could not sleep all night, but kept sending out orderlies in all directions, and conversing with the staff over the telephone wires. Every one wanted to know what was happening on the hill. During the night several two-wheeled carts came up with hand grenades, which I ordered to be stored in the bomb-proofs near the dressing station.

At about 4 a.m. gun fire again commenced, and the stream of wounded began to come down from the crest to the foot of the hill and beyond.

The Japanese had made many vain attacks, and we could live through everything but heavy gun fire. But the moral effect had to be considered ; our men were accustomed to the shells and to heavy losses, and to these they had become quite indifferent, but the infantry attacks upset their nerves. And now one of them was in progress : hand grenades were bursting in the left breastwork, and an orderly ran up asking for reinforcements, officers, and hand grenades. Grenades then began to burst on the right breastwork, and our men there also sent for a supply. I sent up all they required, and asked Colonel Irman to send me officers from the staff. In response Captain Bielozerov was sent to me. Serious work was at hand, for the roll of rifle fire broke out, foretelling an impending attack. I ordered the company at the foot of the hill to come up to the upper road, and asked for yet another company by telephone. The reply came that there was none available. I then telephoned for our 5th Company to leave its lines on Division Hill near Fort Yi-tzu Shan, to which it had only just returned, and to come up at once to 203 Metre Hill. The firing and bursting of grenades increased, while the bombardment ceased —truly a bad sign.

Indeed, our men were already flying out of the left breastwork. I brought up my company of sailors, sent it to meet the fugitives, and shouted myself hoarse, " Stop, stop ! reinforcements ! " Nevertheless, they would not stop, and the sailors also wavered and came to a standstill. There was a good deal of confusion, and what I cried out, what I actually did, I do not now quite remember. It seems, however, I succeeded in rallying the men, for those of my own regiment began to gather round me ; and when I found that I was at the head of a considerable number of men I led them against the left breastwork. Riflemen and sailors rushed forward and swarmed on to the work with Captain Bielozerov, who was the first in. Much the same happened as regards the breastwork on the right, but the state of affairs was not quite so bad there, as no panic had occurred, and they had simply sent me word that the Japanese had taken it, but that our men were still holding the rear rampart. With the other officers I led a detachment of sailors up through the communication passages into the work. The Japanese made a poor resistance, and in a few minutes we had captured the place at the point of the bayonet.

THE LAST RESERVES FOR 203 METRE HILL, DURING THE FIGHTING IN NOVEMBER.

p. 240]

I sent off a long written report, shell fire having destroyed the telephone wires, which, however, our sappers connected up again within ten minutes.

Here I should like to say a word or two about our sappers. I had only very few of them, either on 203 Metre Hill, or in my section of defence, but they were all fearless and beyond reproach. Notwithstanding constant danger, they worked with perfect unconcern. Many of them were placed *hors de combat*. One shell fell into a bomb-proof where they were working and severely wounded eight of them, in spite of which the energy and daring of those left were in no way diminished. They were always seeking opportunities to make themselves useful, and, indeed, their services to their country and their Tsar had a great effect on the soldiers with whom they came in contact.

Having taken command on 203 Metre Hill, I could not, of course, exercise control over the other de-fended hills, so Colonel Irman undertook this duty. Being thus in ignorance of what was going on beyond 203 Metre Hill, I felt very uneasy about Akasaka Yama, which the enemy was again attacking. Sap-ping up as far as the ravine in front of 203 Metre Hill, the Japanese had driven one sap-head from this ravine straight towards the foot of Akasaka Yama, then, stopping work about 70 feet from it, they had run across in groups to a small stretch of dead ground under the cliff facing Namako Yama and had begun to do something there, as we could plainly see. Although I had had abattis constructed above this cliff, and our trench ran along behind the abattis,

16

this point was the most vulnerable in the whole of the defences of Akasaka Yama, and my fears were realized, for the enemy chose this very point for his attack.

I was the more concerned about Akasaka Yama because, if it fell into the hands of the enemy, communication with 203 Metre Hill from the rear would be interrupted, the latter could then be enfiladed from all sides, and it would become impossible to hold it any longer. On the other hand, as long as Akasaka Yama remained ours, it gave strong support to 203 Metre Hill and prevented the enemy from attacking it from the front and right flank. The Japanese made one attempt to do this and suffered very severely, several hundreds of men falling on the northern slopes of 203 Metre Hill under the fire of the rifles and machine guns on Akasaka Yama.

Having received a severe check, the enemy ceased attacking, but continued to work at his parallels and to make a zigzag to the right. This was very serious for us, as it brought the Japanese up to a point on the hill from which they could observe the fall of their shell within the harbour area. Without doubt, we should have to make a sortie in force.

By hurling at least three companies on the enemy in the night, we could drive him out of his parallel and destroy it. The casualties would be heavy, but the success gained would be large in proportion. As it was, we were only just able to hold the hill, and our losses were severe. We could only get reinforcements with the greatest difficulty, as they were wanted for General Gorbatovski's section, which was also being attacked. But it was impossible to hold the hill without reserves ; either several companies a day would have to be sacrificed, or else the hill abandoned.

The fearful effect of the 11-inch shell made us think it expedient to dig caves out of the hill-sides to give the men cover, and we began to do so, but it was then too late. Those we had time to make were only large enough to shelter a few men.

Evening was already drawing in on November 29. The bombardment slackened (the Japanese must have run out of ammunition), and curls of smoke were to be seen in places covered from fire under the hill, where the men were making fires for their tea. Everything seemed to point to the day ending quietly, and I felt quite satisfied, not having the least suspicion of what a trick the sailors in the left breastwork were going to play upon me. I had sent my orderly there (I do not remember what for) ; ten minutes later he came running back to me and reported that there was not a single man in the breastwork—it was absolutely empty.

" But where are the sailors ? " I cried.

" I don't know, sir ! They must have gone away."

I immediately sent for the naval officers and ordered them to find their men and send them back to their post, and in the meantime I sent to the breastwork all the men near me—about ten riflemen and scouts, who were acting as my orderlies.

I always kept near me a few men thoroughly acquainted with the fortifications on the hill. This was essential, as a man who did not know every feature might very easily lose himself in the labyrinth of trenches and communication passages, and thus fail to take my orders to those for whom they were intended.

An hour later the sailors were all collected, and I only forgave them their foolish action in consideration of their splendid previous attack, and the way they had driven the Japanese out of the breastwork. I ordered the naval officers to be always with their men and not to stay in the bomb-proofs, reminding them that this was the second time the sailors had been guilty of leaving their post.

Night had already fallen—for me always a trying time, as it is impossible to exercise effective control in the darkness—and the only thing I could do was to walk about the hill and encourage my men by talking to them. But my voice had almost entirely gone, from constantly shouting in the daytime.

When it had got quite dark, some sappers arrived, bringing sand-bags. Reinforcements—two companies—also came up. I decided to let those actually in the fighting line sleep, and to make those who had just arrived work; but what sleep and what work were possible under a hail of every kind of shell? We had available for night work, besides Lieutenant Fenster and Acting Ensign Yermakov, Lieutenant Reinbott of the Fortress Mining Company. Though I was really dog-tired those last two days, still I did not feel as if I wanted either to eat or sleep.

As soon as day broke on the 30th, the firing increased in volume, and we witnessed the utter destruction of the right face of the left breastwork by the agency of several well-aimed 11-inch projectiles. Luckily, the enemy failed to do much

damage to the side which was open to his constant
attacks, but the inner ditch was completely filled
with dead bodies, both of our own men and the
Japanese, which we were unable to remove. It was
impossible to do so, as in the daytime this face of
the work was swept by shrapnel from the flank
and rear, and at night our men there were always
on the "qui vive" for an attack, and could not
leave the cover of the breastwork; besides which a
great many men would be needed to carry away
the dead, and we had no one to spare.

At 8 a.m. the Japanese suddenly attacked the
left breastwork, captured the front portion, and
raised their flag. The sight of this flag always filled
our men with fury. I knew this, and, pointing
to it, shouted to the reserve: "Go and take it
down, my lads!" and, like one man, our sailors
rushed into the work. I led them for some distance, and a moment after there was no sign of the
Japanese or their flag to be seen. Twice more the
hostile flag made its appearance on top of the
hill, but each time it was torn down by my handful
of reserves.

At about 11 a.m., or a little earlier, I was in the
telephone bomb-proof with the commandant, Major
Stempnevski, Acting Ensign Yermakov, and several
naval officers. Suddenly we heard shouts and ir-
regular rifle firing. I rushed out on to the road,
and this is what I saw. Our men were in full flight
from the centre of the hill and the left flank, and
many of them were simply tumbling head over heels
in their hurry to get away. Not far from the bomb-
proof I had to jump over the body of a Japanese,

apparently just killed. I began to shout "Stop, stop!" and in order to enforce my words I drew my sword and hit one after another (with the flat, of course), Lieutenant Podgourski and the other officers with me doing the same. The men heeded my voice, and, stopping where they were, opened a straggling fire on the top of the hill. I was then anxious to go to the reserve, as, owing to the firing, my voice could not carry so far, but fearing that my men might follow after me, I did not myself go back, but sent Yermakov.

By this time we could see Japanese soldiers springing up on to the top, and they began at once to fire along the road. At the same moment several dozen men scrambled up to me from below, and, standing round me, began to fire and shout hoarsely "Hurrah!" In the midst of all this noise and firing I felt that matters had passed beyond my control, while all the time the number of the Japanese on the hill was growing and growing. Luckily, the reserves were not more than 10 paces from me now, and I already saw Yermakov and Fenster ahead of me; they both had rifles. The only thing to be done now was to make a rush with the new-comers and the men I had round me, and this we did. Those who had retreated, finding they were reinforced, threw themselves on the Japanese with a deafening shout, and we were once again masters of the hill.

Had not the reserve come up at the critical moment, we should have been driven off the hill, and then, indeed, it would have been impossible to retake it, as the Japanese were being strongly

RUSSIAN DEAD ON 203 METRE HILL AWAITING INTERMENT.

reinforced. Once on the summit again it was quite easy for us to throw down hand grenades. They rolled down and caused fearful havoc among the retreating enemy. Our rifles and artillery, which both opened a heavy fire on the foot of the hill and the neighbouring ravines, were a helpful addition to the grenades. In less than ten minutes the Japanese had disappeared into their trenches, and once more we breathed freely.

Without waiting for the enemy's guns to open fire, I took my men back into the reserve bomb-proofs; and it was fortunate I did so, as almost immediately shells began to burst over the top, covering it with a cloud of poisonous black smoke. Once again our slightly and badly wounded men began to hobble, or be carried, away from the summit.

It was a terrible sight; still it was wonderful to behold how these heroes died fearlessly or suffered without complaint.

The number of corpses on the road rapidly increased, and in consequence it was difficult to breathe, from the offensive smell.

The time had certainly come to ask for men to collect the dead.

I sent a report of all that had taken place, and then went with the commandant and some other officers to our observation position near the dressing station, where there was an enormous number of wounded, keeping the surgeons hard at work.

I remember as if it were to-day that I had turned with my face to the rear and was looking at the crowd of men who were standing near the lower dressing station, and wondering where they all came from. Suddenly there was a fearful explosion, and I was thrown with terrific force to the ground. The shock was so great, that for a time I was stunned. When I at last got up, scattering the earth which covered me, there in front was a great pile of bodies, and beneath them all lay the commandant, Major Stempnevski. All were motionless, but ghastly gasping sounds and heartrending groans filled the air. I turned round. At my feet were several dead, and on them, face downwards, lay Acting Ensign Reishetov and the sergeant-major of the 2nd Company, while a young naval mechanic was sitting on the ground, crying aloud with pain and clutching with both hands his left side. Others, like myself, were now coming to themselves, and we began to separate the dead from the wounded. An assistant-surgeon ran up to the young mechanic and carried him down, and we put Major Stempnevski into the splinter-proof. He was conscious. Blood was pouring from his head and face.

" Where are you hurt, Stanislav Youlianovitch ? " I said to him ; and he replied : " My back is injured, and I can't breathe."

" They will take you down below," I said.

" No, no ; wait till the firing has slackened."

So I left him lying in the splinter-proof. Probably the shell had struck the cliff near which we were standing, but I, luckily, was a little farther off, and had only received a bad blow on the right shoulder. An hour later they carried our gallant commandant away to the lower dressing station, and I felt myself very much alone.

I reported what had happened, and asked for one

of the other officers to be sent up to take the place of the commandant. Although the Japanese had had more than one good lesson from us, they were not satisfied, and here and there came out of their trenches in considerable numbers, but were immediately driven back again by rifle and machine-gun fire from 203 Metre Hill and Akasaka Yama. However, with demoniacal persistence, they twice crawled through our wire entanglements, and on the left flank even got as far as the breastwork, but, decimated by hand grenades, they broke and fled, strewing the slopes of the hill with their dead.

This was a red-letter day, both for us and for the Japanese. At about 8 p.m. I had just gone up to a bomb-proof to have some food, when I heard shouts of " Hurrah ! " and renewed bomb explosions, which told me of yet another attack. I rushed out of the bomb-proof, and saw our sailors and riflemen crowding on the parapet near the gorge of the breastwork, and throwing hand grenades down into it. This looked bad, as the Japanese must have driven them out of the work. I told the other officers to place the few dozen men who were on the road behind the stones and boulders near the breastwork, so as to prevent the enemy from seizing the road, and to mark at the same time the extreme point beyond which our men must not on any account retreat.

I immediately sent for the reserve, which consisted at that time of our 1st Scout Detachment. It was not an easy matter to climb such a hill as 203 Metre, nor could it be done in a moment, so a considerable time elapsed before Captain Vaseeliev came up with his men. The handful defending the gorge of the breastwork above had dwindled away considerably, and I reported that the Japanese had got as far as the left flank of the connecting trench, now completely wrecked, and had established themselves there. But apparently they had not secured a very firm foothold, and the interior of the work was unoccupied. That meant that our men, surprised by the suddenness of the attack, had evacuated the work, the front face of which had been captured by the enemy. I shouted to the defenders ordering them not to retreat another step, but to hold on for all they were worth, as I was coming immediately with the scouts to their support. An officer, who had remained in the bomb-proof in the centre of the work, sent an orderly to tell me that the enemy had occupied the parapet, but were afraid to come down into the work. Unfortunately, I was not able to find out this officer's name.

Having told Captain Vaseeliev where to make his attack, and the necessary dispositions being made, I addressed the men briefly, and then set out with them against the point which I had decided to attack—the right flank of the left breastwork, and the left flank of the connecting trench. Of course, the gallant fellows outstripped me, and the rush of these men, together with the few left who had defended the gorge of the breastwork, and some other riflemen who appeared from somewhere on the right, drove the Japanese out of their trenches. It does not take long to tell this, but it was not done quite so quickly.

The detachment under Captain Vaseeliev, and all those who rushed forward with him, for a long time kept on shouting "Hurrah!" firing, and throwing hand grenades. The Japanese on the parapet made a stubborn resistance. Together with some other officers I remained in the gorge of the breastwork, and heard our men shouting "Hurrah!" and saw them running along the narrow trenches to the front face, which the Japanese still held. Then two explosions were heard, followed by others, and the next moment our men were on the parapet. Dozens of hand grenades were hurled after the retreating enemy, so that the very hill seemed to quiver from their violent explosions. I immediately went down to the road to give orders that all those who had descended the hill should be brought up at once. Whenever the alarm went a fair number of men were always there.

But I had anticipated matters, for a whole company—about a hundred men—were coming up the hill towards me, sailors and riflemen, led by their field-cornet, who received the St. George's Cross from me on the spot. This was a pleasant surprise for him; but a disagreeable one was awaiting me.

Feeling that the hill was now safe again, I was standing on the road in the centre of my positions, when Captain Vaseeliev came quickly up to me and reported: "I am badly wounded, Colonel, and I can't command any longer. Allow me to go down to the dressing station."

"Very well," I said. "From my heart I wish you rapid recovery. The Cross of St. George is yours."

The regiment had lost yet another gallant officer, but God grant! not for ever.

Everything being now quiet on the hill, I sent a report to Colonel Irman and desired him to ask General Kondratenko to give me permission to leave the hill to get some rest and have my wound dressed. I also asked for sand-bags and men to repair damages. Everything I asked for was sent up, and three engineer officers also arrived. There was no need to show them where the work was to be done, and I had just sat down to rest—it was now about midnight—when I saw Colonel Irman and my adjutant, Lieutenant Kostoushko-Valeejinitch, arriving. Having made a full report and explained the present situation, I took them into the commandant's bomb-proof, where Colonel Irman at once expressed the wish to inspect the hill and thank the men for repelling the attacks.

He disappeared into the trench with Lieutenant Kostoushko, and I lay down to rest, as I was worn out through want of sleep. Loud talking in the bomb-proof awoke me. Opening my eyes I saw a crowd of naval officers, some of them old friends, but some new arrivals, who had been sent to the hill from headquarters.

Here I may mention that the naval detachments were frequently commanded by heads of the Naval Department or by ensigns of the fleet. Many of these were splendid fellows, among whom Losev and Morosov were particularly distinguished for their unsurpassed bravery.

I had eaten hardly anything for four days, and had scarcely slept.

MAP OF THE WESTERN DEFENCES OF PORT ARTHUR.

REFERENCE.

1. Advanced Hill
2. Three-headed Hill
3. (Side Hill) Height 426
4. Panlunshan
5. 174 Metre Hill (Angle Hill)
6. Division Hill
7. Namako Yama (Long Hill)
8. Akasaka Yama (Flat Hill)
9. 203 Metre Hill (High Hill)
10. Connecting Ridge
11. False Hill
12. Fugazay Hill
13. Red Hill (Rigi Hill) showing Fir Wood on right
14. Interval Hill
15. Extinct Volcano
A. 1st. Position of Headquarters of 5th Regt.
B. 2nd.   „   „   „   „
C. 3rd.   „   „   „   „

Scale of English feet

Enlarged from a Russian Map

London. Hugh Rees, Ltd.

CHAPTER XI

DECEMBER 1 ran its course in the usual way, until it had grown dark, when something rather serious occurred. Owing to the constant alarms, and my fears for the safety of the hill, I could not think of eating, but, taking advantage of a period of comparative quiet, and hoping that the Japanese would take some time to recover from the severe lesson they had had, I had gone out into the open air (it was fearfully close in the bomb-proof) and was sitting on the slope of the parapet, when suddenly the alarm was raised. Rifle firing broke out, accompanied by the roar of bursting hand grenades. I sprang to my feet and saw that our men were flying out of the left breastwork—fortunately, however, only a few of them as yet. Midshipman Soimonov was there with the sailors.

" What's all this about ? " I shouted.

" The hand grenades were too much for us. Every one has gone, and the Japanese have captured our work."

" You fools ! " I yelled after them. " You have been asleep again. Get back at once and tell Midshipman

Soimonov that I order him to turn the Japanese out again."

Upon this, the sailors turned and ran past me. Ten minutes afterwards there was a splutter of firing from the left breastwork, next a loud "Hurrah!" and then, a moment afterwards, silence. An orderly from Midshipman Soimonov ran up to me and reported that they had regained the trench, but that the Japanese were still in possession of the work itself, from which I concluded that the sailors alone were numerically too weak to retake the place.

I sent a telegram to the staff, "Send me one fresh company," but probably there were none available, as I did not even get a reply. Everything was now quiet on the top of the hill. I was at a loss what to do under these trying circumstances. At about 2 a.m. I received a message: "The non-combatant company of the 12th Regiment is coming up under Sergeant-Major Kournosov. Organize a counter-attack at once and drive out the Japanese."

Before very long these reinforcements arrived. Taking in addition a small body of men found at the foot of the hill, I myself showed them the way (no one else knew the disposition of the fortifications so well), and then went round with Kournosov and from all sides inspected the left breastwork.

The Japanese in it were keeping very quiet.* I posted my men, appointed leaders for each column (one was to attack from the rear, and one from the

---

* Our Official History (Part III., p. 96) states that the Japanese held the summit (of the southern peak) for some time, but were driven back at 3 p.m. From the present narrative it is evident that some at least remained there till after nightfall.

THE LAST RESERVES GOING TOWARDS 203 METRE HILL. IN THE DISTANCE IS SEEN 203 METRE HILL IN THE CENTRE, FALSE HILL ON THE LEFT, AND AKASAKA YAMA ON THE RIGHT.

p. 254]

right flank), and indicated to them their points of attack. On a given signal both columns were to make their attack simultaneously. Before, however, the signal had been given, the men suddenly began to fire and shout "Hurrah!" There was such a medley of noises, that it was impossible to make one's voice heard, and, owing to the darkness, personal example was out of the question. For a long time there was much intermittent firing and disorderly shouting, and then at last all grew quiet again for a brief space, only to be followed by renewed shouting and firing a few seconds afterwards.

" Well," I thought to myself, " we shall never do anything with these non-combatants," and the darkness and maze of trenches over the scene of action combined to make all attempts at control useless. I decided to wait till dawn, and sent a report to that effect.

Everything grew quiet again, so Soimonov came up and reported that the riflemen had started firing and shouting, and that his sailors had rushed upon the parapet, but were met by shots. It was quite dark, and the men had thrown themselves down on the slope of the parapet and would not advance any farther. They thought there were a lot of Japanese in the work, and some one could be seen smoking just inside the entrance to the bomb-proof.

" Why do you think that there are a lot of Japanese in the breastwork ? " I asked.

" I don't know, I'm sure, how many there are, but I personally think that there cannot be very many, as their volley was a scattered one ; but our men lost confidence owing to the darkness."

"Take some grenades and throw them into the work," I said, and I sent about a hundred grenades up to them.

In a few minutes the grenades burst in the work, and then all was silent again. This silence lasted a long time. I could stand the suspense no longer, so sent an officer to Soimonov to find out what was happening.

About two hours afterwards, the officer returned and reported that he had been all round the work along the lower line of trenches and had not met a soul. He had then crawled into an embrasure and looked into the work, where nothing was to be seen but a heap of smouldering planks and beams, with the charred head of a man amongst them. Our men had then immediately reoccupied the breastwork.

Apparently, the Japanese had been driven out by our hand grenades and the place was empty. I at once sent a report of what had occurred, and replaced the sailors by a company of rifles which had just arrived.

I unfortunately forgot the name of the plucky young officer who had climbed into the breastwork, but it is not too late for him to come forward now, and, if he does, he will certainly receive the St. George's Cross.

My back began to ache a good deal with a kind of burning sensation. All the time I had not undressed to see if my wound from the bursting shell was serious or not, and, besides this, I was absolutely worn out. I felt I ought to try and regain my strength, and eagerly awaited a reply to my request for permission to leave the hill to have my wound examined and properly dressed. Sanction was at length given, and Second-Lieutenant Organov was sent to take my place; but he told me before I left, that, as he knew nothing whatever about the fortifications on the hill and their disposition, he could not, therefore, hope to be an efficient commandant, and begged me to come back as soon as possible. I promised to return the following morning, and then went off to the staff headquarters.

Dr. Theodore S. Troitski examined me, and found a small punctured wound from a splinter, which had been driven some distance into my back, and also a large blue bruise. When my servant, Peter Ravinski, shook out my grey wool-lined jacket, quite a quantity of small splinters fell out. The thick wadding and cloth had prevented them from penetrating, and they had lodged in the lining. Only one—probably larger than the others—had gone right through and caused the wound. After a short conversation with General Kondratenko, I lay down to sleep.

The following day (December 2) the senior doctor in the fortress came to the staff quarters in the morning and had me taken to Field Hospital No. 9, where Dr. Krjivetz operated, but failed to remove the splinter. He said that to look for it would involve tearing open the wound, and as the splinter was very small, judging by the puncture, he thought it better to leave it for the present.

After the operation I returned to the staff. General Kondratenko, who was already there, seemed to be in a very uneasy frame of mind.

" They have already been asking for you on the

17

hill. All is not well up there, and the commandant seems very anxious. Please go as soon
as ever you can, Nikolai Alexandrovitch."

I at once ordered my horse and rode off.

Apparently everything was quiet on the hill, and
there were no signs of disorder. When I had reached
the foot of the hill, I found a crowd of men of various
units and corps, which Captain Prince Nikoladtse
had collected and was trying to organize. Having
wished the men "Good morning,"* I began to
climb the hill.

The firing was very desultory, and I reached the
road in rear without mishap. The commandant
met me with undisguised pleasure and reported that
everything was all right.

"Why have you been so alarmed ? " I asked.

"I feel as if I were lost in a forest, sir : I
don't know the officers, or the men, or the place.
Nobody slept last night," answered the young commandant, evidently very much concerned at his
helpless plight.

As a matter of fact, things could not have been
better. Every one was at his post. Several detachments of sailors had arrived, that under Lieutenant
Lavrov being composed of a really splendid lot of
men. All the sailors were in the very best of spirits,
like Lavrov himself. He at once came and reported
to me that his men were ready for anything. These

---

* A Russian officer always addresses his men on parade by using
two words which mean "Good morning, men"; and the men answer
all together in two words signifying "We are glad to be able to serve
you."

men, who had originally constituted a balloon section, had made a balloon, but, as there was no means of producing hydrogen, it could not be made to rise. How useful it might have been to us!

" If you call for volunteers," said the Lieutenant, " my fellows will respond to a man." And he spoke the truth.

Late in the evening, wishing to reconnoitre the empty lower trench and the Japanese trenches in front of the hill, I called for volunteers, whereupon every man in the detachment stepped forward. Then they drew lots, and three men, delighted with their good fortune, came into the commandant's bomb-proof; they were Quarter-Master (artificer) Yakov Artouk, and two 1st class A.B.'s—Ivan Nefedov and Theodore Pilshchikov. One of them especially, a beardless boy, impressed me by his obvious joyousness. I explained to them what they had to do and sent them off.

Everything was now quiet. About ten officers had collected in the bomb-proof. We discussed what was to be done to protect our road in rear (where we always had a number of men) from the direct fire of a battery which the Japanese had placed near the village of Shui-shih-ying.* Eventually we came to the conclusion that the only way to effect this was by destroying it with the guns from the forts.

I immediately sent to General Kondratenko asking that this might be done. I gave orders that no one was to leave the trenches except on duty. Then we decided to make traverses in order

---

* The Japanese eventually had six batteries firing from the neighbourhood of this village at the rear slopes of 203 Metre Hill and Akasaka Yama. (See Map III.)

to give some sort of cover to those who had to be on the road. The men usually left the trenches for water or hand grenades, of which we required a very large number, and, thank God! Lieutenant Melik-Porsadanov and Midshipman Vlassev kept us regularly supplied with them.*

As I had not had sufficient rest at the staff headquarters, by this time I felt an overpowering drowsiness, so lay down on a mattress and fell soundly asleep.

At 2 a.m. I was awakened. The sailors who had been sent to reconnoitre had returned unharmed, and reported that they had gone to the farther Japanese trench. There they had found only one sentry, whom they had killed, but not a single Japanese was in any of the trenches (of which there were many) in front of the hill. Our ruined circular trench was also deserted, but it was impossible to walk in it, as it was quite full of earth, stones, and splinters of wood and iron.

I congratulated the men and awarded them crosses (General Kondratenko had supplied several to be given on the spot to those who should distinguish themselves). This method of prompt reward made a deep impression on every one.

I then sent three more volunteers to find out where the Japanese were on the left of the hill, those selected being Bereznouk, 1st class A.B., Semen Boudarev (he had a mother and wife), and Kholodenko, also a 1st class A.B.

---

* Grenades were made in three factories, capable of turning out about 1,000 daily, working the usual hours, and about 2,500, working day and night. (A. Bortnovski, *Voenny Sbornik*, Jan., 1910.)

I had reason to think that our round trench on the left, which we had evacuated, was still unoccupied by the Japanese. If this were the case it was essential to occupy it as far as possible, as it was an excellent *point d'appui* from which to make sorties against the enemy's sap-head.

For a long time we awaited the return of our gallant three, but there was no sign of them.

Day broke (December 3). On the left flank hand grenades were bursting, accompanied by the roar of 11-inch shells. Many of the latter fell over the crest near the telephone shelter ; some did not burst at all, but, striking the earth, slowly ricocheted away towards False Hill, turning over and over in their flight. It was a striking display, and the soldiers watched it with much interest, joking about the bad laying of the Japanese gunners.

A non-combatant detachment (I do not remember of which regiment), under a quarter-master, came up to make good our losses of the preceding day. The men were placed in the trenches allotted to the reserves, and the officer stood looking at the road, and the piles of dead lying on it. I suggested to him that he should sit in the trench or stand close up under the almost perpendicular bank of the road. But the young fellow said he was not afraid of such missiles, pointing with his hand to an 11-inch shell which was hurtling away after having ricocheted off the ground ; but just at that moment there was a terrific roar, and he was hidden in the black smoke from a large shell that had burst just where he stood. When the smoke had cleared away, he was no longer there.

A message came from the left breastwork to say that there was hardly a man there, and asking for at least a few reinforcements, as the Japanese were beginning to make a move. I sent up Second-Lieutenant Shakovskoi and twenty men with hand grenades. At about 12 noon the cannonade was so terrific that it was impossible to speak in an ordinary tone of voice, and one had to shout to be heard. Our lower road was swept by shell, but we had not many casualties. A new commandant arrived also—Major Veselevski, a brave and intelligent officer, who had more than once rendered me good service, and was always quick at carrying out my instructions.

It is always good to see an officer calm and collected in a post of danger—one feels stronger somehow, both morally and physically. The commandant's smiling face and his quiet orders made a forcible impression on the men. Such a commander always inspires them with unlimited faith—they look at him with a kind of superstitious awe, and feel that they *must* obey him, even in moments of extreme peril. I will even assert that, the greater the danger, the more blindly will the men submit to the will of a commander who has won their confidence and respect.

A good officer stands for much in battle, just as a bad one may cause irreparable harm.

Officers should be very carefully selected, and unreliable ones eliminated by every possible means. Expert knowledge of military science is not essential; what really matters is the spirit, the individuality, of a man; but it is difficult to define in exact language the characteristics required, and to recognize them in peace time is yet harder, for few men display them outwardly. Unfortunately, a commander does not himself choose his officers, but has them pitched at his head willy-nilly, and how, indeed, can one expect to have *all* officers of the best type ? Still, governors and instructors at military academies and colleges can be of great assistance by judicious recommendation.

Honourable pride, nobility of thought, a sense of the high calling of an officer's profession—this is what every military man should have ingrained into his nature from his youth upward. For this reason officers must be recruited from families bearing noble traditions.

Physical strength and health are also important factors ; therefore, officers must be encouraged to indulge in sport of all kinds, in order to develop their quickness of movement and strength of limb.

An officer should enjoy a cultured and even fastidious life, and thus tone down the roughness of our average army officer. Officers should occupy a high position in society, but at the same time they should be trained to endure the hardships of a war willingly and with equanimity. And to this end they must always bear in mind that their profession, even in its smallest details, is one of great national, and even Imperial, importance.

A really talented officer is priceless, but such a man is a hundred times more rare than a talented painter, professor, or other civilian.

The day * was now far advanced, but the bombard-

* December 3.

ment continued without slackening and shells fell very close to our bomb-proof on the lower road. All this was the work of the battery at Shui-shih-ying, which our guns had not yet succeeded in silencing. Although our bomb-proof was built right up against the steep cliff, with 8- and 9-inch beams, the roof was composed only of 8-inch baulks, with a layer of big stones, cemented with clay, about an archine thick. Though this was proof against 6-inch shell, as we found when one struck it, the 11-inch howitzer projectile was quite another matter.

So we sat in this bomb-proof and quietly talked. We were surprised at the foolishness of the Japanese —who were only now beginning to scale 203 Metre Hill, when they ought to have done so much earlier. They had been breaking their heads against our strong central forts, and had lost a whole army in trying to take them.

What was to prevent them making a landing-in-force in Pigeon Bay, occupying Lao-tieh Shan, destroying our fleet from there, and then taking the New Town, which was very poorly defended from the Lao-tieh Shan side ?

It is absurd to credit them with exceptional knowledge and skill in military science. Neither do I acknowledge that they are exceptionally brave, in which opinion my riflemen agree with me.

The Japanese are very cautious, and they have no reason to boast of their daring. True, they attack without flinching ; for this there are many reasons : first of all, their initial success ; secondly, the numerical inferiority of our garrison ; and thirdly, the fact that they may be peppered with shrapnel if they do not advance.

I am absolutely convinced that in a future campaign, when we have a double line in Manchuria, when Vladivostok has been strongly fortified, when we have twice the number of guns, besides Maxims to every company, we shall utterly defeat them and drive them off the Continent.

Thus we held forth, sitting in our bomb-proof till evening. The firing died down, and, following the example of the men, we were able to bring out our samovar and have tea.

Our losses on this day, in spite of the heavy gun fire, were comparatively small. The men had got to know the place, and had learnt how to avoid splinters and to find corners immune from fire.

At 8 p.m., as usual, dinner was served with 1 lb. per head of horse-flesh. The samovars sang, and the men walked freely up and down the hill, some of them bathing in the stream at its foot. All then turned in, except the sentries, who stood with hand grenades ready and kept a sharp look-out for the enemy. If a grenade was heard, every one stood to arms. The men in the trenches were relieved in turn in small detachments.

The engineers, who were with the reserves that came up at about 8 p.m. under Acting Ensign Yermolov, started work by repairing, or I should rather say by rebuilding, the trenches with their sand-bags, and in addition began to cut a communication trench along the rear of the hill. As usual there was but little of the old trenches left, and it was fortunate that I had had a considerable number of bags stored in the regimental depot, ready for such emergencies.

At 12 midnight I made a tour round the left breastwork and other fortifications. The former was completely wrecked, except for its left face, and the inner ditch was filled with dead bodies. Providentially everything was quiet, so I gave orders for them to be carried away. All that remained of the central battery with its flanking pieces were piles of rubbish and torn sandbags.

The right breastwork had not suffered so badly, and was fully capable of being defended. The Japanese refrained from attacking it, as the fire from Akasaka Yama barred the way. One attempt to attack this part of 203 Metre Hill had cost them more than a thousand men, and their approaches were still far from the top.

The left flank of the lower round trench was quite whole, and the men were perfectly comfortable there. They had built up a thick, solid wall between themselves and the ruined portion of the trench, and had decided to make a small sortie that night.

On the morning of December 4, owing to the ill-success of this sortie, there was a good deal of cross firing and grenade-throwing. The battery near Shui-shih-ying still gave us considerable trouble, and three officers and several men were wounded.

At about 8 a.m. heavy rifle firing and a number of explosions were heard on the left breastwork—an ominous sign.

I went outside and called up the reserve. It was

reported to me that the Japanese were attacking, and the commander asked for reinforcements, so, in order to encourage them, I sent up a few men.

To my surprise I heard shouts from the work attacked, and saw our men flying down the hill. They had been driven out and were in full retreat. With the other officers and the reserve I rushed up to meet them, hoping to stop the fugitives, but it was already too late and I was carried off my feet. The men from the breastwork fled down as far as the lower slopes of the hill. The reserve, however, stood fast. I shouted for the commander of the latter, but he was not to be found, and I had to take his place.

It was fortunate that the reserve consisted of one of my own companies. We charged up the hill and drove the Japanese out of the breastwork with our hand grenades, but those of the enemy inflicted heavy loss on us. By my orders the breastwork was then occupied by the reserve.

At this time the commandant was away inspecting the left flank of the hill, and thus did not see what was happening. The workmen who were renewing the central battery between the breastworks assisted materially in the defeat of the Japanese by attacking their left flank. I do not know who the officer was that led them to the attack.

I passed through some bad moments during this panic, and was thankful that the enemy was not in force. Afterwards I learnt that the Japanese had crawled up unnoticed and hurled several grenades right amongst our men. An officer was killed and many men either bayoneted or blown to atoms; the rest broke and ran.

All my reserves were now used up, so I sent a request for as many sailors as possible. As a determined attack now appeared to be imminent, I went earlier than usual to my observing station. Rifle firing again broke out in the left breastwork, a sign that the Japanese were collecting in their parallels.

The battery at Shui-shih-ying caused us ceaseless annoyance. In order not to attract its attention, I gave orders for the dressing station to be removed to a point near the foot of the hill. I withdrew half the men from the right breastwork to form a reserve. But they only sent me ten men, saying that they were half a company. The men in the left work were standing firm.

The rifle and grenade duel continued for a very long time.

Evidently the Japanese had decided not to attack, being deterred by our hand grenades, and the bombardment continued without abatement. The 11-inch " portmanteaus "* (as the men called the 11-inch shell) were bursting continually in the right breastwork. The right flank of the hill was completely wrecked by them, and the only sign there of what were once fortifications was the crest-line covered with splinters and fragments of beams. But, as I have already said, they did not like attacking this flank, as it was swept by the flanking fire from the trenches on Akasaka

* This name was probably borrowed from the sailors, who called the 12-inch shell of the Japanese battleships " portmanteaus." (See the " Battle of Tsu-Shima," by Semenov.)

ROAD BEHIND 203 METRE HILL AFTER THE FIGHTING ON NOVEMBER 28.

Yama of which the Japanese had a great dread owing to their previous fearful losses.

Many wounded were coming from the left breast-work, and some, who were not able to walk, were rolling themselves slowly down. The sight of these men painfully dragging themselves down the steep slope always affected me deeply. From time to time several orderlies had been sent to me asking for reinforcements and hand grenades. I could not give them much help, but sent up five men from the reserve with grenades, which I hoped would give them some encouragement.

At last, thank God! some sailors arrived, and with them a number of officers. I at once sent a detachment into the breastwork under a naval ensign. They reached it without loss, and climbed in over the parapet, the entrance having been destroyed. Suddenly I saw the ensign running out of the work with about twenty sailors and riflemen in his train. My heart sank. While I watched them the ensign lay down, and the sailors, doing the same, began to fire. As, however, they were in the very place where the 11-inch shell constantly fell, I sent the ensign an order to return to the breast-work. I saw the orderly reach him and give him my order, but nevertheless they all remained lying where they were.

My ire rose, and I sent to the ensign to say that if he remained where he was, I would shoot him like a dog. In another moment I felt that I had been too hasty, but the orderly was already gone. About a quarter of an hour later I received in reply the information that a part of the ditch had fallen in and the parapet had been demolished, making it impossible to remain there any longer. So I sent him an apology for my hasty reprimand, and thanked him for his enterprise and bravery. A non-commissioned officer, who had come back for hand grenades, took him this message.

Though many shells fell round the little band of sailors and the naval ensign, who remained on one knee with his drawn sword in his hand, no casualties occurred. Many were wounded, even near the bomb-proof and on the road, but these men seemed to bear charmed lives, and all the officers standing near me marvelled at their extraordinary luck.

Then suddenly there was the scream of an 11-inch shell. With a deafening roar it burst right over them, and thick black smoke shut out the awful picture, while all of us held our breath. The smoke cleared away, and we saw the sailors still lying there and the ensign kneeling as before. Once again we breathed freely. Unfortunately, I forgot to find out this officer's name.

The firing began to die down—a sure sign of impending attack. Our hand grenades burst over the breastwork in still greater numbers. I sent a party of sailors towards the work and another into the central trench to be ready in case of need to charge with the bayonet from the flank. But no attack came. The Japanese could not, apparently, bring themselves to face the shower of grenades.

Evening came on, and we were still awaiting the attack. Then an alarming incident occurred. A detachment of our 3rd Company, under Acting

Ensign Moskvin, was stationed in reserve in a gun emplacement. The men were sitting right at the bottom of the emplacement, but the Acting Ensign's head could be seen over the top. Suddenly a large shell burst, as it seemed to me, right over him. When the smoke cleared away, he was lying motionless on the steps of the emplacement. He was immediately carried to the road, and found to be stunned, but apparently unwounded; how it was that he was not blown to atoms passes my understanding.

It transpired afterwards that Moskvin had been injured internally in the chest and head, in consequence of which he completely lost his hearing and power of speech, and was paralysed down the right side. He was a brave lad, and I felt very sorry for him. About a month afterwards, he regained his speech and power of movement. Later on he became a prisoner of war, and eventually died here in Kiev. I was unable to attend his funeral in person, but my wife followed his remains to their last resting-place.

The day was now over and there had been no assault. It was almost incredible. Had I indeed made a mistake regarding the intentions of the Japanese?

That evening a great number of units had collected on 203 Metre Hill, and, in order to prevent overcrowding, I sent half of them down to the place where the kitchens were situated.

Any one who carefully reads these lines might very well ask the question "How is this? Men are constantly being sent up to the hill, but none seem to leave it?" But it must be remembered that

203 Metre Hill cost us 4,000 men.* Units arrived in good order, but, as soon as heavy losses occurred, they were usually mixed with later comers.

The senior of those left alive would come to me and report that such and such a company or detachment had practically been wiped out, that there only remained so many men, and could they have a rest ?

I always commended these detachments for their heroic behaviour, and granted the request provided there were fresh units on the hill who had had time to become thoroughly acquainted with its fortifications and their disposition.

Soon after Moskvin's unfortunate experience we became easier in our minds, and collected in the commandant's bomb-proof † to drink tea. The samovar was singing on the table at which the commandant and I sat. He gave every one tea in turn, for we had only two glasses ‡ left. The naval men who had just arrived told us of all that had happened in the centre, where we had brilliantly beaten back all the Japanese attacks. Every one was convinced that there would be no more big assaults of that description, as the enemy had lost more than 10,000 men.

They told us about Losev, who, on being ordered to drive the Japanese out of a trench captured by them under the glacis of Fort Erh-lung, had adopted a very simple method of carrying out the order.

---

* Our Official History states " about 3,000," but the author ought to be in a better position to give the correct number.

† Situated in the centre of the right breastwork. (See Map. V.)

‡ The Russians always drink tea out of glasses.

BOMBPROOF IN THE REDOUBT ON THE TOP OF 203 METRE HILL.

p. 272]

Accompanied by a few men, he took several grenades in his arms, climbed straight up on to the glacis and hurled the grenades into the trench. The Japanese, thrown into confusion, jumped out of the trench and retreated, whereupon our men at once re-occupied it.

Captain Sirotko, commanding our 9th Company, related all that had happened on Akasaka Yama during the last few days.

As will be remembered, this important hill was defended by a trench and a large redoubt on the summit, called by us Karmenny (the Stone Redoubt). This redoubt was further strengthened by abattis. Companies of the 5th and 27th Regiments held the hill under the command of Lieutenant-Colonel Boudiarnski, a strikingly enterprising and daring officer.

Concurrently with the attacks on 203 Metre Hill the Japanese assaulted Akasaka Yama, having first wrecked the trenches in front of the Stone Redoubt by gun fire.

On November 27, previously sweeping the intended point of attack with a terrific artillery fire, they rushed the trenches in front of the Stone Redoubt, driving out a Scout Detachment and the 4th Company of the 27th Regiment. Lieutenant-Colonel Boudiarnski took the left half of our 9th Company out of the trenches which were not being attacked, and ordered it to go to the support of its discomfited comrades.

At 7 p.m. this half-company reached the position indicated, and found a Scout Detachment already there, on whose left the Japanese were established.

18

They immediately occupied this trench to the left of the Scout Detachment of the 27th Regiment, driving the Japanese before them, and thus cut off the retreat of those who were near the Stone Redoubt and already throwing hand grenades into it.

The even numbers of the left half-company were ordered to stand up and fire to the front, while the odd numbers were to turn about and fire on the Japanese near the Stone Redoubt. This unexpected fire from their rear, combined with the rush of our 12th Company and of the 7th Company of the 14th Regiment from the front out of the Stone Redoubt, caused a panic among the enemy, who retreated into the trench occupied by the 9th Company, where they were bayoneted to a man. The various units now occupied their former positions and the men of the left half of our 9th Company returned to their own trenches.

On November 28, at 1 p.m., the right half of the 9th Company was sent to the Stone Redoubt to the assistance of the 8th Company of the 27th Regiment, which was being hard pressed by the Japanese. At 2 p.m. this half-company, under the command of Sergeant-Major Platonov, reached the 8th Company, whose commander immediately gave them an order to extend along the left flank of the Stone Redoubt, taking cover behind the boulders there. At this time the Japanese were swarming up 203 Metre Hill, and had driven back a part of the 4th and 8th Companies of the 27th Regiment from the col between 203 Metre Hill and Akasaka Yama. The men of these companies were retiring, but the right half of the 9th Company opened fire on the attacking Japanese and compelled them to take shelter in the trenches. Then, assisted by the retreating companies, they all rushed in with the bayonet, drove the enemy out of the trenches they had occupied, and seized the ones on their left flank.

At 6 p.m. the Japanese again attacked and took the trenches occupied by the 4th and 5th Companies and Scout Detachment of the 27th Regiment, together with the 12th Company of the 5th Regiment. The companies retreated in disorder, but the left half of the 9th Company, under Captain Sirotko himself, was sent up at this moment and reached them in time. Extending the 4th section, Captain Sirotko barred the retreat of the fugitives and turned them back, while the men of the 3rd section hurled themselves on the captured trenches, and, swinging round to the left, drove out the Japanese. Step by step the other companies then took up their former positions. The men fought not only with bayonets, but even with naked fists.

After this decisive repulse of the Japanese the danger zone was held by the 9th, 10th, and 12th Companies of the 5th Regiment, who beat off more than four attacks during the night.

On November 29 the 9th Company was allowed a well-deserved rest and relegated to the reserve.

On the 30th the Scout Detachment of the 27th Regiment was driven out of its trenches. The enemy attacked Akasaka Yama furiously, and as the commandant was afraid that their local success against the Scout Detachment might become a

general one, he sent the 9th Company to occupy
the heights in rear,* where it stayed until 12
noon. When, however, the 3rd, 10th, and 12th
Companies of the 5th Regiment had successfully
resisted the Japanese attacks, and the assault had
been abandoned, the 9th Company was sent to
strengthen the left flank and to keep touch with
203 Metre Hill.

In the evening the left half of this company
received orders to relieve the 3rd Company of the
5th Regiment. About the same time the right half
of the 9th Company, which was holding the lower
line of trenches on the left flank of Akasaka Yama,
repulsed another attack on the col between the
latter and 203 Metre Hill.

On this day three men of the 9th Company, who
had been wounded, returned to their company as
soon as their wounds had been dressed. General
Stessel met them, and rewarded them all with
St. George's Crosses. Captain Sirotko stated that
these were the only rewards received by the 9th
Company after nine days' incessant fighting. Many
received rewards afterwards, but it is better to give
them either during the actual fighting—the right of
doing so being given to commanders of companies
beforehand—or directly afterwards. Such immediate recognition goes far towards raising the spirits
of the various units. General Kondratenko, with
General Stessel's permission, frequently awarded our
soldiers crosses, and expressed his regret that he
had not more to distribute.

On December 1 the Japanese scaled 203 Metre

* Of Akasaka Yama.

Hill, and, lying under the steep cliff on the right flank, began to enfilade the trenches on Akasaka Yama, but the 9th Company drove them off with its fire.

To man the trenches near the cliff itself was the most dangerous duty of all. The enemy constantly rushed them from their sap-heads, and the men occupied them very reluctantly. Observation, too, was extremely difficult, and the place was often left entirely undefended.

Captain Sirotko drew the commandant's attention to this as soon as he learned the state of affairs from men sent there by him.

On December 2 the 9th Company was ordered to occupy the practically ruined trenches on the plateau in front of the Stone Redoubt, a position of the greatest peril. They were full of bodies, both of our men and the Japanese, the result of three attacks made by the 9th and 10th Companies of the 5th Regiment on November 27 and 28.

The Japanese saps were but 20 to 30 paces from these trenches.

The 9th Company remained in this position until 2 p.m. on December 4.

Throughout this fighting the companies resisted innumerable attacks with the help of pyroxylin grenades, which were brought up to the firing line by men specially detailed for the purpose.

At 2 p.m. on December 4, after nine days' ceaseless fighting, the 9th Company was withdrawn, having lost in killed and wounded 60 per cent. of its strength. During these nine days the men of the company, sleepless and worn out, held the trenches under a hellish artillery fire, drove the Japanese out of those they had taken by rifle fire, hand grenades, and bayonet charges, and beat off every assault of their persistent enemy, never, even for a moment, showing the least sign of faltering under this terrible ordeal.

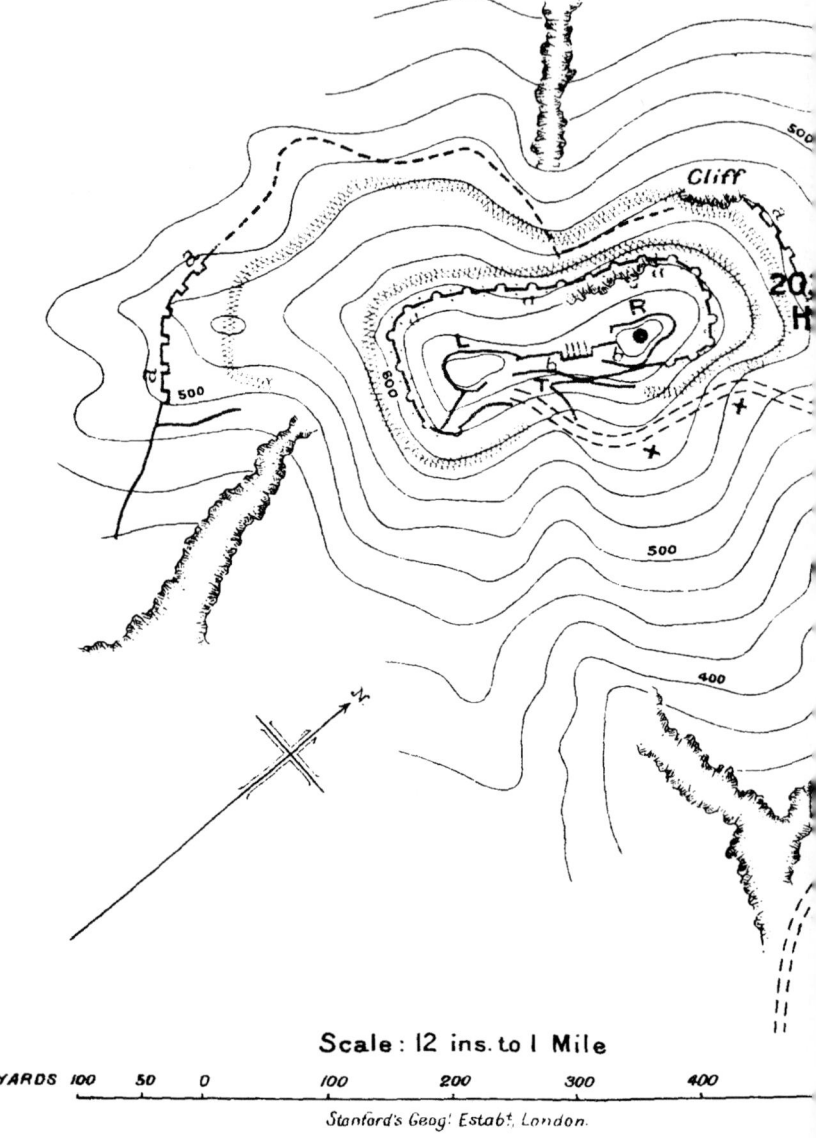

Cliff

500

R

20,
H

500

800

500

400

Scale: 12 ins. to 1 Mile

YARDS 100   50   0   100   200   300   400

Stanford's Geog.ˡ Estabᵗ, London.

3 METRE HILL

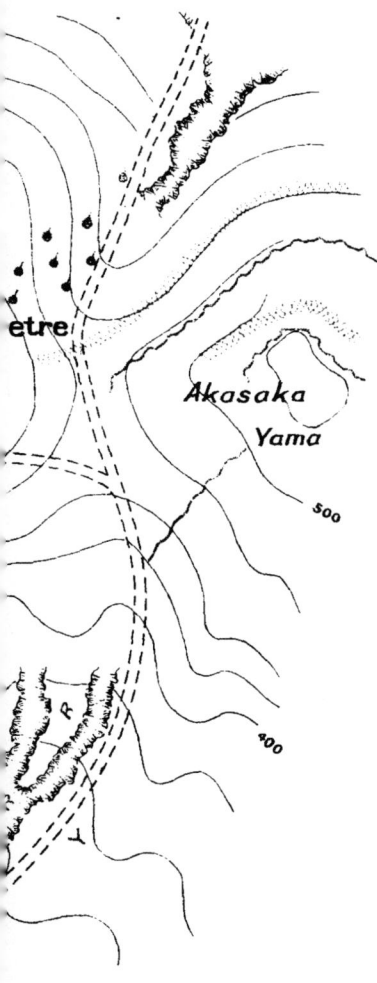

Akasaka Yama

500

400

YARDS

Near the telephone cabinet (marked T)
on the upper road were small bomb-
proofs and dug outs, and a local
dressing station.

R	Right Redoubt
L	Left Redoubt
	Wire Entanglements
	Trenches unoccupied
	Traversed trenches occupied
	Lower (circular) trench
	Central Battery with connecting trenches
	Trench on crest-line with communi- cation trench to the upper road
X X	Upper road
Y Y	Lower road
	Commandant's bomb-proof
T	Telephone Cabinet
D	Dressing Station
R R	Ravine where the reserves were usually kept
	Fougasses

CHAPTER XII

HAVING finished tea and exhausted our conversation, we decided to have a rest, but shouting and firing quickly brought us out of the bomb-proof. It turned out to be a false alarm. I climbed into the connecting trench and made sure that all was right, though the men seemed to be in a restless condition and were obviously anticipating serious fighting. I went back to the road and joined a group of officers there.

We all of us noticed how the Japanese batteries at Shui-shih-ying were sweeping the whole of our rear. Just as I was ruminating over this ominous fact there was a tremendous roar. . . . I felt a fearful blow on the left side of my head, and was thrown into the ditch.

Dazed and all but unconscious, I was unable to struggle to my feet again. However, I was happy in the thought that I had not been killed outright. Some one assisted me to my feet and held me up, and I then saw Major Veselovski and several other officers lying dead near me, the former having half his head blown away.   To my left, most of the men of the dressing station were lying piled one on another, and the remainder were already at work among their fallen comrades.   Lieutenant Rofalovski, a very brave fellow, who had formerly been my orderly officer, suddenly appeared on the scene and helped to carry me below.   I thought that I could walk, but was hardly in a fit state to judge.

So I was carried down to the lower dressing station, feeling a stream of warm blood trickling down my neck, and on arrival there my head was bandaged. Of what happened after that, I have not much recollection, but I remember people talking from time to time as I lay in a semi-conscious condition. Finally I lost all consciousness, until I heard some one say: "That is Colonel Tretyakov." I then opened my eyes, and at the same moment felt a sharp, stabbing pain on the left side of my face and head.   I was being carried along on a stretcher.   Some one was riding behind me, and the sound of hoofs on the hard road beat painfully into my head.   " Who is riding ? " I asked.   They told me I heard my own chargers, which were always kept under shelter near the kitchens when I was on the hill.   By the time we reached the town, consciousness had completely returned, but the pain in my head and neck increased, and one of my eyes throbbed badly.   I thought that it must have been put out, and touched it with my hand, but it seemed to be all right.   I could not see with it, because my head and that side of my face were covered with bandages.

A few minutes afterwards, my stretcher was put down, and a doctor bent over me. " How do you feel ? " he asked. " My head is very painful." The doctor examined me and said that I was going on well. Feeling somewhat encouraged by this, I sat up on the stretcher, but my head ached terribly and I felt dizzy. I heard some one say in a whisper: " Well, there's no hope; the brain is severely lacerated."

I involuntarily felt my head, but it seemed to me to be all right. Then it dawned upon me that they were referring to the unfortunate commandant, Veselovski. Soon afterwards, I was taken to the Red Cross Hospital and comfortably installed there.

On examination the surgeons found a number of small splinters in my head and neck, as well as a very large one in my eye, which they removed at once. There was one big splinter in my neck, which had lodged near the spinal column and prevented me from turning my head. I could even feel it with my hand. Then they applied the X-rays and extracted it, but a bit of splintered bone was left, which I can feel even now.

For three days I lay racked with pain, but after that the pain grew less and I began to take an interest in what was going on around me.

But I am going on too fast.

Lieutenant-Colonel Saifoolin took my place on the hill, but he was wounded in the same arm, and almost in the same part, in which, during the battle of Nan Shan, he had been wounded before.

On the evening of December 6 I heard a rumour that 203 Metre Hill had been captured, and on the 7th my adjutant arrived and confirmed this disastrous intelligence.

On the fall of 203 Metre Hill we abandoned Akasaka Yama, as well as Division and False Hills. Division Hill was an irreparable loss to us, as it was not only capable of being defended step by step, but, moreover, it protected Ta-an-tzu Shan Fort. Without doubt, the defenders could have held out for some time longer. Colonel Irman himself tried to recapture it, but was unable to collect sufficient men for the purpose. I also heard that the following men remained in the commandant's bomb-proof: Lossev, a telephonist, Second-Lieutenant Goudkov, the wounded commander of our 6th Company, and part of our 1st Scout Detachment, who refused to leave the hill and remained at their post in the right breastwork.

With these men in the work it might have been possible to drive out the Japanese once again, but apparently General Kondratenko considered it inexpedient to continue holding the hill at a possible cost of 500 men per day, and this, perhaps, was a sufficient reason for evacuating it. Colonel Irman had to send several men to the breastwork with direct orders to the 1st Scout Detachment to leave the hill, before they would forsake their post.

The following is the account of the final struggle for 203 Metre Hill as I heard it from Captain Sirotko.

About 1 p.m. on December 5 the 9th Company *
was moved from the staff headquarters to 203
Metre Hill. Thirty-six men of the Medical Corps
had just been added to it, so that it now consisted
of one company officer, two acting ensigns, and
102 rank and file. General Kondratenko in person
gave the company an order to reach the hill as quickly
as possible.

Under a heavy rifle fire, which caused several
casualties, the company reached the foot of 203 Metre
Hill about 2 p.m. Just as it reached the hill,
the Japanese captured the whole of the crest-line
and began sweeping the road in rear with rifle fire
and throwing down stones and hand grenades. Our
6th Company, posted on the reverse slopes, suffered
heavily from these missiles.

The trench above the road was full of riflemen of
various companies and units, but they could not be
induced to leave their cover.

Therefore, Lieutenant-Colonel Saifoolin ordered the
9th Company to advance across the open to the left
of the trench. Under a hail of bullets, stones, and
grenades, the company charged up with the bayonet
and drove the enemy out of the ruined trench on
the crest-line. Then the remainder of the men,
encouraged by their comrades' success, made a rush
for the summit.

The company, with Captain Sirotko, Acting Ensigns
Lesenkov and Grouzdev, and the squad and section
commanders at its head, then rushed out of the
position it had just taken, and charged over the crest,

---

* This company had been withdrawn to the reserve at 2 p.m. on
the 4th. See preceding chapter.

supported on its right flank by the 6th Company under Captain Sazonov and Second-Lieutenant Goudkov. They were, however, met by such a storm of bullets, shrapnel, and grenades, that in a few moments they lost half their men, Second-Lieutenant Goudkov being very severely wounded.

Captain Sirotko was badly wounded in the head and arm, and, losing consciousness, fell backwards down the hill. When he came to himself, all the men had again retreated into the trench, which was wreathed in flames on its left flank where the telephone bomb-proof stood. All the officers were now *hors de combat*, except on the right flank, where Lieutenant-Colonel Pokrovski, who had replaced Lieutenant-Colonel Saifoolin, badly wounded while commandant of the hill, was still unhurt. Two more attacks—one led by Lieutenant-Colonel Pokrovski, the other by Colonel Irman—were equally unsuccessful, and cost us dear. Nevertheless, our men still clung to the rear slopes of the hill.

About midnight, when Captain Sirotko had been attended to and had somewhat recovered, General Kondratenko, who was at the staff headquarters, sent him four midshipmen and an acting ensign of the 27th Regiment, under whom another attack on the Japanese above might be made. By this time, however, the enemy had succeeded in dragging some machine guns to the top of the hill, which was now strongly held. Realizing this, and that enormous losses would be incurred in any further attacks, Colonel Irman decided to evacuate the hill, and gave the order for a general retreat.

It is a pity that we did not adopt the Japanese

tactics, of overwhelming the enemy with gun fire and then seizing the hill without loss.

During this fighting the 9th Company lost all its officers, and 60 per cent. of its men were killed or wounded. From September 6 to December 22 this company lost 253 men killed and wounded, *i.e.* 60 per cent. in excess of its actual war strength of 155 men. It had performed the following duties: covering the retreat from Namako Yama; three bayonet attacks on the enemy occupying the trenches on the left flank of Akasaka Yama—all of them successful; the repulse of numerous attacks on the left flank of Akasaka Yama; and the three last gallant, though unsuccessful, attempts to recapture 203 Metre Hill.

The Red Cross Hospital was abundantly supplied with everything necessary for such an institution in a besieged fortress.

Thanks to the number of nurses, and their tender care of the wounded, the hospital was more or less like one's own home, and the patients felt themselves very comfortable there after life in the trenches.

In the evening numbers of officers came in from the fighting lines to have their wounds dressed, and they had much interesting news to tell us. The stories I heard from them, and from those who were lying there wounded, were so interesting and so detailed, that if it had been possible to write them down, I could have compiled a full and instructive account of the whole siege. But, as it was, I was too weak to attempt the task.

What depressed me and every one else was the thought that we were being beaten without being able to defend ourselves.

Taking into consideration the enormous superiority of the enemy in guns, and the scurvy that was raging in the fortress, one could almost with certainty fix the period within which the final stand must be made. In my own mind I allowed about two months. News from the Manchurian Army was far from reassuring, and gave us no hope of relief.

For three days after the fall of 203 Metre Hill the Japanese bombarded our ships. The naval men who came in said that the fleet was now doomed. It would soon be at the bottom of the sea, and without it the squadron coming from home would be useless in view of the enemy's strength.

I cannot understand how any of us could have buoyed ourselves up with the hope that our Far Eastern Fleet was a match for the Japanese.

Was it, indeed, impossible to have foreseen that they would sooner or later protect their own interests ? Had we realized the situation and sent three or four more battleships * to the Far East, there would have been no war and above all no triumph for the Japanese.

To our own mistakes, to our own blindness, and not to the enemy's valour, I attribute our *débâcle*. When we have made good our shortcomings, victory will be ours. Of this I am assured, for I know

---

* Admiral Wirenius, with a squadron of one battleship and two cruisers, was actually on his way to Port Arthur when war broke out.

GENERAL VIEW LOOKING SOUTH FROM 203 METRE HILL, SHOWING THE NEW TOWN AND THE HARBOUR.

p. 286]

the characteristics of the Japanese, I know their army, and I know their men.

I did not notice any despondency among our officers, but good ones were becoming scarce.

An officer from Fort Chi-kuan told us that the Japanese had for some time been masters of the ditch, but, fearing to attack us, remained on that side of the parapet.

Our men were rolling 10-lb. naval mines into the ditch, and I can imagine the effect of the explosion of these implements of destruction. The Japanese tried to drive us out of the caponier of this fort by burning in it material soaked in arsenic. Our men were stifled by the fumes, and the sentries in the casemates had to be relieved every few minutes. Fort Erh-lung was in a similar plight.

On the evening of December 16 a report reached us that General Kondratenko had been killed. I refused to believe it, but a few minutes afterwards some wounded eye-witnesses were carried in—a young artillery officer, and an ensign of a Reserve Engineer Company, named Schmidt—who verified the rumour.

It seems that about 8 p.m. on the 15th, General Kondratenko went to Fort Chi-kuan, nearly all the senior officers of that section of the defence being already there, amongst others Lieutenant-Colonel Rashevski, Major Zedginidzi, and Lieutenant-Colonel Naoomenko. They had been summoned to discuss the question of further defensive measures at that point, as the defenders were in desperate straits from the poisonous gases they encountered during mining operations.

The casemate where the conference took place having been struck more than once by 11-inch shells, the ruined part had been shut off by a stout partition made of baulks, and a hole, made by a shell, in the vaulted roof had been filled up with loose stones, resting on a pile of mortar and heavy fragments of beams, with which the interior of the casemate was strewn. This I had myself noticed during occasional visits to this ill-omened fort.

General Kondratenko sat at the table with his back to the partition, while other officers were seated on forms. The rest were standing near the entrance to the casemate. Suddenly there was a terrific explosion, and the latter, who were the only ones that escaped alive, were blown through the entrance, while the whole of the interior fell in. When they recovered their senses, soldiers were already in the casemate removing the dead. With the General perished the flower of the officers of that section.*

The death of General Kondratenko made a lasting impression on the garrison; every one lost heart, since we knew there was none to take his place.

A few days afterwards, our fleet ceased to exist, and although the ships' companies went to swell the numbers of our reserves, from that moment misfortune dogged us.

On December 18 the Japanese exploded a mine under the parapet of Fort Chi-kuan. It did not make a very large breach, and the garrison retreated

* Seven were killed on the spot, and seven more wounded.

from the parapet to the retrenchment behind, and thus prevented the enemy from seizing the former; but in spite of this, at 11 p.m. we evacuated the fort. Captain Kvatz, the commandant, told me when he came into hospital that he had withdrawn his men in pursuance of General Fock's orders, and that he himself considered that further resistance was not justified. Although, according to him, 100 lives were sacrificed daily in the effort to hold this position, nevertheless I could not accept his conclusion, since there was still one casemate in the fort which was absolutely untouched. However, the loss of this fort was not so very serious, because it was on a very low site, and behind and above it was the Chinese Wall, which had already rendered us great service during innumerable attacks.

By December 24 I had quite recovered, and my eye no longer pained me. Dr. Mirotvoretz had operated successfully, and removed a splinter from my neck.

Everything had been quiet in my section during my illness, as the Japanese were concentrating against the eastern front and taking no further action against us.

I was discharged from hospital on December 25. On reaching my section, I found that the staff headquarters had been moved, and was now placed behind the crest of a hill, near Battery No. 4, where it was completely protected. With Colonel Irman's staff I found many of the town officials, among them Colonel Vershinin, the head of the Kuan-tung Peninsula district. Messing arrangements had been made, and there was plenty of everything, but as the

19

charges were exceedingly high, our officers preferred to dine separately. I felt very well during the evening, but the wound in my neck became so painful that night, that in the morning I had fever, and had to return to hospital for three days.

Having had my wound disinfected, I again rejoined my regiment.

During this time the Japanese had attacked Interval Hill, where our 2nd and 3rd Companies, under Lieutenant Ivanov, were posted. The attacks began at 2 a.m. on December 25, but they were all repulsed by our fire from the trenches and from a lunette occupied by the 7th Company. About ten of the enemy, however, succeeded in climbing up a hill somewhere in rear, where they dug themselves in. Lieutenant Ivanov reported this to Colonel Irman, and said that he would turn them out. This was quite unnecessary, as they would probably have retreated later of their own accord; nevertheless, Colonel Irman ordered the companies to leave Interval Hill and take up a position behind our line, in touch with our 11th Company.

On December 26 we evacuated Solovev Hill, near Pigeon Bay.

The 5th Regiment was now concentrated on our main inner position and occupied the space between two permanent forts, presenting a considerably stronger front than before; it had also been brought up, for the third time, to its full complement. The Japanese were now faced with a problem similar to that previously presented by 174 Metre Hill, but rendered additionally difficult by the existence of permanent fortifications.

KUROPATKIN'S LUNETTE.

They wisely decided not to repeat their rash attacks of the past, and contented themselves with remaining in the positions they had occupied. Thus everything was fairly peaceful, and I availed myself fully of this interval of quiet, feeling that it was safe to leave the staff headquarters occasionally.

First of all, I went to see Colonel Grigorenko, but, being unable to find his house, I went on to the commandant's. There I met Colonel Khvostov, who had just arrived with a report. We had a long talk about the situation, and I carried away with me the impression that no disaster was threatening us for some time to come.

It seemed that, in the event of the capture of Fort Erh-lung, the commandant had a second line of defence, which we could hope to hold against the enemy for a considerable time.

One would have thought that the rocky ground would have prevented the enemy from mining beneath Forts Erh-lung and Sung-shu, but nevertheless by now they were making rapid progress there. We could not make a very stubborn resistance at these points because we had no miners, and, consequently, no system of counter-mining. The counter-scarp galleries were merely blocked with stones and cement, which became so solid that it would have taken about three days to destroy, as proved to be the case at Fort Chi-kuan.

Some time before this, General Kondratenko had asked me to come and make an investigation. One night (I do not remember the date) I went with Colonel Grigorenko to Fort Erh-lung, where I found

General Kondratenko in the counterscarp gallery. After listening attentively to the Japanese working on the other side, we came to the conclusion that they were tunnelling in three separate parts of the outside wall of the gallery. They evidently wished to make breaches in this wall by exploding several small charges, and thus get through into the gallery. As we could only offer a passive resistance, we determined to block the gallery with a large boulder and cement it hard against those portions of the wall where the Japanese was working. This plan was carried into effect at once.

All this took place some time before, and the enemy were now right under the breastwork of the fort and ready to explode several charges. In anticipation of this the fort was evacuated except for sentries on the parapets. Imagine the frame of mind of a sentry who knows that at any moment he may be blown to atoms! The commandant, having made arrangements for further resistance in case of the destruction of the fort and subsequent Japanese attack, was quietly awaiting events.

Having breakfasted with the commandant, and heard a full account of the state of our defences, I returned to the headquarters of the regiment. The Japanese were directing a somewhat heavy fire towards the road along the shore, but the shells mostly fell into the water beyond.

On December 28 I again rode into the town. While crossing the bridge over the Lun-ho, I felt the earth tremble slightly and then heard a loud

KUROPATKIN'S LUNETTE.

rumble in the distance. Looking up, I saw a huge column of black smoke hanging over Fort Erh-lung. "Well," I thought to myself, "the fort is blown up, and possibly taken, but there is not much harm done, as the Chinese Wall is behind it."

When I reached the staff, all the details were known. It turned out that the explosion had not been entirely successful, as we were still masters of the retrenchment, but we had lost heavily owing to the rain of shells into the fort. Rumour said that the Japanese themselves had suffered heavy losses from the explosion, that the whole of the trench nearest the fort had been wrecked, and that the men of the attacking party, who were waiting in it, had perished in the ruins.*

In my section everything was quiet, and we spent the evening quite happily, congratulating ourselves that the Japanese had not broken down the defence of the fort, which they could have done if they had exploded their 150-lb. pyroxylin charges under the parapets.

But our joy was premature. The following day we learnt that Fort Ehr-lung had been evacuated in the night; all *matériel*, cartridges, and shells had been removed beforehand. Besides the fort, we had also abandoned that part of the Chinese Wall which ran straight to the rear from both flanks, and had occupied a position on a rocky crest-line behind, and on a height to the left of it.

---

* This proved to be an exaggeration. The storming parties were protected by roofs of boards and scantling, and only a few casualties occurred (see Official History, Part III., p. 116).

Our perilous situation in the centre of the line, the deadly artillery fire, the constantly repeated attacks, and the endless vigil wore out our men, and their spirits began to flag in a marked degree.

In a great battle, soldiers may make a stubborn fight, especially if victory may yet be snatched or some great prize won for the Fatherland. But if after constant fighting there is no apparent gain ; if they are, each moment, exposed to deadly peril; if from each individual heroic effort is demanded, not for one soul-stirring moment alone, but cease-lessly, with certain death the only reward,—it is pardonable if hearts grow faint, if men are at times found wanting in energy and slow to carry out orders.

Then is the time for reliefs ; but for us there were none available.

Scurvy, moreover, claimed its victims, bringing in its train suffering and weakness. Nourishing diet was necessary, and I do not know why we spared the artillery horses. Long ago we had lost all hope of any offensive action, so ere this the gun horses might well have furnished the men with meat once a day. They may perhaps have been utilized in other ways, though the fact remains that by this means we might have kept, fit and well in the trenches, more than another thousand men !

On December 30 we were dining peacefully, when suddenly tremendous firing burst forth from all our batteries, and the rattle of musketry along the front told us that the Japanese were making a determined attack.

We all rushed up on to the hill, but nothing was visible save the smoke from our own batteries and from

GUN IN KUROPATKIN'S LUNETTE.

bursting shrapnel. All our forts were smothered with shell, though we could not see the enemy's infantry. I tried to get some news through the telephone, but it was already overtaxed and continuously in use.

Only in the evening did we learn that the Japanese had made a fierce attack on the Chinese Wall and Naval Ridge beyond. This attack had been repulsed with enormous loss to the enemy, who had, however, succeeded in fortifying themselves at the foot of Naval Ridge, and thus enfiladed the Chinese Wall. Still, even that was not of supreme importance, since the Chinese Wall had a number of traverses and splinter-proofs along it.

In my section all was quiet. We had not a single man in reserve, but even so we believed we could beat back every attack. This was not the case, however, on Lao-tieh Shan, where Major Romanovski had practically only our mounted Scout Detachments. The enemy constantly attacked them, and captured another hill near Pigeon Bay. This was decidedly serious, as now the Japanese had nothing but these scouts between them and the other half of the western front, where there was but a remnant of the 27th Regiment, the main portion of it being required on the front attacked, which was held by only a few men.

Fortunately, the Japanese seemed content with the success already gained, and settled down for their usual long rest, or, possibly, their men were also required on the front of attack.

On December 31, after tea, we received news of a further disaster. Yet once again in this disastrous war had fortune favoured the Japanese. Fort

Sung-shu had been blown up, and, what was worse, in one stroke the whole garrison had been annihilated. This is what had happened : About a thousand hand grenades had been stored in an excavation which the garrison also used as a shelter. A Japanese shell burst, detonating these grenades, and the whole place collapsed on the garrison. This was a fearful blow to us, and we deeply lamented the death of our gallant comrades and their commandant.*

Fate had indeed played us a sorry trick !

We were all dispirited, and few cared to partake of dinner that night.

On the evening of the 31st we evacuated the Chinese Wall † and took up positions at Wang-tai and on the Mitrofanievski, Vladimirski, and Laperovski Hills.‡ It now became very difficult for us to hold out on the front exposed to attack. We ought to have begun fortifying the New Town on the side facing the Old Town, but no orders were received to that effect. What were our commanders doing ?

That night we were all very depressed. Every one discussed plans for continuing the defence, if only till the new year.§ This was the universal wish, and could certainly have been realized. We dispersed at a late hour, to be aroused in the morning by heavy firing. On climbing the hill, we saw

* Mention of this incident is made in Official History (Part III., p. 119), where it appears that the Japanese had actually sprung their mines before this accidental explosion took place.

† Attacked by the 6th Brigade under General Ichinohe. (See Map III.)

‡ Eminences flanking the Wang-tai position, probably named after the officers charged with their defence.

§ The corresponding Russian date was December 18.

SHELL BURSTING IN KUROPATKIN'S LUNETTE.

Wang-tai literally swept with shell, and so covered with smoke that it was impossible to see its summit. The bombardment continued for a long time. We could not follow exactly what was taking place, but learnt in the evening that the Japanese had captured it. Our reserves had at first quickly driven back the enemy, afterwards repulsing five further attacks, but towards evening, when there were only three or four of the defenders left, the sixth assault was successful.

That evening, by General Fock's order, the whole of our front from Wang-tai to Chi-kuan Battery was evacuated.

The same night the Japanese attacked Signal Hill, near Takhe Bay, but were repulsed.

On January 2, 1905, the majority of the officers were collected at the staff headquarters to hear the latest reports. Suddenly an officer came galloping out of the town and informed us that he had himself seen two officers riding out beyond our lines with a white flag.

My heart froze at this news. We all remained silent for some time, seeking to hide our discomfiture.

" Can that mean surrender ? " said some one at last.

" Doubtless," answered another.

After a full minute's silence conversation broke out noisily on all sides. Every one asked what was to be done under the circumstances, and as they were all talking at once, it was impossible to understand anything. But general indignation against General Fock was apparent, and every kind of accusation was heaped upon his head. I do not remember how long this continued, but I know that we had not yet sat down to dinner, when we received the fateful news by telephone: " Arthur surrendered. The officers are allowed to keep their swords and return to Russia after giving their parole not to take any further part in the present war."

There was a tremendous commotion at the receipt of this news. The majority had no wish to surrender, and vehemently attacked our seniors for surrendering the fortress without the consent of all the officers. Some of them wanted to set out immediately for Lao-tieh Shan and continue the defence there; others proposed to hire Chinese junks and leave the fortress, so as not to become prisoners of war; only a few decided to bow to the will of their commanders. As each one insisted on his opinion being accepted, the discussion soon became very heated, and there was a danger of untoward results.

Eventually those who wished to defend themselves on Lao-tieh Shan gave up the idea, as owing to the lack of water and fortifications of any kind it would be impossible to hold that position. Those who had thought of escaping in junks could not do so, owing to contrary winds.

How long this stormy scene lasted I do not remember, but at its very height some one rode up and told us that the senior officers had sent a telegram to the Tsar asking whether the exemptions obtained by the authorities for the officers were to be accepted or not. This news seemed to have a quieting effect, but with one accord every one determined to express his disapproval of the action of the authorities by an absolute refusal of all exemptions that had been granted as the price of the capitulation of the fortress. All were resolved to share the fate of the men and endure with them the humiliation of becoming prisoners of war. It was a praiseworthy decision, and I expressed my approval, but at the same time several arguments against it presented themselves. Many of these were unheard, as there was much loud discussion. The two chief points advanced were :

(1) As prisoners of war, the rank and file would be separated from their officers and distributed in various places throughout Japan, hence the presence of the latter would be of no help to them, nor would it lessen their hardships.

(2) As an enormous number of officers had been withdrawn from Russia in order to make good the losses sustained in Manchuria, the need of them at home was a very urgent one, and in the event of war in Turkestan, which was more than probable, we should find ourselves in a most critical position. Even without war the want of officers would jeopardize the efficiency of those regiments and reserve battalions that were left. Some 500 officers were in question, and these in Japanese prisons could render no service to their country in her hour of need.

Besides all this I added : " Gentlemen, people in Russia might think that we officers became prisoners of war in order to spend a pleasant time in beautiful Japan, free from all duty and hardship, at a time when disturbances are taking place in the centre of our own country, and she has great need of all those who are anxious for her welfare."

The officers of my regiment agreed with me and decided to return to Russia, and I can add now that they were far from being of no use here at home, as the regiments in the south were almost without officers, a deficiency which led, as is well known, to serious disorders in the reserve battalions; so that their arrival was most timely.

When the surrender of Port Arthur became an acknowledged fact, we had great difficulty in preserving order in the fortress.

The soldiers felt that something beyond belief had happened, something savouring of disgrace to the brave Russian Army and the Russian Empire as a whole.

" Have we got to surrender, sir ? " cried my men when I inspected the companies for the last time.

" Yes, my lads," I answered. " We have been ordered to surrender; but no blame attaches to the 5th Regiment, and you can with a clear conscience tell each and every one that the 5th Regiment has always looked death bravely in the face and has been ready to die without question for its Tsar and its Country. Every one knows this, and no one will dare to cast a word of reproach at you. As you have always been, so you remain, true heroes, known to the Japanese, to our great and dear Fatherland, and to the whole world. Your conscience is as clear as the sky above you."

Many of them burst into tears, and I could hardly speak for the sobs that choked me.

A wrinkled old man who was standing near me,

and was the sole witness of our emotion, snatched his cap off his head, and, waving it triumphantly in the air, shouted : " To the honour of the 5th Regiment, hurrah ! " But there was no one to follow his lead.

Even now I feel overcome as I recall these sorrowful moments, and I can dwell no longer on a scene so heartbreaking.

NOTES

No. 1

ORGANIZATION OF AN EAST SIBERIAN RIFLE REGIMENT

EACH regiment consists nominally of four battalions.

Each battalion consists of four companies, the war strength of each of which is 240 N.C.O.'s and men.

The war strength of a rifle regiment of four battalions is :

Officers	79
Officials	7
N.C.O.'s and men (combatant) .	. 3,855
Non-combatants	. 442
Total . .	. 4,383 all ranks.

No. 2

GENERAL REFERENCE OF NAMES OF COMMANDERS AT THE BATTLE OF NAN SHAN (pp. 41–61)

Commanding 5th Regiment : Col. TRETYAKOV.

,, 1st Battalion : Lieut.-Col. SAIFOOLIN.

,, 2nd Battalion : Lieut.-Col. BIELOZOR (killed) ; replaced by Major STEMPNEVSKI (jun.).

,, 3rd Battalion : Lieut.-Col. DOUNIN.

Company Commanders

No. 4. Capt. SHASTIN.

,, 6. Major GOMSIAKOV (killed); Capt. SICHEV (superseded); Lieut. POPOV.

No. 7. Major STEMPNEVSKI (jun.).

,, 8. Capt. MAKOVEIEV (killed); Capt. SAKAROV.

,, 9. Major SOKOLOV.

,, 10. Major GOOSOV; Half-Company, Second-Lieut. MER-
KOULEV.

,, 11. Capt. BOOCHATSKI.

Scout Detachments

No. 1. Lieut. VASEELIEV.

,, 3. Capt. KOUDRIAVTSEV and Lieut. CHOULKOV.

Mounted Detachment: Capt. ANDREIEVSKI and Lieut. SIETCHKO.

Guns

Field Batteries : Lieut.-Cols. ROMANOVSKI and PETROV.

Machine Guns : Second-Lieut. LOBYREV.

Naval Guns : Midshipmen SHIMANSKI and DOUDKIN.

Mountain Guns : Lieut. NAOOMOV.

Bullock Battery : Second-Lieut. SADYKOV.

13th Regiment

1 Company (not numbered): Capt. LUBEEMOV; Capt.
TEEMOSHENKO.

No. 2 Company : Capt. ROTAISKI.

Scout Detachment : Lieut. BANDALETOV.

14th Regiment

No. 3 Company : Capt. USHAKOV.

1 Company (not numbered) : Capt. KOUSMIN.

Scout Detachment : Lieut. ROOSOI.

No. 3

According to our Official History none of the Japanese divisions
landed near Terminal Point itself, but in the first place made
use of Pi-tzu-wo and Hou-ta-shih, and afterwards Dalny. There
are two Ta-scha rivers, 15 miles apart, the most northerly one
being that indicated in the text.

No. 4

The Japanese went down into the water on the right flank as the tide receded, and sat or lay there until ready for their final attack. Their opponents apparently thought them dead, and later were surprised by an attack from that quarter.

Ying-Cheng-tzu

Shuang-tai-kou

Eight Ships
Bay

Chang-ling-tzu

Lieh-shu-fang

Feng-Huang Shan
(Wolf Hills)

II° Verst.
Station

Louisa Bay

Kan-ta
Shan

Headquarter
Hill

Waterworks
Redoubt

Ta-ku Shan

Hsia-chia-tu

Temple
Redoubts

Hsiao-ku Shan

203 Metre Hill

W. Pan-Lung
E. Pan-Lung
Chi-kuan
Wang-tai
Chi-kuan Battery

Lung-wang-tang

PORT
ARTHUR

Pigeon Bay

Lao-tieh
Shan

London

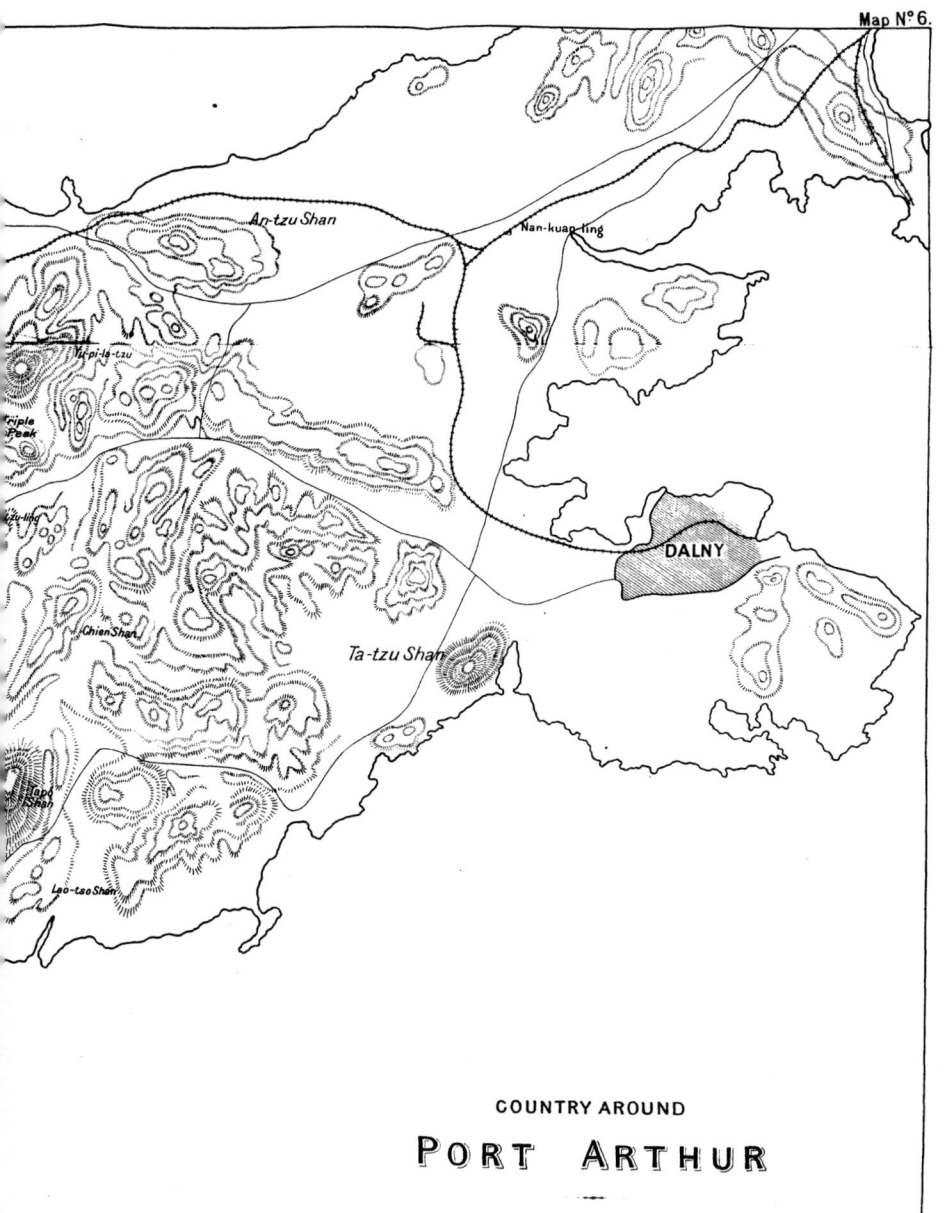

An-tzu Shan

Nan-kuan-ling

Mi-pi-la-tzu

Triple
Peak

tzu-ling

Chien Shan

DALNY

Ta-tzu Shan

Itao-
Shan

Lao-tso Shan

COUNTRY AROUND

PORT ARTHUR

SCALE

Yards 1000   0   2000   4000   6000   8000   10000 Yards

INDEX

312 INDEX